Passing the Baton

Managing the Process of CEO Succession

Richard F. Vancil
Harvard Business School

Foreword by Alonzo L. McDonald

Harvard Business School Press
BOSTON, MASSACHUSETTS

© 1987 by the President and Fellows of Harvard College

All rights reserved.
Printed in the United States of America.

90 89 88 87   5 4 3 2 1

Library of Congress Cataloging-in-Publication Data

Vancil, Richard F.
  Passing the baton.

  Includes index.
  1. Chief executive officers — United States —
Succession.   2. Directors of corporations — United
States.   3. Industrial management — United States.
I. Title.
HD38.25.U6V36   1987   658.4   87-11962
  ISBN 0-87584-182-1

Contents

4   *Management Teams*   105

Foreword

ALONZO L. McDONALD

E ven the term CEO carries an aura of mystique. Although not a traditional corporate title, it infuses new body and blood when attached to the more familiar title of chairman, president, managing director, or vice chairman. CEO signifies the ultimate legal authority and responsibility entrusted to a single individual in today's corporate hierarchy.

Chief Executive Officer—and its initials, more often heard in executive suites—means much more than its legal designation. Surrounding those three initials is a growing body of meaning that defies simple definitions or translations. Like the term "marketing," "CEO" is linked with a spectrum of individual impressions, reactions, experiences, and emotions that varies with each person who hears the term spoken. Yet the literature surrounding the concept of the CEO, unlike the literature on marketing, is mostly oral. It consists of a lot of folklore. Even the valid parts reflect more the personal sharing of experiences among members of this exclusive club than objective descriptions of its more profound meanings.

Legal descriptions and requirements aside, even more mysterious than the workings of a CEO is the process of planning and managing the naming of a successor. It is for this reason that the topic became an important research focus at Harvard Business School and a natural subject for exploration in the experimental Senior Executive Sessions at the School. These sessions bring together for one to two days about a dozen chairmen, presidents, or vice chairmen with two or three faculty members to exchange experiences and debate issues among themselves. They focus on some current topic of central interest and importance to participants, normally one in which practice runs ahead of theory or business literature. These discussions, during three sessions on CEO succession moderated by Professor Richard Vancil, led to this welcome breakthrough in management literature on a topic rarely ventilated in public.

The subject of CEO succession is particularly intriguing because of its many facets and the large numbers of lives and careers it touches. As a preamble to the story itself, a few reflections on its often unspoken implications may add to reader appreciation.

Fundamentally, this is a story of power. Although immersed and rationalized in a maze of worthy motivations, the quest for power — both personal and institutional — is a primary drive for high achievers who press to reach the top rung of the corporate ladder. With power comes most of the rest that one seeks in the quest for career advancement, both the ego-satisfying rewards and the opportunities for more responsible service to society.

Power spawns recognition, latitude for personal action and influence, maximum leverage for one's efforts, high compensation, convenient support infrastructures, and public reputation. In addition, power brings the challenges of leading major commercial enterprises in new directions, imparting new vitality to them, realizing new and greater opportunities for their people, and fulfilling societal needs in a more efficient and satisfying manner.

Naturally, therefore, the passage of power makes for a fascinating story. This is particularly so in the United States, where we encourage, expect, and still marvel at the actual passage of power from individual to individual. We watch with awe when this happens in our governments and our great institutions in a relatively peaceful and constructive manner with a minimum of conflict and negligible violence. Historical precedents for this way of transferring power were rare before our founding fathers laid down principles of self-government and made them real by example and action during the early decades of our search for governing patterns in the new North American society.

This is also the story of matching extraordinary talents with very complex and challenging situations. Each side of the equation represents part of an enormous puzzle with needs to balance, fit, assess, and ultimately to match. Then add the uncertainties of the rapidly changing business scene and the need to envision the future corporate situation and its needs along with the likely leadership profile best suited to understand and do the job needed.

This is also a story of corporate cultures. Each enterprise has a distinctive set of values, operating precedents, traditions, and expectations for its leaders. Will and should the new CEO fit the old culture? Will he or she attempt to change or to adapt it? Or, will the culture abandon the new leader heading out increasingly alone in unexpected and therefore strange and frightening directions?

Adding to the excitement, this is a story of personalities and interrelationships. It concerns real people with real strengths and weaknesses, motivations, idiosyncrasies, and individual visions of the future for the enterprise and their role in it. Choosing between these people, or going outside for another, can make for real drama and an emotionally charged atmosphere that can touch the lives of every corporate constituent.

The process that leads to CEO succession can be a long and complicated one. A lot of people are involved or have vested interests in it. The process can be random or thoughtful, logically pursued step by step over time or precipitous and immediate. It can be equitable or arbitrary. It can strengthen an organization enormously or leave it weakened and competitively vulnerable.

The process of choosing a successor CEO provides the final test and perhaps the most demanding one for a CEO. The incumbent's role is critical—as planner, animator, nominator, evaluator, decision maker, any combination, or none of these.

Ironically, the selection of a successor CEO, even with its recognized and acknowledged importance, is normally handled by novices. Most CEOs only get one chance to think through, manage, or assign this task essential to future corporate continuity and vitality.

The process is also intriguing because it is usually carried out in privacy, if not complete secrecy. Hints, movements, suggestions all trigger suspicions and speculations, often leading to protracted grinding of the rumor mill. Many people like to anticipate, discuss, watch, and bet on a horse race. It generates considerable interest, whether the process is an open contest or simply the movement upward of a likely corporate prince from among one's peers.

There are some basic principles that the reader may glean about this process, but its character is highly individualistic and personalized. Therefore, the case method of exploration, research, and study, which is a hallmark of Harvard Business School, is particularly useful in dealing with CEO succession. The author has used the mini-case method heavily to make his points, thereby bringing into the open the subject for current and future CEOs and other participants in the process so they can profit from the specific experiences of others.

Because of the fundamental importance of the subject to corporate well-being and our society's economic prosperity — and the added fascination of the interplays between power and personalities at the top — it has been a great pleasure to assist Dick Vancil in a small way on this project. I hope the reader enjoys the stories and comes away with enough good ideas to lead better or counsel in the critical choices of our future corporate leaders.

Preface

This is a very personal book because it is focused on very private matters — matters that are usually discussed only in one-on-one conversations or in executive sessions of the board of directors. In order to bring you into those discussions, I have persuaded twenty-nine collaborators, mainly current or prior CEOs to share their experiences with you. Collectively, our objective is to help "you," a current or prospective CEO, and your senior officers and directors enhance your understanding of the issues that must be addressed in managing the process of CEO succession in your company.

Reginald H. Jones

My initial interest in the topic of this book is attributable to Reginald H. Jones, chairman and CEO of General Electric from 1972 to 1981. In the Advanced Management Program at Harvard Business School, we frequently invite senior executives to visit the campus and engage in a question-and-answer session with the participants. At my invitation, Jones agreed to come in April 1982, a year after he had retired from GE. The selection of his successor, which had been widely covered in the press, was a natural topic for discussion.

I was intrigued by the story Jones told, not because of its inherent drama, but because Jones clearly had thought carefully about the *process* by which his successor should be selected. That behind-the-scenes look at how the succession process could be managed was clearly separable from the specific choice that would ultimately be made, and yet the process obviously affected the result. We had videotaped Mr. Jones's comments, and I became preoccupied with his story, studying it, on and off, for more than a year, trying to understand how he had done what he had done, and why. Jones's story — told in his own words — and my analysis of it are presented in detail in chapter 6.

Seminars on CEO Succession

The impetus that led me to undertake a major study of the topic occurred, like my initial interest, almost by happenstance. In 1983, Alonzo L. (Al) McDonald returned to the School to serve as an informal ambassador to high-level executives in the business community. The School offers no formal programs for CEOs, and Al's idea was to draw on that group as a resource to assist faculty members in their research. My topic was a natural for that purpose, and Al persuaded me to run a program. The first seminar on CEO succession was held in April 1984. We then held another a year later and a third in October 1985. Each group of about a dozen CEOs (thirty-seven in total) convened at 6:30 p.m. on a Monday for cocktails and dinner at the Dean's house, and the group broke up by 4 p.m. the next day. The credential required for an invitation was experience as a current or prior CEO. No homework before the meeting was required, and the discussions were almost totally unstructured.

The seminars were a great success from the point of view of the participants, and far more productive for my research than I could have anticipated. They were useful for the CEOs for three reasons. First, the setting invited candid discussion: a small, relaxed group of peers talking in the Dean's living room was unlikely to pontificate. Second, although coming from different situations, the members of the group faced an important common problem; each knew that, sooner or later, he must yield his title to a successor.[1] Third, each member of the group had already given some thought to the matter and identified many of the issues he would need to address. After dinner on Monday evening, I asked the group to identify the topics it would like to discuss the next day. It took about an hour to go around the room, but the group had no trouble producing a list of more than fifteen issues. What each member lacked was a breadth of experience in the various ways those issues might be handled. Pooling the participants' experience, including that of the two or three prior CEOs in each group, was synergistic; the whole was clearly greater than the sum of the parts.

1. All participants in the seminar, and all the collaborators, were males. I will use masculine pronouns in this book, except when commenting on boards of directors.

Those discussions also identified the issues I address in this book. In one sense, the purpose of the book is to provide a conveniently packaged version of the seminar so that more CEOs can "attend" it. I have written this book for the incumbent CEO, but it will also be useful and understandable for his senior officers and for the directors who work with him during the process of CEO succession. I know my target audience. They are experienced, sophisticated, and eager to understand the clinical details of how CEO succession has been handled in a number of situations.

Historical Diagrams of CEO Succession

The third serendipitous event that convinced me that I could — and should — write this book was the accidental invention of succession diagrams. A dozen CEOs swapping stories in a seminar was educational, but the context was sketchy, and we had no framework for comparative analysis. Hicks Waldron at Avon, an early collaborator, provided all the data I requested, and I played around with this information, on and off, for several months before it fell into place. The Avon diagram, Exhibit 1.3, is not simple, but it is an efficient way to display a lot of data and, fortuitously, the succession pattern at Avon was starkly explicit. Subsequently, I designed a survey that provided more than two hundred such diagrams, as described in Appendix A.

For my research, the diagrams provided two important benefits. First, in preparation for my interviews with CEOs, I sent each one a copy of the diagram for his company. Every CEO recognized the relevance of history as a starting point for a discussion of CEO succession, and in many cases I learned a great deal about the traditions of the company. Even more important, the demographic data I gathered in my survey of large U.S. companies paid off. Defining three modes of top management organization permitted us to do a better job of comparative analysis across companies, and the definition of eight departure routes for incumbent CEOs provided valuable insights into the issue of CEO tenure.

Research Design

The unvarnished label for my research design is "networking." The seminars defined the list of issues to be addressed, and the organization of the book seemed obvious: the best way to help you would be to deal with the issues chronologically, starting with the first minute that you assume the CEO title and ending on the day when you transfer that title to your successor. It was also clear that I would need a large number of collaborators to help me in this task—CEOs who had faced one or more of the issues and dealt with them effectively. My final, most crucial design decision was to insist that the stories I gathered be presented undisguised, spoken in personal pronouns by the individual involved. From the seminars, I knew that undisguised stories were feasible if they focused on the *process* of CEO succession rather than on the individuals involved and the outcome. During the next eighteen months I spent the equivalent of one man-year gathering stories, first from CEOs that I knew or had met at the seminars and then, following my nose, from random targets of opportunity.

In total, I had one-on-one discussions about CEO succession with forty-eight executives, more than half of them incumbent CEOs, but also including a few in three other categories: prior CEOs, outside directors, and candidates to become CEOs. I learned something from every member of that set, and even if it was too sensitive or personal to appear in print, it added to my mental data base. My oral data base, the stories told by my twenty-nine collaborators, is the bedrock on which this book is constructed. Each story is different, and some of them range over a variety of topics, but collectively they should give you considerable comfort as you wrestle with the same issues other CEOs have faced. Each story is analogous to a tile in a mosaic; its value and meaning are increased by the array of adjacent pieces. My role in this enterprise is to string the stories together in a way that adds value, presenting my analysis of the links and my interpretation of the overall design.

Caveats

The research was designed to fulfill the objective stated in the first paragraph above, period. The costs of that choice are not trivial, and I want to alert you to the trade-offs and omissions I grappled with.

First, the stories told here must be viewed as self-serving. I interviewed each collaborator, one-on-one, in one or more wide ranging sessions that ran from forty-five minutes to three hours or more. The conversation was not recorded, but I took copious notes. I then selected the focal points of greatest interest and drafted a statement for the CEO to review and approve of. The subsequent negotiation, involving one or more phone calls, was amicable, but my only choice was to accept his changes or to delete the story from the book. Several stories were deleted, but as you will see, the stories are remarkably candid. The twenty-nine men who agreed to work with me understood my objective and wanted to help me achieve it.

The risk inherent in such personal stories is that the speaker tells it as he remembers it. The protection for the reader is that the speaker knows what he says will be read by other people who were on the scene at the time, so he can't wander too far, at least in terms of facts. The benefit of first-person stories is that the speaker can give us his opinions on why and how the events unfolded as they did. The cost of such stories is that we have only one person's version of what happened in what is frequently a messy, dynamic process. Furthermore, even that person's story is only partial; the public version of a private turmoil is not the whole story. More was involved than meets the eye, particularly in terms of the trauma, frustrations, and disappointments that inevitably occur when the stakes are so high.

Mitigating these risks to some degree is my belief that in the most tumultuous situations there is simply no "truth" about how the selection decision was resolved. In the few cases where I talked to several of the people involved, my only conclusion was that what each person saw, including the incumbent CEO, depended on where he sat. The stories here are not the whole story, but the whole story may not exist. In any event, I'm sure you'll find these stories compelling—and useful.

Acknowledgments

My formal collaborators are listed below. Without their help— and the assistance of the seminar participants and other CEOs who talked privately with me—this book would not exist. I view their help as a desire to contribute to the professionalization of corporate management. I thank them for trusting me to provide a vehicle for that task.

The support and critical comments of my colleagues at Harvard Business School was invaluable. My debt is particularly high to Kenneth R. Andrews, Gordon Donaldson, Michael C. Jensen, and Rosabeth Moss Kanter. In addition, I received numerous constructive suggestions from Fred K. Foulkes (now at Boston University), Regina E. Herzlinger, George Hollenbeck, Paul R. Lawrence, Theodore Levitt, Jay W. Lorsch, John B. Matthews, Jr., Thomas R. Piper, Walter J. Salmon, Richard S. Tedlow, and Abraham Zaleznik.

The people who run the apparatus supporting faculty research at Harvard Business School are a world-class team. It starts with Dean John H. McArthur who sets the standards and marshalls the necessary resources. Professor E. Raymond Corey, the Director of the Division of Research when this study began, was an immediate advocate, and urged me to conduct the demographic survey. More than a score of others were involved in the two years that followed, but I owe special thanks to Barbara Ankeny, Audrey L. Helfant, and Joanne F. Segal. The bedrock of the entire undertaking, from beginning to end, was my secretary, Marianne D'Amico, and there is no way I can thank her sufficiently for her assistance.

Richard F. Vancil

April 1987
Boston, Massachusetts

List of Collaborators

Robert E. Allen, President and COO, American Telephone and Telegraph Company

Earle B. Barnes, former Chairman, Dow Chemical Company

Roger E. Birk, former Chairman and CEO, Merrill Lynch & Company

Ronald E. Cape, Chairman and former CEO, Cetus Corporation

E. Paul Casey, Chairman and CEO, Ex-Cell-O Corporation

John T. Connor, former Chairman and CEO, Allied Chemical Corporation

T. Mitchell Ford, former Chairman and CEO, Emhart Corporation

Lawrence E. Fouraker, Outside Director, Jewel Companies

Richard L. Gelb, Chairman and CEO, Bristol-Myers

John W. Hanley, former Chairman and CEO, Monsanto Company

James A. Henderson, President and COO, Cummins Engine Company

James R. Houghton, Chairman and CEO, Corning Glass Works

Reginald H. Jones, former Chairman and CEO, General Electric

Robert D. Kilpatrick, Chairman and CEO, CIGNA Corporation

William E. LaMothe, Chairman and CEO, Kellogg Company

C. Peter McColough, former Chairman and CEO, Xerox Corporation

Alonzo L. McDonald, Chairman and CEO, Avenir Group, Inc.

J. Irwin Miller, former Chairman and CEO, Cummins Engine Company

Richard W. Miller, Executive Vice President, RCA

David W. Mitchell, former Chairman and CEO, Avon Products

Richard J. Munro, President and CEO, Time Inc.

Paul F. Oreffice, President and CEO, Dow Chemical Company

Donald S. Perkins, former Chairman and CEO, Jewel Companies

Donald C. Platten, former Chairman and CEO, Chemical New York

Henry B. Schacht, Chairman and CEO, Cummins Engine Company

William A. Schreyer, Chairman and CEO, Merrill Lynch & Company

Michael S. Scott Morton, Outside Director, Emhart Corporation

Walter V. Shipley, Chairman, Chemical New York

Hicks B. Waldron, Chairman and CEO, Avon Products

PASSING THE BATON •

Findings and Conclusions

I have asked myself, retrospectively: What have I learned as a result of writing this book? Because this book is not a suspense story, I'll summarize my answers in the beginning. Some of what I learned you may already know, and vice versa, so reading this section is not a substitute for reading the book. Nevertheless, having pulled together a list of items that seem useful to me, I want to share it with you.

The insights listed below are the result of my analysis of the demographic and oral data bases I have constructed. Each item is expressed concisely, so that you can scan the list quickly, and I cite the chapter(s) and/or story(ies) that elucidate my analysis. The distinction between findings and conclusions is, I believe, important. The findings are a description of current practice, which I did not invent, although I have the privilege of a discoverer in reporting what I found. The conclusions I draw are, inevitably, personal, but I offer them as a starting point for your own analysis of how to improve the process of CEO succession.

Findings
The Relay Process
The most common pattern of CEO succession in large U.S. corporations is to select an overt heir apparent several years before the incumbent CEO is expected to step down. Analogous to a relay race, these two executives work in tandem until the CEO passes the baton (the CEO title) to his teammate. The other succession process, less common but more widely reported in the business press, is a horse race, an exciting event yielding a winner — and several losers. In the relay process, the promotion of the heir apparent is almost a nonevent. (For the relay process, see the Cummins Engine story in chapter 4; for the horse race, see GE's story in chapter 6.)

Role of the Board in Selection

The CEO title is used almost universally, but the number of executives involved in top management varies from one (the solo
CEO) to three or more (a team). The duo mode of top management—two executives engaged in the relay process—is most
common. As the time for succession approaches, it is not uncommon for the solo and team modes to select an heir apparent in
order to have the benefits of the relay process. The distinction
between the duo and team modes can have a major impact on the
role of the board in selecting the new CEO. In the duo mode, the
incumbent's recommendation is likely to be accepted because he
will continue to serve as CEO for several years. In the team mode,
the CEO retires when his successor is named and becomes a lame
duck. After his departure the board of directors will have to live
with the new CEO. In this situation, the board is far more active
in selection than in those companies using the relay process. (For
three versions of selection in the team mode, see AT&T in chapter 5, GE in chapter 6, and Chemical Bank in chapter 7.)

CEO Tenure

At the seminars (described in the preface) each group spent considerable time discussing the "right" tenure for a CEO. The rough
consensus was for ten years, plus or minus two, with a minimum
of five years. A particular concern was that some CEOs stayed on
too long. Subsequently, my demographic analysis revealed that
the tenure issue is managed by selecting a new CEO who is the
"right" age when appointed. The median age of a new CEO is
nine years before his expected retirement date. The concern over
"curmudgeons" who stay on too long is overblown; my analysis
shows that only 4 percent of all CEOs fall into that category. (See
exhibits in chapter 3.)

New CEOs from Outside

The single most striking trend in CEO succession during the last
twenty-five years is the frequency with which an "outsider" is
appointed to that post. Defining an outsider as an executive who
has been employed by the company for five years or less, the
percentage of CEO appointments going to outsiders has tripled
during this period. In the late 1960s, only 8 percent of new CEOs

were outsiders; by the early 1980s, the percentage was up to 25. In contrast, insiders who are appointed CEO have typically worked for the company for more than twenty years. The trend is a reflection of the massive change in the international business environment during this time (chapters 2 and 8).

Transition

The major benefit of the relay process is that it provides a flexible interval for the final grooming of the next CEO. The interval, called transition, begins with the selection of an heir apparent and ends with his validation when he receives the CEO title. In the interim, he must demonstrate his leadership by coalescing a team of his former peers who are willing to work with him, and he must develop a corporate perspective with particular emphasis on dealing with external constituencies. At the same time, the transition interval provides other senior managers with adequate time to reassess their own ambitions and expectations. (See Exhibit 7.1 and the AT&T story in chapter 7.)

Conclusions

Summary Appraisal

Subject to the caveats mentioned in the preface, I believe that the process of selecting new CEOs in large U.S. corporations is serving our country very well. The objective of the process, shared by the incumbent CEO and his directors, is to pick the "best" person *and* to accomplish that while minimizing the internal disruption that inevitably occurs when there is a change of leadership at the top. The incumbent CEO is, appropriately, the manager of the succession process. He is the one who has groomed a small group of candidates to succeed him, and is the best informed to assess their qualifications. More important, there is no conflict of interests between the CEO and his outside directors; he knows that the ultimate measure of his own performance is that he produced a successor who was even better than he was.

Continuity and Change

The trend toward appointing an outsider as the new CEO has major implications for the governance of large U.S. corporations. The issue is best cast as the inevitable tension between continuity and change. Every corporation must achieve both in order to survive in a competitive world. Organizational continuity, all the way down to the shop floor, permits efficiency, dedication, and confidence. Environmental change requires that old tasks be done differently — or not at all — and new tasks must be learned. Managing these two forces is the CEO's most important job. For the board, the task is episodic; as the time for succession grows near the board must decide whether the need for major change is so pressing that an outsider should be brought in. (See AT&T in chapter 5 and the analysis accompanying Exhibit 1 in chapter 8.)

The Selection Process

Mindful of the two broad objectives of the succession process, the incumbent CEO is the designer of a *selection* process that ultimately produces his successor. The design choices can be viewed as a spectrum, ranging from an overt, prolonged horse race to the quiet, perhaps unannounced, early selection of an heir apparent at the other extreme. In choosing a process somewhere on this spectrum, the CEO must be concerned about the equity among the candidates and the disruption that frequently occurs in a horse race. Viewed from the perspective of the candidates, the internal trauma of a selection decision can be mitigated if the pool of candidates is not explicitly defined and if the decision is made earlier than expected. This is more common in companies that have a strong family culture. Other companies, with the traditions of a meritocracy, find the equity of a horse race necessary. (See the analysis accompanying Exhibit 2 in chapter 8.)

Exit Barriers and Transition

The four-phase career of a CEO moving through the relay process works well until the final phase. When the chairman/CEO passes the CEO title to his successor he is, in effect, demoted to chairman only, and serves the remainder of his career as a lame duck, finally retiring when the president/CEO selects an heir apparent. The final phase is necessary, albeit awkward for the chairman, to permit an orderly succession for the next generation. Voluntary early retirement is an option, but the barriers to exit are enormous.

My conclusion is that the exit barriers should be lowered, particularly in companies using the team mode of top management where the chairman/CEO usually retires at the time that he passes both titles to his successor. The nonfinancial barriers — the loss of status and perquisites, and the specter of unemployment — are formidable enough. Most CEOs stay on until mandatory retirement for those reasons, and because they enjoy the power and action at the top. There is, however, another major barrier to early retirement: the loss of a few years of compensation at the peak of a career. Given the stakes, in terms of energy at the top, my recommendation is that the financial barriers be mitigated or eliminated. (See Exhibit 1 in chapter 7, and the analysis in chapter 3.)

Disappointing CEOs

My analysis suggests that roughly ten percent of all newly appointed CEOs are fired, with half of them failing within the first three years. Deposing an incumbent CEO is an almost impossible task for the board of directors as a group and the result is that most boards have a high tolerance for mediocrity. Senior officers find it easier to leave than to foment a revolution, and the president/COO may be faced with a moral dilemma. The prior CEO, retired but still on the board, is in the best position to assess the situation and discuss it privately with the COO and two or three senior directors. If they agree, then, like a junta in a political coup, they inform the incumbent that he should resign. Opinions vary on the issue of whether the prior CEO should continue to serve on the board of directors. I feel that keeping him on the board is a relatively cheap insurance policy for the one time out of ten when it is necessary to dis-appoint the incumbent. (See chapter 3.)

The Partnership Board

The dramatic changes of the last few years are reshaping the face of corporate America; the buzz words are unfriendly takeovers, voluntary restructurings, and international competitiveness. The performance standards for CEOs have gone up substantially in this new era, and the performance standards for directors must too—not just for legal reasons—because the survival of their corporation is threatened more than in the past. Making the transition from current practice to a partnership between the board and the CEO is a formidable task, impossible in some situations. Getting from here to there requires two steps.

First, structural changes are required to enhance the independence of the board from the CEO. (My five prescriptions toward that objective are outlined in chapter 8.) In order to develop a partnership board, the partners must be equal. The second step cannot be achieved by structural means. It turns on the character of the CEO: his personal style, ego, and willingness to listen to a group of people he regards as peers. Some CEOs cannot do that, but a CEO willing to nurture the independence of his board is more than halfway there. An effective partnership, with a board and a CEO working together on major corporate issues, is our best defense to ensure the continued vitality of our industrial establishment.

1

Overview

O n the broad landscape of corporate management there is one small piece of turf that has not been systematically explored. The reason is simple: it is forbidden territory for all but a few selected members of the corporate tribe. There, almost like witch doctors retreating to a secret cave to conjure up a new elixir, those few develop and act out a ritual that ultimately produces a new CEO. The decision is then announced with grave solemnity. It is a rite of passage celebrating the old and the new; a combination of an Irish wake and a Jewish bar mitzvah.

The secrecy preceding the event is appropriate. A corporation is not a tribe, it is a voluntary society of individuals. But a corporation is not a democracy that chooses its leader by popular vote. It has many constituencies that must be served, and the board of directors is the body empowered to select the new leader. The board proceeds discreetly, in partnership with the incumbent CEO, because the stakes are large. The decision affects both the future of the corporation and the careers of the senior managers from among whom the next CEO will (usually) be chosen. These officers and the outside directors, a dozen or so of each, have all the relevant information and, somehow, their collective judgment coalesces to produce a successor.

My purpose is to sketch the first crude map of this territory. I am intrigued by the process by which this small band of travelers sets out to reach a decision that few, if any, have been involved with before. They know a successor must ultimately be chosen; the big questions are who and when. For me, trying to pull together a body of accumulated wisdom on this topic, the specific event is of only passing interest. Buried beneath those two simple questions are dozens of tougher, prior questions that must be faced. My mission is to identify those questions — the process issues of CEO succession — and to describe and explain the various ways they are resolved.

In this chapter I briefly survey the landscape. First, by way of backdrop, I discuss the changing patterns in corporate governance during the last twenty-five years. Next, I define the most common patterns of CEO succession, describing both the *structure* of top management in each case and how that structure affects the *process* by which succession decisions emerge. Finally, I turn to the cast of characters involved in the succession process, discussing in broad terms first the role of the board of directors and then the critical role of the incumbent CEO.

The remainder of this book is organized in rough chronological order, from the moment a new CEO is appointed until the moment that title passes to his successor. Each of the next six chapters contains several stories in which one of the participants in the process explains why and how certain actions were taken. My role in these chapters is to comment on the stories as they cumulatively unfold, trying to make the whole greater than the sum of the parts—no mean feat, given the diversity of the situations. The closing chapter summarizes the stories across two main topics, the criteria for selection and the selection process. My conclusion is that CEO succession is handled thoughtfully and well in the United States, but that boards of directors need to increase their independence from the CEO, and I offer some prescriptions toward that end.

Corporate Governance: Patterns and Trends

The governance of large publicly held U.S. corporations has received considerable attention during the last two decades. The debate, which I will not rehash here, has focused on the role of the board of directors, but the core issue has been the division of duties and responsibilities among the board, the CEO, and other senior officers. Using this broader definition of the cast of characters, I have gathered data about CEO succession events during the last twenty-five years for a random sample of 227 corporations. Findings from this survey are presented throughout this book. For the immediate topic, the survey provides some provocative data about trends in the human resources involved in corporate governance. I present those data, and comment on some of the forces that appear to be driving the change. Then I discuss how those trends have affected the organization structure of corporate management.

Resources for Corporate Governance

For each company in the sample, I traced the career of each parent-company executive who was a member of top management during the twenty-five years from 1960 through 1984. I defined a top manager as an executive who held one or more of five titles: chairman, CEO, vice chairman, president, and COO. By recording the data of each title change for each executive over time, I was then able to draw a diagram of the twenty-five-year succession history for each company. The value of these diagrams will be apparent in the next section of this chapter, but individual items from the data base are also useful.

Slicing the data chronologically allowed me to calculate the number of top managers employed by each company in each year. In 1960, the average company in the sample had 1.66 executives holding one or more top management titles; by 1984 the mean for the sample was 2.12 executives. The total number of executives devoted to the tasks of corporate management increased by 28 percent during that period.

I also gathered data on the size and composition of the board of directors for each company in each year. The average board in 1960 had 13.4 members, and that number increased less than 6 percent, to 14.2 members in 1984. The composition changed radically, however. In 1960, 49 percent of the directors were "insiders," current or retired officers of the company, and that ratio held constant for a decade. In the next fourteen years, the number of insiders dropped by 25 percent and the number of outside directors rose 30 percent, giving the latter group a 66 percent majority.

Top managers and outside directors, the men and women responsible for minding the store in corporate America, have increased the managerial resources devoted to that task by 28 percent and 30 percent, respectively, during the last twenty-five years. One causal factor is simply the growth in size and scope of these large corporations; there are more people and more assets to be managed.

An even more important factor, I believe, is the explosion of knowledge about industrial organization and microeconomics, and its effect on the technology of management. It is useful to list some of the major events affecting U.S. corporate management during this era: diversification and decentralization, foreign direct investments, worldwide competition, oil shocks and inflation, government programs (e.g., EPA and OSHA), deregulation, worldwide capital markets, restructuring, and perennially, improvements in information processing.

Management, initiating some of these events and responding to others, had to invent new tools in order to cope. The more useful and enduring of these were the formalization of strategic planning and analysis, first at the corporate and then at the business-unit level, and the design of explicit programs and policies for the development of the management cadre itself. Perhaps the best single statistic to document the professionalization of U.S. management is the number of people taking MBA degrees: 4,814 in 1960 and 71,000 in 1984, an increase of more than 1300 percent.

I have no standard by which to gauge the efficiency or effectiveness of corporate management during this period, but an increase of only 28 percent in the number of top managers does suggest that there were, at least at the top, some economies of scale. One effect of that increase, however, was to cause a change in the organization structure at the top. I describe that next, and then explore its implications for the process of CEO succession.

Modes of Top Management Organization

The trick in finding patterns in a mass of data is to set the lens on the right focal length, yielding a picture that is sharp and clear. My objective was to divide the sample into a few categories that would be (1) realistic, in terms of describing how corporate managers structured their tasks; (2) unambiguous, making it easy to assign each situation to a category, and permitting a reader to determine his or her own current category; and (3) useful, providing a context to make it easier to understand the process of CEO succession in each company. The solution was as simple as one–two–three or more.

The most common mode of top management organization in large U.S. corporations during the last twenty-five years has been to have only two executives holding any of the five top management titles. Typically, one person is chairman, the other is president, and one or the other is also CEO. If the chairman is CEO, the president may also carry the title of COO. One or two senior officers may be members of the board of directors, but they do not carry the title of vice chairman. I call this two-person structure the "duo" mode of top management organization.

In 1960, the second most common form of top management structure involved only a single executive, the "solo" mode. This person might carry only the title of chairman or president, with the other titles not assigned to anyone, or he might carry two or three titles, including CEO. The COO and vice chairman titles were not used. By 1984, the second most common structure consisted of three or more executives, each carrying one or more of the top five titles — the "team" mode of top management organization. The most typical arrangement is like the duo mode, but with one or more executives serving as vice chairmen.

The first thing to be said about these three modes of top management is that, in any single company, they may be quite dynamic over time. If the president of a duo-mode company dies or departs, the position may go unfilled for a few weeks or a year or two. During that time, the company is classified in the solo mode. Nevertheless, most companies do have a policy or tradition of using one of these three modes most of the time. Finally, over a period of twenty-five tumultuous years, policies governing top management organization do change, and the trend is clear. As the tasks of top management have grown in size and complexity, more executives have been needed to share the load.

The magnitude of this change within large U.S. corporations is displayed in Exhibit 1.1. In the early 60s, these companies, collectively, used the solo mode 36 percent of the time and the team mode only 8 percent; by the early 80s, the team mode had grown to 25 percent and the solo had dropped to 21 percent. For most companies, the transition was from solo to duo or from duo to team, with a few companies doing both. More than one-half of the companies changed their dominant mode of management during this period. As you would expect, however, in 1984 there was still a strong correlation between the size of the company and the management mode: smaller companies were more likely to use the solo mode; very large ones the team mode.

Recognizing these dynamics, both company-specific and the underlying trend, is important in analyzing how the different modes of top management affect the process of CEO succession.

EXHIBIT 1.1

Top Management Modes of Organization

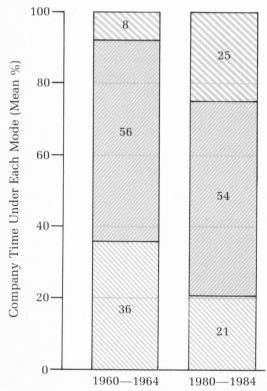

Using the date of "succession events" defined in Exhibit 1.3, the number of executives holding top management titles at any point in time was calculated for each company in the sample. The first and last five-year intervals are plotted on this chart. During a five-year span, many companies used more than one mode of organization; the dominant mode (most commonly used for each company in each interval) is shown here, as a percent of all companies in the sample.

Patterns of CEO Succession

The majority of large U.S. companies use the duo mode of top management organization, and the primary reasons for its popularity are that it is efficient, and it facilitates the process of CEO succession. The duo mode, in fact, is more pervasive than the statistics above would suggest; in many companies there are, from time to time, a vice chairman or two, nearing retirement, and serving out their final years with dignity. Such situations are "teams" according to my classification, but are not the teams I discuss in chapter 4. The succession process used in duo companies is so common that I will discuss it in some detail below, and then discuss succession patterns in the team and solo modes.

The Most Common Process

The process of CEO succession usually ends with a terse announcement so unremarkable that only the size of the company allows it to claim space in the "Who's News" column of *The Wall Street Journal*. The reporting of the event at CPC International Inc. on June 21, 1984 is almost stereotypical.

Here, in a pattern we will see frequently, the chairman passes the CEO title to the president, who is six years younger. "No one is surprised" at this "normal succession." The chairman will probably retain that title until he retires three years from now, and the new CEO doesn't have "an obvious successor."

This book focuses on these unremarkable events. Each such event, obviously, is of major importance for the future of the particular company, yet the *process* of selecting the new CEO has apparently been managed to minimize its significance. Accepting this intent (for the moment), I will label these "healthy" successions because they achieved the objectives of the officers and directors who were responsible for the result. The process used most often to produce a healthy succession is most easily described in the context of a specific situation. I will use Avon Products, Inc. as an illustrative example.

The Avon Story. Avon Products, Inc. was one of the darlings of Wall Street in the "two-tier" stock market of the

EXHIBIT 1.2

CPC Names Eiszner
As Chief Executive
To Succeed McKee

By a WALL STREET JOURNAL Staff Reporter

ENGLEWOOD CLIFFS, N.J.—CPC International Inc., a major food processing concern, said James R. Eiszner was named chief executive officer, effective Sept. 1. He will succeed James W. McKee Jr., who will continue as chairman.

Mr. Eiszner, who is 56 years old, has been president and chief operating officer of CPC since 1979. He will continue as president; the chief operating officer job will be left vacant.

Mr. McKee, who will be 62 in August, said the change is being made to provide for an orderly transition at the top. Mr. McKee has been chief executive for 12 years.

Mr. McKee has a financial background, while Mr. Eiszner's strengths are in technology and marketing.

Despite those differences, Mr. Eiszner said that he and Mr. McKee are "philosophically very much attuned" and that he didn't expect to make any immediate changes.

"This is absolutely a normal succession," Mr. Eiszner said. "I think no one is surprised, except at the timing." Mr. McKee could have remained in the chief executive's job for another three years. "He just felt it was time," Mr. Eiszner said, because 12 years is a long tenure in the job.

Because there won't be a chief operating officer, division heads will report directly to Mr. Eiszner, which means there won't be an obvious successor to him in the organizational structure.

---

late 1960s. When Hicks B. Waldron was suddenly named president and CEO in late 1983, I asked him to contribute his experience to my research. I first met Waldron in 1976 when I joined him on the board of Connecticut General Corp. (now CIGNA Corp.), so we knew each other well enough that he agreed. With his help, I subsequently produced the first diagram of a CEO succession history, shown in Exhibit 1.3.

The diagram has proven to be a very useful tool in this research. Based solely on public information, the diagram reports a great many facts in a concise format. More important, it captures the dynamics of succession over a twenty-five-year period and presents a pattern that conveys the basic situation almost at a glance. (See Appendix A, "How to Read and Interpret the Succession Diagrams," for a detailed explanation of the diagram format.) Most important, each diagram is unique, based on the specific events in a single company. Much can be learned about the succession process by examining the differences in the patterns across a set of companies. If nothing else, the diagrams drive home the fact that CEO succession is situationally specific. The common succession process, one level of abstraction removed from the set of diagrams, is conceptually useful, but ultimately it is the collective judgment of the officers and directors involved that produces the *name* of the new CEO.

The Avon succession diagram is a good example of the common succession process, and illustrates why I have chosen the analogy to a relay race as the title of this book. In a relay race, a teammate runs briefly at the same speed as the baton-carrier, awaiting the moment for a smooth handoff. In a corporation, the president "runs" in tandem with the chairman/CEO for several years. And, just as a runner who has passed the baton gradually slows down before retiring to the sidelines, so a chairman who has relinquished the CEO title may work beside his successor before retiring completely. Ewald, the new Avon CEO in 1961, carried the baton, but always had a running mate (first Rooks, then Hicklin). The baton (the shaded area in the diagram) was passed to Hicklin in 1967. Ewald then retired, and Fusee ran alongside. The race continued in that fashion until 1983, with handoffs to Fusee and then Mitchell.

EXHIBIT 1.3   Avon Products, Inc. • CEO Succession History

The dates beneath each name are sequenced: year of birth; year of first full-time employment; year appointed to the board of directors; year retired from the board of directors. Succession events = changes in title(s) held by an individual: Chairman (CH), President (Pres), Chief Executive Officer (CEO), Chief Operating Officer (COO), Vice Chairman (VC), Executive Vice President (EVP). Retirement as a full-time employee is also a succession event (Ret.). For convenience, the age of the executive at each event is in lower left corner of box; eg, Mr. Clark retired at 75, but stayed on the board until 1976, retiring as a director at 89. Mr. Waldron joined the board in 1980, but did not become a full-time employee until 1983, at 60.

Timeline (years): '60 '62 '64 '66 '68 '70 '72 '74 '76 '78 '80 '82 '84

Mr. Chamberlin '28/'85/'85
- Pres (56); CCEO

Mr. Waldron '23/'83/'80
- CH Pres CEO; PCEO (60)

Mr. Chaney '32/'55/'75
- Pres–COO (45); Pres (50); EVP (51)

Mr. Mitchell '28/'47/'71
- Pres (43); CH–CEO (49); CH (55); Ret. (56)

Mr. Fusee '17/'45/'65/'77
- Pres (50); CEO Pres (47); (CEO?) CH (56); CH Died (60)

Mr. Hicklin '11/'28/'60/'80
- Pres (50); CH–CEO (56); CEO VC (54); CH (60); Ret. (62)

Mr. Rooks '06/'26/'52/'62
- P Died (55)

Mr. Ewald '01/'17/'25/'80
- Pres (59); CH (61); CH CEO (65); Ret. (66)

Mr. Clark '87/'22/'25/'76
- CH (73); Ret. (75)

For the first twenty-two years of this chronology, Avon used the "relay process" to provide an orderly succession for four CEOs. Then, suddenly, that process failed and Waldron was brought in as CEO. The important question, given the inevitable disruption that occurs when there is such an abrupt change, is why.

The Story Behind the Diagram. Facts are facts, but when it comes to the question of what really happened in any particular succession event, there is no such thing as the truth. Opinions about, and perceptions of, the truth are the best I can do. In the situations discussed in this book, the perceptions are provided by one or more of the key players involved. At Avon, Waldron asked the former chairman and CEO, David W. Mitchell, if he would be willing to discuss the issue with me. Mitchell agreed. We met in New York City in early June 1984, and this is what he told me:

My abilities and experience were primarily developed in the direct selling business. As I saw Avon's future having to be diversified into other areas, I felt that a man with an entirely different background was needed to head up the corporation.

Avon was founded as a simple, direct sales business that was unique only because it became fully integrated and very large. Even in 1977, when I became chairman after Fusee died, it was still a simple business. Bill Chaney really knew that business. He was young, smart, aggressive, a good administrator—really the only guy that was likely to succeed me. So we made him president and chief operating officer.

Then our business suddenly matured. In 1976, the first full year that I was CEO, our return on equity peaked at 23 percent, and then declined steadily to 10 percent in 1983, when I retired. Chaney began to show some weaknesses as a leader, and some of his people came to see me, concerned about him. By 1980 I was telling the board that Chaney was iffy as my successor—and that I wanted to retire sometime between age fifty-five and sixty.

The acquisition of Mallinckrodt in 1982 was a major strategic move for us, and also gave me a chance to try to broaden Chaney by moving him to run Tiffany, which we acquired in 1979. I put Jim Preston in charge of the Avon business, because he was looking like a contender, and told Chaney that he didn't have a lock on my job. But I didn't tell him he wouldn't win. Looking back, I probably failed to move fast enough to develop other candidates. Some of the directors wanted me to look outside, but as a group they felt it was my problem. I waited too long, but the board could have pushed me more.

I asked Hicks Waldron to join our board in 1980. He was CEO of Heublein, and a great marketing talent. When Heublein was threatened by a takeover in 1982, I started to think about him as my successor. He wasn't too happy working for the white knight that bought his company, and finally agreed. I met individually with each director to discuss the proposal, and everyone was relieved. Chaney and Preston were hurt, but Waldron's age, sixty, helped a little.

I also wanted Waldron's perspective on the succession issue. Our initial conversation was in mid-March 1984, after he had been in office about eight months. At that point, he really wanted to talk about how he took charge of Avon, and that turned out to be a story in itself. Subsequently, in July 1985, we met again, discussing a range of topics. Here is what he told me about Mitchell's retirement:

I was totally surprised when Dave Mitchell came to me in May 1983, asking if I was interested in becoming the next CEO of Avon. As a director, I knew that Bill Chaney and Jim Preston were considered to be very live candidates, but I also accepted Mitchell's analysis of the situation, as stated in his quote above. In fact, some of us on the board were becoming concerned about the future of Avon's core business, and as CEO of Heublein I had loaned my strategic planner to Avon on two or three occasions to help them get a better fix on the nature of the problem.

Mitchell also suspected that I might be interested because Heublein had been acquired by RJR Industries in
mid-1982, and I was now head of their Food & Beverage
group, which included Heublein and Del Monte. RJR was
in the final throes of its own CEO succession, and I was
one of the candidates in that situation. So, I told Mitchell I
might be interested in a couple of months. But the more I
weighed RJR versus Avon, tobacco and liquor versus cosmetics, fashion, and health care, Winston-Salem versus
New York City, the RJR management team versus the
Avon management team, the more I leaned toward Avon.
Finally, in July, I called Dave, told him I'd like to come,
and then advised Paul Sticht that I was leaving.

Mitchell stepped aside early because he was tired. He
told me, "I've come up from shipping clerk to CEO, but after thirty-six years I just don't have the new ideas to deal
with our situation. I want to get out of this rat race and
retire to California with my new bride. If you take my job,
my legacy to Avon is that I left a terrific guy in charge." I
had to respect his candor, and I couldn't argue with his
good judgment in picking me, so I took it.

The Avon succession, I think, is a case of "All's well that
ends well," and I have to admire Mitchell for assessing his own
limitations and for recognizing that Waldron's situation was a
rare opportunity.

The Avon story also serves to introduce one of the major
themes running through this book: the tension between continuity and change. Every corporation must achieve both if it is to
survive in a competitive world. Organizational continuity, all the
way down to the shop floor, permits efficiency, dedication, and
confidence. Environmental change requires that old tasks be
done differently—or not at all—and new tasks be learned.
Managing those two forces, really, allowing both to evolve simultaneously, is perhaps the most important job of a CEO.

For Mitchell, the massive environment change was over-
whelming. Suddenly, in just a few short years, more women
joined the full-time work force, including many of Avon's door-
to-door distributors. Turnover among those people increased at

the same time that the "Avon ladies" found there were fewer women at home to answer the door bell. An irreversible social sea change had occurred. Fresh eyes were needed, and, as soon as he found them, Mitchell walked away.

Elements of the Relay Process. The first twenty-two years of the Avon chronology provide a good example of the CEO succession process in publicly owned corporations. Look back over the last twenty-five years in such companies and you will see that the typical company has had from two to five CEOs. Looking forward, that pattern will continue, almost like a monarchy.

In a corporation, however, unlike a monarchy, where the genealogy of blood lines is carefully prescribed, no bylaws impersonally determine who the next CEO will be. If the corporation is to survive, a new leader must eventually take office, but the process by which he or she is selected must be determined by the incumbent officers and directors. There is a process with some common elements, but practice varies widely, because the circumstances in each case are different. The most important elements are the objectives of the process, the events of selection and validation, and the process of transition that occurs between those two events.

OBJECTIVES. The basic purpose of the succession process is to pick the "best" person to be the new CEO. The only problem is in agreeing on who is best in a specific situation. I find it useful to specify another objective that, in many instances, appears to be of overriding importance: the succession process should be orderly, designed to minimize the organizational disruption that is almost inevitable when a change in leadership occurs. This objective is the primary reason for having two events in the process of CEO succession rather than one.

The cost of disruption is not trivial, as any manager — even three or four levels from the top — who has lived through the turmoil of a messy succession can attest. Those are the situations the newspapers report with lurid details of who did what to whom, a story usually cast in terms of winners and losers. But the real loser is the corporation itself, not because the linen is washed in public, but because many of the top managers are so preoccupied with the battle for succession that their productivity suffers. The selection of a new CEO is a high-stakes poker game, with the chips denominated in terms of personal careers of the contenders, but almost everyone involved would prefer to have the issue resolved quietly and smoothly with no headlines, thank you. In one sense, the goal of an effective succession process is to allow that to happen — and still pick the best person.

Two implications of that goal are worth noting. First, the process must be carefully planned and managed so that all parties concerned, primarily senior officers and directors, will believe that it was thoughtful, objective, and fair. The word consensus is too strong, and compromise has implications of mediocrity, but there should be wide agreement that the candidate chosen was the best of the lot. Second, the disruption is likely to be less if the new CEO is well known to many members of the organization. This establishes an automatic bias in favor of promoting an existing officer rather than bringing in an outsider. All things considered, this bias is probably appropriate in most situations, but it does mean that the "best" is defined in local terms, thus increasing the potential for internal conflict.

SELECTION AND VALIDATION. The two-event process is surely familiar to most readers. The corporation is run by two top officers, the chairman and the president, and one or the other carries the title of CEO. Using Mitchell's career at Avon as an example (see Exhibit 1.3), the event of his election as president will be called his selection as heir apparent to the CEO. A few years later that initial choice was confirmed when he became president and CEO, an event called validation.

The primary virtue of the two-event process is that the validation of the heir apparent is almost a nonevent. In one sense, nothing has happened; the same two people still occupy the same offices. But the baton has been passed, even though both runners are still on the track. The invention of the CEO title occurred, I believe, because it was needed for an orderly succession process. In 1962, only 25 percent of large U.S. corporations used the CEO title. By 1970, 74 percent had adopted it, and in 1984 it was almost universal (96 percent).

These two events are episodic, but continuing. In the third stage of his career at the top of Avon, Mitchell became chairman and CEO, participating in the selection of his prospective successor, who was named president. Finally, even though that president did not become CEO, Mitchell ultimately passed that title to Waldron, the new president and CEO, and Mitchell then served briefly in the fourth stage as chairman only.

Those changes in titles, events that can be marked on a calendar, are the dates when decisions are announced to the organization and the public. The timing of those announcements is, in itself, a major decision in the succession process, and the interval between one date and the next may vary from a few months to more than ten years. Even more important are the decisions made during those intervals: Who should be the new president (the likely successor)? and, Is the current president the right person to become CEO? This latter question is at least as important as the former, and is resolved in a process I call transition.

TRANSITION. Having just been selected, the new president now becomes a partner with the CEO/chairman and they begin a more or less gradual transfer of power from the older person to the younger. If the transition period runs for several years, as it frequently does, the growing power of the president may be recognized officially by occasional realignments of the division of duties between the two executives. Finally, when the time is right, the CEO title is transferred to the president and the succession process is complete.

Transition is a time of final testing for the new president. He is not quite a crown prince, because he must still prove his mettle on two crucial dimensions. First, he must use the time available during transition to gain broad support for his leadership within the organization. Second, he must demonstrate to the CEO/chairman and to the board of directors that he has a corporate perspective and the promise of being an effective external spokesman for the firm. If he succeeds, as all parties hope he will, that fact is validated by the transfer of the CEO title.

Succession Within Teams

The team mode of top management organization embraces a wide variety of situations, and as a result, no single succession process is applicable to these companies. Searching for patterns, I have identified three.

CEO succession at IBM might be defined as a "modified duo" process. IBM usually has a president and a chairman, with one or the other named CEO, but Frank Cary in 1973 was "solo" for several months, and during the last ten years the company had a vice chairman on two occasions.

IBM has two formal policies that help manage the tension between continuity and change. First, key executives are required to vacate their positions at age sixty, a policy intended to infuse the corporation with new views because turnover at the top is expedited. Second, prior CEOs are permitted to continue on the board of directors until age seventy. The result is that a new CEO will have two or three of his predecessors on the board during his entire tenure. IBM clearly emphasizes continuity.

The other two patterns in the succession of teams are a reflection of the company's policy for the replacement of team members; some do it in an evolutionary manner, others replace the entire team as a episodic event. I provide examples of each later: Dow (chapter 4) and AT&T (chapter 5) use the evolutionary approach; Chemical Bank (chapter 4) and General Electric (chapter 6) select the new team members as a group. As we shall see, the latter process is considerably more complex.

Succession with a Solo CEO

The succession process for replacing a solo CEO has not revealed itself to me, despite my persistent efforts to discover it. One fact is clear: many companies in this category are still controlled by the family of the founder, and the incumbent CEO is a member of that family. As long as the dynasty continues, there is little need for a formal succession process; the incumbent will decide which member of the next generation will succeed him and when that event will occur. The infighting that sometimes occurs among family members could be called a succession process, but it has dimensions I do not choose to study.

The breakup of the dynasty, however, is worth examining and will be a minor theme in this book. Every company has a founder, and once the family decides to sell stock to the public, it is almost inevitable that, someday, an unrelated executive will become CEO. This is a one-time-only succession event that requires a unique process in each situation. One example, Ford Motor Co., is given below, and in subsequent chapters I discuss Cummins Engine and Corning Glass (chapter 4), Xerox (chapter 6), and Cetus Corp. (chapter 7).

Henry Ford, 2d, served as the CEO of Ford Motor Co. for thirty-four years, finally relinquishing that title in 1979 and resigning as chairman a year later. During the last twenty years of his tenure, five presidents served under him without becoming CEO, and the last two of those, Knudsen and Iacocca, departed with more than the usual amount of publicity.

Using my classification scheme for modes of top management organization, Henry Ford chose duo most of the time (he almost always had a president) and team sometimes (when he also had a vice chairman). But any businessman-in-the-street would say that, during those twenty years, Henry Ford was de facto a solo CEO. If nothing else, this example illustrates that my categories are only a starting point for thinking about the process of CEO succession. Far more important than the number of executives holding top management titles is the CEO's positioning of those managers as the time nears for his succession. The incumbent CEO is the manager of the succession process, but the board of directors has the legal responsibility for making the choice. A discussion of that relationship forms the concluding section of this chapter.

The CEO and the Board of Directors

The preceding description of the facts and events of CEO succession captures the dynamics of the process, but it is impersonal and therefore sterile. More interesting than who should be the next CEO and when he should take office are the questions, Why was this person selected? and, How was that decision arrived at? Recasting that slightly, the issue I now address is the role of the CEO and the board of directors in choosing the next CEO.

The Partnership Board

In the growing literature on the controversial topic of corporate governance, there is perhaps universal agreement on only one item: The board of directors is responsible for selecting the next CEO. The perennial surveys of corporate directors consistently report that their number-one concern is "picking the next CEO." But such surveys, and most of the other articles that purport to address the issue, offer precious little advice about how that obligation is to be fulfilled. The obvious reason, of course, is that the process is interpersonal between a CEO and his directors, and it is difficult enough to describe such interactions, much less to prescribe how they should be conducted. I have defined some patterns in the succession process, but am not able to provide similar precision on the relationships between a CEO and his directors.

Instead, faced with a broad spectrum of behavior, I will rely on models at various points across that spectrum. Fortunately, the existing literature does provide two such models, which I shall adopt as the polar extremes. One, espoused by Dr. Harry Levinson in his widely read article, "Don't Choose Your Own Successor,"[1] I will call the active board. The other, described by Myles L. Mace in his book, *Directors: Myth and Reality*,[2] I will call the passive board. Somewhere in the big middle between those two extremes lies a third model, which, I believe, represents current good practice in the United States today; I will call it the partnership board.

In healthy situations today the board of directors is neither in charge in an activist sense nor a mere puppet. Rather, it is a partner with the CEO, working in a positive fashion to find the best successor. An effective partnership, evolving as the cast of characters slowly changes, is not easy to achieve or to maintain. A partnership between a CEO and his board, almost like a marriage, requires that each party devote explicit attention to the

1. Harry Levinson, "Don't Choose Your Own Successor," *Harvard Business Review*, November–December 1974, 53–62.

2. Myles L. Mace, *Directors: Myth and Reality*, Boston: Division of Research, Harvard Business School, 1971, 70–71.

needs and expectations of the other, resolving issues as they arise in such a way that everyone maintains a sense of personal dignity. The host of minor rituals designed to ensure that result need not be recounted here.

Rather than affection or mutual need, the CEO/board partnership is based on the common bond of shared responsibility. Each person has voluntarily accepted the personal responsibility to do whatever he or she can to ensure the health and survival of the corporation. The relationships among these individuals, by design, are professional, impersonal, almost aloof; relatively few of these people know each other socially as personal friends. It is easy for such a collection of individuals to be nothing more than that. Pulling them together in such a way that the whole is greater than the sum of the parts is possible, but requires effort and patience.

The bonding element that, over time, creates an effective partnership starts with shared information and the need to agree on actions that must be taken. Emerging from that endless agenda is a more or less overt set of shared values and objectives that can greatly facilitate the decision-making process. And, finally, there emerges an unspoken sense of trust in those around the table, and particularly a trust among the directors that they and their CEO are working toward common ends. In such an atmosphere of mutual respect and trust, the CEO and his directors can then work together effectively to choose the next CEO.

How is that partnership achieved? Slowly. A partnership between the CEO and his board in choosing a successor is simply a manifestation of the broader professional relationship among that group of individuals. And that relationship, in turn, is determined by the characteristics of the individuals who, incestuously, select new members to join the group. I do have one good story to illustrate a partnership board and will return to this topic later. At this point, let us return to the issues related solely to CEO succession.

Building Trust

Shared information, and an open discussion of its implications for action, ultimately permit the development of trust among the

CEO and his directors. For the succession decision, the critical information is of two sorts: the efficacy of current corporate strategy in a changing environment, and the qualifications of the available candidates to become the next CEO. Neither set of data is "factual," but periodic discussions, every year or two, of each topic may yield a rough consensus on the current situation, and that consensus evolves over time. Both sets of data are dynamic; the world continues to change, and individual candidates blossom, fade, or depart. These two topics, almost unrelated during the early years of the incumbent CEO's tenure, are finally merged in the succession decision.

What major strategic challenges will face the next CEO? Who, if any, among our internal candidates is qualified to meet those challenges? Answers to both questions require fairly long-term forecasts of environmental change and personal growth. Both questions are important, but they are sequential. First, the CEO and his directors must reach some consensus on what I call the strategic mandate for the new CEO. Then they must make a choice. Several years of working together on those two topics does, at least, facilitate the discussion that finally results in a decision.

Strategic Mandate. The mandate for the new CEO, in one sense, is generic: maintain and improve the health of the corporation in order to ensure its survival. A strategic mandate, more specifically, is a forecast of the future environment facing the corporation, an assessment of the degree and rate of change that will be required to cope with that environment, and an identification of the skills, experience, and foresight required of the next CEO if he is to create and execute a successful strategy for the next era.

There is a major difference between a mandate and its fulfillment. The incumbent CEO, much less his directors, cannot tell the next CEO what strategy should be pursued. Their purpose, in fact, is to select a new leader who will have the vision to define for them what should be done. Their mandate itself may not be fully articulated, but it is expressed implicitly by the selection of an individual to be the new CEO. That person accepts the responsibility, and then creates his own strategic agenda. If the selection was well conceived, the incumbent and his directors may be somewhat surprised by the new initiatives, but not disappointed.

Assessing the Candidates. The result of succession is a new CEO, a CEO facing the problems of the future, which may be quite different from those dealt with by his predecessor. The best candidate is the one who best combines the personal characteristics that will be needed during the tenure of the next CEO. Carefully selecting the best from an internal set of candidates, however, is not good enough if he is the best of a bad lot. One major issue here is simply the determination by the CEO and his board that one or more sufficiently qualified candidates are available. That decision was negative at Allied Chemical in 1979, and it triggered an external search that produced Ed Hennessy as the new CEO. His predecessor, John Connor, describes that situation in some detail in chapter 5.

On the positive side, promotion from within surely helps to attract and retain a strong management cadre. The incumbent CEO needs those people during his own tenure in order to be effective. He wants them in place to provide a successor. And, perhaps less recognized, he knows that if his successor thrives it will be, in part, because he has inherited a strong team of colleagues to work with him. This is why the never-ending task of developing subordinate managers is so important to CEOs. For the same reasons, it is also important to the board of directors. To the extent that the board's committee concerned with management compensation and development can help the CEO build a strong team, everybody's job will be easier when succession time rolls around.

I am skeptical about the value of trying to define the criteria for the "perfect" new CEO, particularly if there are two or more qualified insiders. Instead, selection involves predicting how each candidate will respond to the prospective environment. The choice, then, is the candidate whose predicted response best matches the response that the CEO and his board believe is the most appropriate. This is the reality of selection, and it is the reason that most directors agree that their biggest impact on corporate strategy lies in the selection of the next CEO.

Role of the CEO. Building trust among a disparate group of directors and their CEO takes time, patience, and — most of all — a desire on the part of the CEO to create a partnership with his directors. To do this, he must not only share information and seek counsel, but also earn the confidence of his directors by committing his management team to a set of performance standards the directors approve, and then achieving those results.

It is rare for a board to lose confidence in its CEO to such an extent that it dismisses him and seeks a replacement. At the other end of the spectrum, and probably typical of a majority of companies, is a board that is completely confident of the talents of its CEO; it trusts his business judgment, agrees on the strategy he is pursuing, and is satisfied with the performance of the firm. Its only concern is whether the CEO's successor can be as good. Boards that are somewhere in between those two extremes, particularly those at the negative end, should worry about succession, and must find a way to intervene — usually by insisting that outside candidates be considered as well as internal ones. But those that have a CEO they trust should have no qualms about relying on him to play the major role in selecting his successor. The partnership is working, and the CEO is the managing partner. Larry Fouraker, formerly Dean of Harvard Business School and now a director of several firms, puts it well: "Shared objectives and mutual respect between the CEO and the board of directors is the crucial element. If that exists, the board can confidently allow the CEO to organize his own succession process."

The incumbent CEO, in some sense, is the tool of his officers and directors; an honest broker seeking to find a solution that the parties involved could not find by themselves. But the incumbent CEO is not an interested bystander, he is the manager of the succession process, and he accepts the responsibility for it the moment he becomes CEO. His objectives are (1) to have an orderly process, i.e., one in which he retains the initiative for taking the next step, thus controlling the pace of the process; and (2) to demonstrate the success of his own administration by turning the reins over to a successor who will be even more successful. His objectives are not inherently in conflict with those of the board.

If, as I believe, an orderly succession process is an important objective in most situations, that result is more likely to be achieved if the process itself is predictable by most members of the management cadre. Such predictions are based on past practice, on the traditional way that succession has been handled. Traditions thus contribute to an orderly process, but at the same time constrain the ability of the CEO and his board to make radical departures. A lot of careers are riding on the upcoming succession — and the next one after that — and changing the rules of the game will be disconcerting for many managers. It is much easier to destroy traditions than to build them.

The relay process, involving two separate events, makes an orderly succession much easier. During his first few years, the new CEO/president is not very concerned about who his successor will be; he is focused on making his mark on the corporation. His partnership with the chairman (the former CEO) continues to evolve, and both will play a role in selecting the next president. Nevertheless, as the decision point for selection approaches, the CEO/president is more likely to be the dominant figure, if only because he is the one who will be in charge until the choice is validated.

The major reason for the CEO's key role in the selection process is that it is intrinsically related to his broader role in developing the management cadre within the firm. He seeks to attract and retain the best talent he can find, and he achieves that, in part, by identifying high-potential individuals and managing their careers to position them for a shot at the top job. He spends a significant portion of his time in personal contact with his direct subordinates, the key line managers who are the most likely candidates to be the next president. As that cast of characters evolves during the CEO's tenure, an increasing number of them are his choices, even though the chairman and the directors must approve his recommendations. The power of the CEO/president in selection is due to the simple fact that he knows the candidates better than anyone else does.

The major benefit of having all this knowledge in the hands

of the CEO is that he can try to achieve the best overall result. Every candidate in the pool has talents that the corporation, and its next CEO, will continue to need. Selecting one person from that group creates risks of losing some of the others. The incumbent CEO must conduct his discussions with each candidate in such a way that all candidates feel they have been treated equitably. At the same time, the CEO must evaluate each candidate on two dimensions: (1) Which one has the qualifications that match up best with the strategic mandate for the new CEO? and (2) Which one has the personal characteristics that will enable him to retain a group of colleagues to work with him? It is a complex analysis, importantly influenced by the peer appraisals of the entire group of senior officers.

The important role played by the board of directors in this process is to provide counsel to the CEO. For such an important decision, he needs to discuss his comparative analysis of the candidates with someone, and he turns to his directors, individually, in committee, and in the full board. Managing the process, he provides for sufficient time in his schedule to permit an evolving analysis, avoiding the pressure to reach an early conclusion. During this period, the CEO and his directors are educating each other, finally arriving at a choice that the CEO articulates first, but that all the directors understand and agree with. Who picked the new CEO? Nobody. Everybody.

2

The Early Years

Chief Executive Officer! The title has a nice ring to it, and now it's yours.

It's no surprise, in one sense. You've worked for the company for more than twenty years, and ten years ago you began to realize that you might have a shot at the top job. Since then, your personal assessment of the likelihood of success has increased steadily. The promotion to president four years ago was a watershed, but even during the last few months you've been conscious of walking on eggs, afraid of blundering at the last minute. And now you've made it! What will you do for an encore?

You've thought about that, too — particularly during the last couple of years as your partnership with the chairman/CEO has blossomed. But, as it turns out, there are two aspects of the CEO's job that were hard to factor into the hypothetical equation you constructed. First is the time horizon. Before becoming president, you changed jobs four times in ten years, obviously being groomed as a candidate, but also being tested on your ability to take hold of a new situation and make a difference in a couple of years. Even after you became president, the occasional calls from executive recruiters caused you to review your options. Now, it's a near certainty that you'll spend the rest of your business career — ten years, more or less — in the same place. That's a major discontinuity in your perspective.

The other new dimension is scope. Until now, you've been responsible for a piece of the action: an ever-larger piece, but still defined by the CEO. Your reaction has been, "Give me a good business and I'll grow it; give me a problem and I'll fix it." But no one tells the CEO what to do. His greatest mistakes are not the occasional errors of commission when faced with a choice, but the sins of omission — failures to identify new opportunities on which he could initiate action. It is the CEO's responsibility to define and redefine the scope of the enterprise and his vision for its future. Determining, in almost unbounded fashion, what the objectives of the organization should be is a task that is different in kind from your prior, limited assignments. The weight of that awesome responsibility, settling itself on your shoulders, feels almost physical. It's sobering.

Alternatively, if you are a new CEO recruited from outside the company, the nature and magnitude of the problems you face are different, challenging, and equally sobering.

Focus of this Chapter

A new CEO, during the first two or three years of his tenure, doesn't spend much time worrying about his successor. His first priority is to establish his leadership, to convert his legal authority to call the shots into a set of relationships that allow him to affect the direction and pace of events with only minimal use of raw power. He must deal with two sets of relationships, usually intertwined: the management cadre, reaching three or four levels down into the organization, and the board of directors.

This is not a book on leadership, nor is this chapter concerned with the tasks and timetables of new CEOs. Those important topics have been dealt with elsewhere.[1] Our concern with succession, however, requires us to explore the behavior of a new CEO as he builds the relationships with the two groups — senior officers and directors — that will participate in the selection of his successor. The board, in particular, lives with the need to appoint a new CEO in the event the incumbent is disabled or dies, even though he may have been in office only a short while. This chapter focuses primarily on that issue, describing the different ways in which several CEOs have met that need, and explaining why such a variety of practice is necessary and appropriate.

The four stories presented in this chapter demonstrate that, even on a fairly specific issue, every situation is different. Despite

1. See John J. Gabarro, *The Dynamics of Taking Charge*, Boston: Harvard Business School Press, 1987; Harry Levinson and Stuart Rosenthal, *CEO: Corporate Leadership in Action*, New York: Basic Books, 1984; and James N. Kelly, "Management Transitions for Newly Appointed CEOs," *Sloan Management Review*, Fall 1980.

EXHIBIT 2.1

The Early Years of a New CEO

	Selected from Inside	Recruited from Outside
Mandate	Continuity	Change
Organizational Response	"Sigh of Relief"	"Show Me" (Savior or Satan?)
Pace of Change	Measured	Rapid
CEO Agenda	Team-building Consolidation	Strategic analysis Restructuring
Board of Directors Need for a Successor	Replacement available and/or contingency plan	Deferred, temporarily

that caveat, it is useful to distinguish between two broad categories of situations: those where the new CEO has been selected
from inside, and those where he has been recruited from outside
the company. The major areas of distinction between these two
situations are shown in Exhibit 2.1.

This crude dichotomy hides more than it reveals, although it
does show that there are important differences between the two
stereotypical situations. To get behind the generalizations, we
must now look at individual situations.

New CEOs from Inside

I have selected three stories to illustrate the activities of new
CEOs selected from inside, one for each of the three modes of top
management organization defined in chapter 1. General Electric
uses a formal Corporate Executive Office at the top, with three or
four members at any time. Merrill Lynch uses the relay process,
with two people at the top. Ex-Cell-O Corp., a smaller company,
has a solo CEO.

Reg Jones at General Electric

In the preface, I described how I met Reg Jones in April 1982, and
how he piqued my curiosity about the succession process. Jones

was the first CEO to tell me a succession story—how Jack Welch was selected as GE's new CEO—and it is retold in chapter 6. But Jones experienced the entire process, and I will also quote him here, at the beginning of his tenure, and in chapter 7, at the end of it.

Reginald H. Jones had thirty-three years of service with General Electric when, in 1972, he was named chief executive officer at the age of fifty-five. He retired in 1981. Three vice chairmen served with Jones as members of the Corporate Executive Office. Each was within one year of Jones's age. I met with Jones in August 1984, and he described the early actions he took regarding succession, emphasizing the importance of traditions at General Electric:

General Electric celebrated its centenary in 1978, and, as befitting a company of that maturity, it has a strong culture and a host of tradition. Some of these historical practices have an impact on succession planning. For example, the company has always had a strong chief executive officer. In earlier days there was a president and also a chairman of the board. Later the company had a chairman of the board and several vice chairmen. But there was never any question in these varying organizational structures as to which individual was the chief executive officer, no misunderstanding as to the person in control. One of the traditions that strengthens the role of the CEO is that the predecessor resigns not only as chief executive officer, but also as a director. While the predecessor is always available for counsel and advice if it is required, he does not look over the shoulder of his successor. This practice has the added advantage of enhancing relationships between the new CEO and the outside directors, many of whom may have been elected to the board during the tenure of the predecessor.

Another tradition at GE that affects succession planning is the practice of early retirement for the chief executive officer. Both Ralph Cordiner and Fred Borch had retired at sixty-two, and I ended my tenure at sixty-three.

The tradition of early retirement and the uncertainty as to exact timing of the event probably has some advantages in terms of the morale of young contenders, but it also does mean that the CEO must concern himself with plans for succession at an earlier date. The CEO must do his planning soon enough in his tenure to provide for the full development over some years of the succession team. Then once they are ready, announce his own retirement so that GE doesn't lose these highly qualified and naturally ambitious individuals.

Finally, perhaps the most important characteristic of GE is that it is run as a true meritocracy. We hire thousands of people each year, and any one of them may end up as the CEO. We have had a strong executive manpower staff for many years, and they currently follow several hundred GE managers who have the potential for upward mobility. When a management job of any significance opens up, we draw on our files to create a slate of four or five internal candidates who seem to be best qualified, and the responsible management chooses one from that group. We have been dubbed a finishing school for CEOs, and it is interesting that several dozen of our alumni serve that role in other corporations today.

Planning Ahead. Realizing all this, I asked the executive manpower staff as early as 1974 to prepare a first cut of those who might be on the slate to succeed me. The result is shown in Exhibit 2.2.

The initial pool of ninety-six melted quickly down to ten, but that's not bad given the time we had for development and the magnitude of the responsibility. My task, then, was to work with that group by testing them in broader assignments, expecting that a few might fall away, and at the same time looking for new candidates who deserved to be in that set. Interestingly, in that initial set of ten, Jack Welch was not one of the contenders. At that point, he was only a thirty-seven-year-old division manager who had not been captured in the original set of crite-

EXHIBIT 2.2

General Electric Company • Initial Slate of Succession Candidates Prepared by Executive Manpower Staff in 1974

Total number of executives at the equivalent of officer level	96
Executives currently age fifty-five or over	44
	52
Less those without top potential	34
	18
Executive just hired from outside	1
	19
Executives not highly rated against the specs	9
Candidates for intensive development	10

ria. If there's a lesson there, it is that succession planning, at its best, is still a very contingent exercise and must be started early if all possibilities are to be found and developed.

Guided by our tradition of early retirement for the chairman, in my own mind I had established a target date for my retirement of 1980 and laid out a road map for the intervening years. The modified version of that map (Exhibit 2.3) reflects some inevitable changes that occurred along the way, but the basic concept of it was very useful. In the original version of that map, we had proposed that a president would be named in 1978 who would serve as chief operating officer and be the heir apparent as my successor. Putting that in the original map really forced us to rethink the pros and cons of a corporate executive office, and we ultimately decided not to tamper with something that was working so well. Instead, we developed the sector concept, which provided an opportunity for a number of high-potential individuals to demonstrate their capabilities for the top job, and the ultimate winner was, of course, Jack Welch.

It is important to stress that the road map was a very personal and private document, much of it prepared directly by me with the help of only one or two assistants. It was far too detailed and contingent for me to burden the board of directors with it in the very early years, but I did open the dialogue on succession in a very general way in 1974, and the board became progressively and very deeply and intimately involved as the time for a decision neared.

Commentary. The board of directors at GE had the right to feel comfortable about succession during the early years of Jones's tenure. The company is renowned for the depth of its management, and Jones had three colleagues in the Corporate Executive Office, from which a successor could be chosen if something happened to him prematurely. Following conventional practice, the Management Development and Compensation Committee of the board no doubt met with him at least annually and obtained his recommendation as to who his successor should be in such an event. The contingency never arose.

Nevertheless, Jones adopted a long view and began his own succession planning six or seven years before his target retirement date. The most remarkable aspect of Jones's planning is the formal road map that he laid out in 1974, looking forward six years. The specific content of his road map is of little interest to us, but the concept of creating such a document is provocative. His plan was substantive: it dealt with the recession in 1974, focusing particularly on cash management; it also focused on the consolidation of General Electric's businesses and the evolving reorganizations that would be needed to implement it.

Maintaining the privacy of a tentative succession timetable is important to its effectiveness. Jones thought through the entire process, identifying (1) the steps to be taken, (2) a plausible sequence, and (3) the likely elapsed time necessary for each step. That original plan then became a dynamic instrument, changing over time to adapt to unforeseen events as well as to revisions in the original estimates. Nobody — not even Jones — knows how many changes were made during the early years as events unfolded. Having told no one about the timetable, he had no need to

EXHIBIT 2.3 *A Road Map for CEO Succession*

	1974	1975	1976
Structure of the Corporate Executive Office (as of January 1st of each year)	Chm. 56 — Staffs; VC 56, VC 57, VC 58; 10 Groups	Chm. 57 — CXOS; VC 57, VC 58, VC 59; 9 Groups / Other Staff	No structural changes.
Key Personnel Changes	None during this period.	During 1975 would have 1–2 Gr. Ex. placement cases due to consolidations. Encourage 1 group ex. to look outside. 1 staff ex. retires at 62.	Key staff retirements to take place, some at age 62. Strengthening Gr. Xs through changes and redeployment.
Key Organization Changes	Consolidate two "Power" Groups. Reassign groups under 1 VC to free him for role as Admin VC. Finance, Legal, Strategic Planning and Executive Manpower = CXOS staff (Corporate Executive Office Staff). All other staffs report to 1 VC.	None during this period.	Two consumer groups to be combined. (A trial of the sector concept.) Corp. development staff to be combined with strategic planning staff. Staffs to be realigned and reassigned to Chairman and 2 VC. Eliminate VC Admin.
Key Process Role Changes	Initiate retrenchment actions for recession. Cash management highlighted. Resource allocation process tightened and tuned. Revamp Exec. Boards.	Revise Ex. Bd. role. Revise strategic review process. Revise info. demands on operations. Tune control process to trigger/contingency points. Chm. to shape CXOS while VC concentrate on results.	Strategic review process to be finalized after study of 1975 revisions. Info. flow refined. Gr. Xs to concentrate on getting investment pulled through to price/income gains.
Key Results	Retrenchment underway. General road map decided.	Chm. span reduced. Corp. staff reduced and retuned to both Corp. and operating units' needs. Operations O/H reduced.	Group consolidation continues to be studied. Staff honing and realignment to be completed. Best Gr. Xs deployed.

Prepared in 1974 by Reginald H. Jones, Chairman and CEO of General Electric Company

1977*	1978*	1979	1980*
Chm. 59 — CXOS — VC 59 / VC 60 — Staff / Staff	Chm. 60 — CXOS — VC 60 / VC 61 — Selected Staff / Selected Staff	No structural changes.	Chm. 62 — CXOS — VC 45 / VC 50 / VC 58 — Each VC had 2 Sectors and Assigned Staff Components
7 Groups, 1 Sector, Utah	6 Sectors		
Mandatory retirements take place at Gr. X & key staff levels. This permits significant personnel changes to test ultimate contenders for office of the Chairman.	Again, key retirements make openings available for succession candidates.	In Aug., 3 of the Sector Execs. were selected by the Board to replace the 2 VC at year-end. This led to 3 key resignations and necessary personnel promotions.	Chm. successor candidates became the 3 VC on 1/1/80. In December the Board selected a VC to succeed Chm. as of 4/1/81. Sectors & staff reassigned to 2 VC 1/1/81.
Group consolidation and reductions to continue.	Sector concept permitted radical reassignment of key candidates to businesses with which they were not familiar. This was one reason this concept was introduced.	Changes in personnel but not in organization except for duplication at VC level during final quarter. This needed for overlap and smooth transition.	None.
Original road map provided for analysis during this year of feasibility of having one executive responsible for all operations as Pres. and COO. (It was later concluded that operations too diverse to make this an effective org. structure.)	The sector concept was needed to unload the corp. ex. office of an excessive burden of strategy reviews. Sectors composed of similar business provided CXO with 6 strategy summaries rather than 43 received from individual SBUs.	The development of strategic plans for the Sectors showed significant opportunities for savings and enhanced results.	During the year the Chm. & Board had great exposure to 3 succession candidates as new members of the Board. This was vital to selection process.
Gr. X's truly conditioned by now to differentiated decentralization. (Autonomy varies by degree of maturity and success in assignment.)	Board exposure to Chm. succession candidates strengthened.	During the selection process the Chm. held interviews with succession candidates that established the "chemistry" among them. This provided a high level of assurance that finalists would be a team that would work together in a harmonious relationship.	New Chm. has 2 VC that are most compatible in forming new team at the top.
*The original road map eliminated the VC Adm. in 1978. An untimely death moved this change up to 1977 as shown above. The Sector concept was not in original road map.	*The original road map showed an alternate structure that could have provided for a Pres. and COO. This was discarded to stay with 2 VC. The sector concept (to evaluate succession candidates) was an added feature.		*Original road map (1974) contemplated Chm's. retirement in 1980. This was delayed to 4/1/81 resulting in 3 months of overlap with Chairman elect.

41

explain, or document, the changes he made. But the evolving plan did serve him, personally, very well, allowing him—and him alone—to maintain his perspective on the remaining events until the time came to share the final prospective steps with the proper committee of his board. A simple lesson for any incumbent CEO, and a powerful tool.

Bill Schreyer at Merrill Lynch

William A. Schreyer became the third CEO in Merrill Lynch's history in June 1984. Large by any standard, Merrill Lynch was not quite fifteen years old as a publicly traded corporate entity, and in sharp contrast to General Electric, it had very few traditions regarding succession.

I met with Bill Schreyer in August 1985, fourteen months after he became CEO, and we talked about what he had done during those first few months of his tenure. It had been a year of unplanned events. Here is Schreyer's account of that year:

> *Merrill Lynch was a hundred years old in 1985, but the modern history of the company really began when it sold stock to the public in 1971. Don Regan was chairman and CEO at that time, and he continued in that position until he resigned in early 1981 to become Secretary of the Treasury in President Reagan's cabinet. Regan had named Roger Birk as president in 1974, and the two of them made a great team. Regan was a hands-on dynamic leader—always challenging the traditions of Wall Street—and Birk was, in effect, his chief administrative officer. When Regan resigned to take the cabinet post, the board accepted his recommendation that Birk should be the new CEO. Birk was then fifty years old and he held both the chairman and president titles for exactly one year and then invited me to become president. One of Birk's first statements to the board of directors in 1981 was that he intended to serve as CEO only until mid-1985, when he would be fifty-five years old. My promotion to president in 1982 made me the logical successor. I was fifty-three at the time.*

In late May 1984, Birk asked if I could spare him some time over the Memorial Day weekend, and we met on Friday and again on Monday. Birk said that he was ready to pass the CEO title to me immediately. The plan was that he would then continue as chairman for another year before retiring. In fact, I know that Birk did enjoy his honeymoon as CEO for the first year or so, but after that he really did not seem to relish the job. With his self-promised early retirement only a year away, he decided to make the move earlier.

The board of directors was scheduled to meet in early June, and Birk arranged to have dinner with the outside directors the night before to tell them of his plans. At the regular meeting the next day, they approved transferring the CEO title from Birk to me.

I hit the ground running, because there was a great deal to be done at that point. We were in the middle of a major cost-cutting exercise, and were also restructuring a number of our business units. I wanted to make some or-ganizational changes, in part because I would also assume the chairman's title in 1985 and at some point shortly thereafter would need to select a president to work with me. I also remembered my father's advice to me many years ago—he was the Merrill Lynch manager in Wil-liamsport, Pennsylvania, until his death in 1952. He said, "If you ever do get into management, remember this: when you take on your first, and any new assignment, don't do anything for six months. Review, observe, smell, feel the whole thing before you start making changes. Your odds for making the right decision will soar."

An Unexpected Event. Then, on July 1, I was playing a hard set of tennis and began to have chest pains. Just what I needed, having been CEO for only three weeks! The doctors said there was no real urgency, but that I would have to have bypass surgery as soon as it was convenient. I decided to postpone it until January 1985, and I didn't even tell my wife of the impending surgery. I did tell Birk, who was shocked, and I also mentioned it privately to the few of our outside directors.

So, I needed to get the house in order sooner rather than later. I moved quickly to make several organizational changes. My intent was to have all of the candidates who should be considered as the next president reporting directly to me. This meant moving several people. The executive vice president in charge of the capital markets was a particularly important appointment, and I had an executive recruiting firm do some scouting for me before giving it to Jerry Kenney. The three key candidates, as I saw it at that time, were Kenney, aged forty-three, Bob Rittereiser, the chief administrative officer, aged forty-five, and Dan Tully, running our consumer markets, aged fifty-two.

With that in place by mid-September, I decided to go ahead and have the heart surgery in October, right after the board meeting that month. I met with each of the three candidates, gave them their marching orders, and then disappeared from the office for ninety days. It was really a great way to find out what each of them would be able to accomplish—who I could count on to get things done when I was away.

The October board meeting had been scheduled to include a long discussion on management succession. None of us really had the heart to talk about it, but of course, we did. The board did want to know who I would recommend as the next CEO in the event that something happened to me. I recommended Tully, primarily because he is a natural leader, and I thought that was what Merrill Lynch really needed at this time. I felt that—perhaps like Harry Truman—he would really rise to the occasion. I did not tell Tully about that recommendation until nearly five months later.

My operation was a success, obviously, so we scheduled the management succession review for the February 1985 board meeting. A week before that date, I scheduled performance review meetings with both Rittereiser and

Tully, the two most visible candidates. I spent four hours with each of them, telling them that I had not yet made up my mind and laying out as explicitly as I could what I expected of them during the next several months. I was quite explicit about their shortcomings and in general simply tried to clear the air with each of them.

Four Scenarios for the Board. The board was now long overdue for a full-blown review of management succession, so I scheduled nearly a full day to discuss it. I started by reviewing the dossier for each of the executive VPs reporting to me, plus a few other promising younger candidates. I wanted them to understand the strengths and weaknesses, and the potential, of the entire cast of characters. Then, turning to succession, I explained that I would discuss it in terms of four scenarios in the form of organization charts. Scenario 1 (Exhibit 2.4) reflected the impending retirement of Roger Birk as chairman. We needed to name a new president sometime soon, but I told them that I was not yet ready to make the choice between Rittereiser and Tully. I promised that I would get back to them on that decision within a few months.

Exhibit 2.5 is the disaster scenario, showing what our organization chart would look like if something happened to me before the new president was appointed. I did make a recommendation regarding this eventuality, explaining that I thought that two appointments should be made immediately to cope with the possible turmoil of such an event. Roger Birk really did not want to get back into harness as chairman, so I recommended that Dak Ferris be named chairman and Tully be named president and CEO. Ferris was planning to retire in a couple of years, but that would give Tully time to get his feet under the desk before having to pick a successor as president and COO.

Next, I lengthened the time horizon and talked about scenario 3 (Exhibit 2.6), in which I would serve as a "one-term" CEO. I said that I wanted to serve at least five years as CEO, but that I would be sixty-one at that point and

EXHIBIT 2.4   *Scenario 1—Mr. Birk's Retirement*

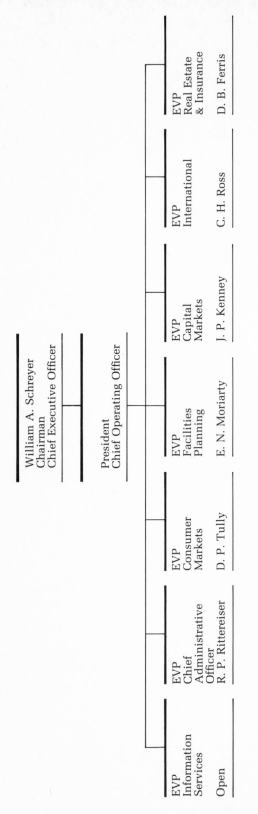

William A. Schreyer
Chairman
Chief Executive Officer

President
Chief Operating Officer

EVP Information Services	EVP Chief Administrative Officer	EVP Consumer Markets	EVP Facilities Planning	EVP Capital Markets	EVP International	EVP Real Estate & Insurance
Open	R. P. Rittereiser	D. P. Tully	E. N. Moriarty	J. P. Kenney	C. H. Ross	D. B. Ferris

EXHIBIT 2.5   *Scenario 2—Disaster*

EVP Information Services	EVP Chief Administrative Officer	EVP Consumer Markets	EVP Facilities Planning	EVP Capital Markets	EVP International	EVP Real Estate & Insurance
Open	R. P. Rittereiser	D. P. Tully	E. N. Moriarty	J. P. Kenney	C. H. Ross	D. B. Ferris

EXHIBIT 2.6 *Scenario 3—One Term*

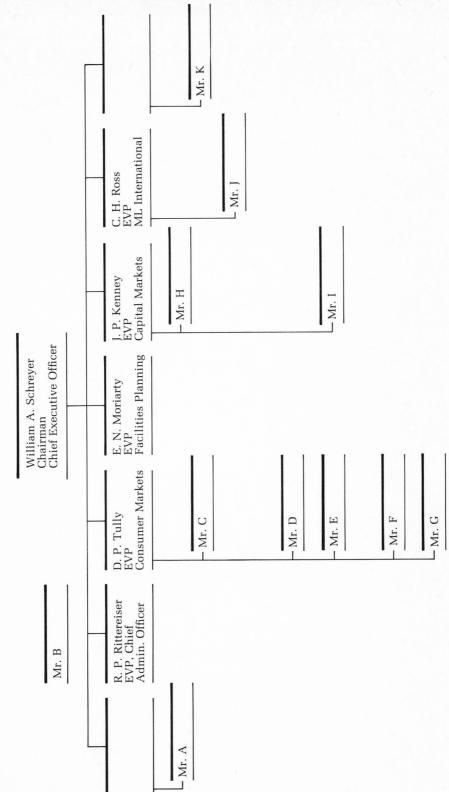

EXHIBIT 2.7   *Scenario 4—Two Terms*

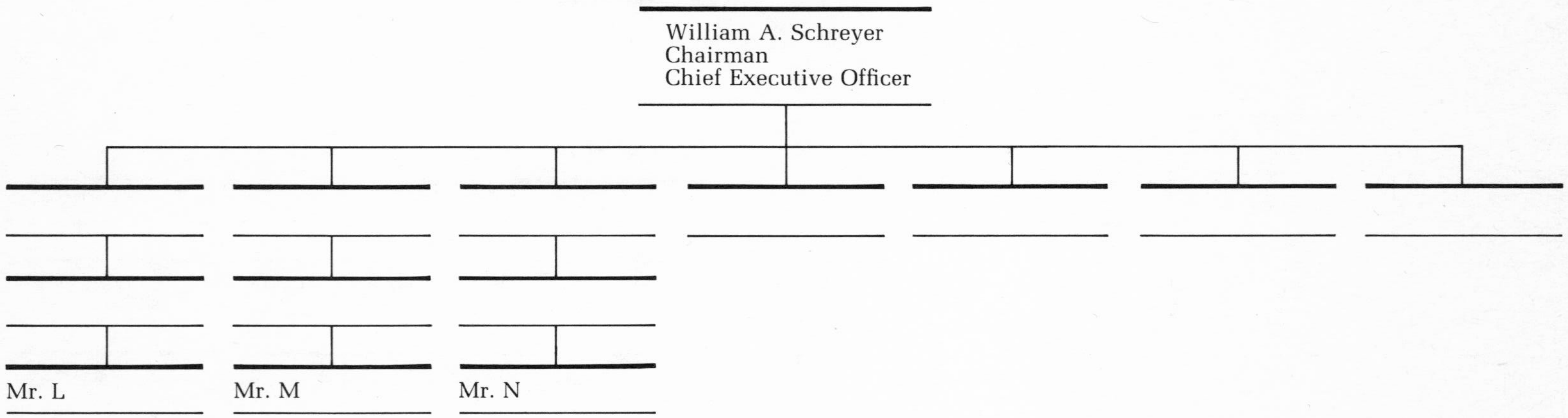

William A. Schreyer
Chairman
Chief Executive Officer

Mr. L

Mr. M

Mr. N

might step down any time after that. Assuming that, the president would then become chairman and CEO, and the board would be faced with the need to select a new president. The diagram listed the candidates that might currently be identified as acceptable. There were eleven people on the chart below the executive vice president level, and we talked about each of them, finally identifying the two or three who seemed the most promising.

Finally, scenario 4 (Exhibit 2.7) reflected the assumption that I would serve "two terms" as chairman and CEO, retiring after nine years when I became sixty-five. This longer time horizon would mean that we might be able to promote someone who was currently only in his early forties, but even casting this wider net, we only added three candidates to the ones shown in scenario 3. The message in this chart was that we really needed to make a serious effort to develop the capabilities of our younger managers.

It was a long day, but the directors seemed very pleased with having devoted that amount of time to it, because they felt they had a much better understanding of what our options were, both imminently and longer term.

Selecting a New President. Then, in late May, on the Friday before our May board meeting, Rittereiser told me that he was accepting a job as president of E.F. Hutton. I was pleased for him, and really thought it was the right solution for both companies. My advice to the board a few days later was that we should not promote Tully immediately, because it would look like a hurried, almost over- reaction to the loss of Rittereiser. The board agreed. A few days after that, in early June, I asked Tully to spend a day with me at my home. We talked all morning and once again I tried to clear the air in terms of what I thought about his performance. As lunch time approached, I asked him if he would like a drink and he said he was ready for one. That was when I told him that I would recommend to the board that he be promoted to president, at the June meeting. He laughed then, and said,

"You bastard, you just had to rake me over the coals one more time." And we both laughed. I also made it clear to him that becoming chief operating officer did not necessarily mean that he would someday become the CEO of Merrill Lynch, but we would have to see how that would play out.

The final event, almost exactly one year from the date I became president and CEO, was the June board meeting at which Birk retired, I became chairman and CEO, and Tully was named president and chief operating officer. At that same meeting, Steve Hammerman was named chief administrative officer, replacing Rittereiser. Tully, Hammerman, and Jerry Kenney were elected as directors, as was John Burlingame, former vice chairman at General Electric. Those actions put my management team into place, and now it is up to us to show how well we can perform.

Commentary. Bill Schreyer had to move fast in dealing with the succession issue at Merrill Lynch, in sharp contrast to the leisurely pace Reg Jones enjoyed. Roger Birk's announced intention to retire early was not a certainty. His promotion of Schreyer to CEO a year before his scheduled announcement made it a reality—and left Schreyer with only a year to produce a new president. Schreyer's sudden health problem served only to dramatize the urgency of putting the house in order for Birk's retirement. Schreyer's first action, after three months in office, was to reorganize the top level of the corporation so that the three primary candidates reported directly to him. For companies using the relay process for succession, it is a fairly common ploy for the president and CEO to reorganize in this fashion. The result, in this case, was to create a more or less overt horse race among the three candidates, and Schreyer intensified whatever competition there may have been among them by disappearing from the office for two and a half months.

Schreyer coped as best he could in keeping his board of directors informed and comfortable under unusual circumstances. Finally, a full-blown review was possible in February, and in my opinion Schreyer did a first-class job. He really focused his board on the central issue, pointing out that he might serve one or two terms as CEO, and illustrating the implications of that choice. Another way of putting the question is, How old should the new heir apparent be? Tully was four years younger than Schreyer, whereas Rittereiser and Kenney were roughly a dozen years younger. Selecting Tully as the new president, with the implication that Schreyer might serve only one term as CEO, would provide the opportunity to appoint a successor to Tully within four or five years. Selecting one of the younger candidates as Schreyer's heir apparent would mean that the next president would not be appointed for eight years or so. This might be a demoralizing prospect for some of the next generation in their late thirties or early forties.

The ages of the individuals involved in CEO succession are important elements in making choices. Cast in the form of a dilemma, the choice that Schreyer and his board faced was whether to promote Tully to president, thereby keeping several options open, while realizing that that act might cause one or both of the other candidates to depart in frustration over the delay. Schreyer defined that choice in the February board meeting, but did not ask the board to resolve it at that point. Then, Rittereiser made the decision for them by accepting a position at E.F. Hutton and the board easily decided that Tully should be promoted.

Paul Casey at Ex-Cell-O

E. Paul Casey and I were both members of the class of 1955 at Harvard Business School, but we did not meet until the fall of 1981. By then, Casey was president and CEO of Ex-Cell-O Corp., a billion-dollar diversified manufacturing company headquartered in Detroit. Casey's career was the central thread in a series of six cases that were used as the opening gun for the Advanced Management Program offered at Harvard Business School. These cases covered a twenty-year time span, and after discussing them for two days, the participants in the program had a chance to meet Casey in a live question-and-answer session. I met Casey when he made one of his semiannual pilgrimages to the campus.

Casey's career is fascinating. Upon graduation, he became

general manager of his family's company, a small firm engaged in manufacturing rubber products. Switching the focus to polyurethane, he went after the automotive market and the company began to grow rapidly. In 1967, he sold his company to McCord Corp., a publicly held manufacturer of automotive parts that was three times Casey's company's size. The transaction was executed as an exchange of shares, and Casey and his family became the largest shareholders in McCord. A year later, at the age of thirty-eight, he became president and COO of McCord. In 1977, he replicated that sequence of events, merging McCord into Ex-Cell-O, and winding up as CEO of the larger entity. Part of the motivation for the merger was that Edward J. Giblin, chairman and CEO of Ex-Cell-O, had not been successful in grooming his own successor, and saw Casey as the solution to that problem.

Giblin, fourteen years older than Casey, had solved his succession problem. Casey, on the other hand, had inherited a succession problem of his own. He knew that early in his tenure as CEO he would face an appropriate concern on the part of his board of directors about who his successor would be. In an interview in early 1984, he described his approach to that issue:

> I joined Ex-Cell-O in early 1978 as president with the understanding with the chairman and CEO, Ed Giblin, that I would be his successor. From the first, he made his intention known to the senior management organization and the board. Ed regularly pointed out to me that "the most important decision any CEO makes is his choice of successor." He cautioned that I would have to face the same issue someday and he hoped I would be as lucky as he.
>
> Ed's succession plan called for me to become CEO on December 1, 1981, one year before his scheduled retirement on December 1, 1982.
>
> In the spring of 1981, Ed Giblin indicated to several board members his growing concern that, since I had no obvious successor, the company would be vulnerable if anything happened to me. The board showed little concern, perhaps feeling that while Ed was chairman he was an obvious temporary successor.

I became CEO as planned. Prior to Ed's retirement, I decided to address the successor issue and thereby minimize what I considered unwarranted and premature concern on the part of any board member. I therefore developed and presented to the board in December 1982 a document entitled Succession Program for the Chief Executive Officer (Exhibit 2.8).

Under the "Concurrent Succession Program to Deal with Emergency," I nominated, in early 1983, our chief financial officer to become vice chairman. He served as my clearly designated temporary successor for two years until his retirement. He was succeeded by our executive vice president, both on the board and as the designated temporary successor candidate. He will retire in three years.

At this point, I still have no identified successor candidate who meets the profile, especially the age issue; so my basic successor problem remains unsolved. Our internal development programs are working, however, and by fall of this year I expect to be able to identify three forty to forty-five-year-olds, either corporate officers or division presidents, who have the potential to be serious successor candidates by 1990, when I will be sixty. In addition, if the opportunity to fill a senior-officer position from the outside arises, I will make as a prerequisite that the person have the basic qualifications to be a successor candidate. In the meanwhile, the existence of the Succession Program provides comfort for the board and has kept the issue in perspective.

I chose to tell the Ex-Cell-O story because, for many readers of this book, it is typical of their own situation. Many of my stories are drawn from larger and more glamorous household names, but for every one of those there are ten Ex-Cell-Os, and in each of those companies, the issues facing the CEO and his board are every bit as important as they are at GE or IBM.

Paul Casey currently holds the titles of chairman, president and CEO, and no board of directors of a publicly held company

EXHIBIT 2.8

**Ex-Cell-O Corporation • Succession Program
for Chief Executive Officer**

Goals

1. Establish and maintain an active and orderly succession program to have available no later than December, 1985, at least two inside candidates each of whom, in the opinion of E. Paul Casey (E.P.C.) and the board of directors, will be qualified to succeed E.P.C. as CEO when he vacates that position at his normal retirement age.

2. Establish a concurrent program to deal with an emergency that might arise before a qualified inside successor is ready.

Considerations

1. E.P.C. is fifty-two years old and in good health. An orderly succession would normally occur in about ten years.

2. No acceptable candidate from inside is now ready to succeed E.P.C. as part of an orderly succession program. However, it is not unreasonable to assume that his ultimate successor is now in the organization and with a development program would be a serious candidate by 1985.

3. An orderly succession program to prepare insiders is appropriate now. Later, if no acceptable candidate has surfaced, it will be appropriate to go outside.

4. Going outside at this point has a number of disadvantages:

    (a) It forecloses opportunity for advancement to the CEO for insiders who aspire to that position. Therefore, it would seriously weaken the corporate-wide Executive Continuity Program which emphasizes the development of internal managers.

    (b) It requires some commitment to an outsider before Ex-Cell-O has adequate direct knowledge of his qualifications.

    (c) Ten years is too long for any candidate who is ready now to be in the wings. Any good candidate won't wait that long.

    (d) A corporate strategic direction for Ex-Cell-O's future has not been developed. The existence of such a plan could influence the selection of a successor.

5. It is possible that a successor may be needed before one is ready under the program for orderly succession either because of E.P.C.'s accidental death or disability, or because he has lost the board's support. Accordingly, a concurrent program to provide for succession in an emergency is needed.

EXHIBIT 2.8 (continued)

**Ex-Cell-O Corporation • Succession Program
for Chief Executive Officer**

Orderly Succession Program

1. Establish a profile of the ideal candidate to succeed E.P.C.

2. Continuously identify and select for development those who have
   the potential to meet the criteria stated in the profile.

3. Establish an individualized development program to prepare each
   candidate for succession.

4. At least annually, evaluate each candidate and report on the status
   of the program to the nominating committee of the board.

Concurrent Succession Program to Deal with Emergency

1. Identify to the nominating committee someone in the organization
   who is a logical candidate to perform as interim CEO until a
   permanent CEO can be selected.

   (a) E.P.C. to keep him informed on all issues.

   (b) Involve him in as many matters as possible, especially
       personnel and board matters.

2. If possible, add to the board one or more outside members who
   could be logical candidates to become the CEO in an emergency.

likes to find itself in such a situation. As you might expect, this
situation is more common in smaller companies—and may be
more serious because there are fewer opportunities to develop a
strong cadre of managers at the next level.

   Casey knows that he "should" have a president standing in
the wings as his replacement. The obvious solution would be to
bring in a seasoned outsider, a few years older than he is, to fill
that role. Following that path would not conflict with his ambi-
tion to develop an internal successor, and meanwhile the board
of directors would be more comfortable with the situation.

   The directors of Ex-Cell-O know that Casey could probably
be persuaded to accept such a recommendation, and might even
rationalize it by explaining that as a solo CEO he is working too
hard and ought to share his load. On the other hand, Casey is in
his early fifties, a proven CEO, and at the peak of his career.

Further, the company is of manageable size (No. 308 in the *Fortune* 500 in 1984), and the decentralized structure of its business units does lessen the need for an immediate backup if something were to happen to Casey suddenly. Finally, the cost of having a president must be measured in terms other than just money; dividing Casey's current responsibilities would, in effect, create an additional layer in the management hierarchy, and might not contribute to running the business effectively.

There is no universal answer to this common dilemma. My own position, in this particular case, would be to continue to bet on Casey. He is aware of the risk to the corporation, and will no doubt continue to designate a temporary successor candidate. Further, selecting new directors with an eye to their suitability to become CEO in an emergency is an appealing tactic—particularly if it could be as successful as Mitchell's selection of Waldron at Avon. Basically, Casey has chosen to rely on his board to handle any unexpected succession problem, and that solution may just come with the turf of being a director in a company this size.

Summary

The selection of a new CEO from inside the company is a signal for the organization that no crisis is impending. There will be new leadership at the top, and of course there will be some changes, but nothing that could be considered a discontinuity. From the point of view of the board of directors, the selection of an insider as the new CEO is a job well done. The next generation is in place, and the board's preoccupation with succession prior to the decision is now relieved, at least for a few years. Even during the early years of the new CEO's tenure, however, the board will want to have a contingency plan. The degree of comfort provided by that plan is importantly affected by the top management structure in the company.

Each of the three stories above represents one of the three common modes of top management organization: team, duo, and solo. The board's comfort with its contingency plan is directly correlated with the number of corporate managers at the top. Team management offers the board two or more people to choose from in the event of an emergency; the solo CEO, at the other extreme, provides the board only with the CEO's recommendation on who his (temporary) successor ought to be. In that sense, the General Electric and Ex-Cell-O stories here are probably typical of current good practice.

Bill Schreyer's situation at Merrill Lynch, however, is not typical of the normal operation of the relay process of CEO succession. Roger Birk's early retirement is the exception, not the rule. In particular, when a new CEO is selected, the prior CEO usually continues to serve as chairman of the board of directors for a few years. Birk served in that role for only one year, thus putting considerable pressure on Schreyer and his board to find an heir apparent. Whether a retired CEO should continue to serve as chairman of the board is a controversial issue, and I will address it in chapter 7.

New CEOs from Outside

The decision to recruit a new CEO from outside the company is not taken lightly. The conventional wisdom in U.S. corporations today is that it is healthy to grow your own CEOs, for a variety of reasons. But sometimes, and particularly in smaller companies, that simply doesn't work. There may be no heir apparent, as in Ex-Cell-O, or the heir apparent may die prematurely, or depart to take a job with another company. In many situations, however, bringing in a new CEO from outside is a signal that major change is necessary and that no insider can bring the fresh perspective that is required.

The single most striking trend in CEO succession in the United States during the last twenty years is the frequency with which an outsider is appointed to that post. The results from our survey of the *Fortune* 1000 companies were interpreted using three definitions of "outsider" in terms of years of employment with the company before being appointed CEO. Using the broadest definition, prior employment of five years or less, the percentage of CEO appointments going to outsiders has tripled during this period. In the late 60s, only 9 percent of new CEOs were outsiders; by the early 80s, the percentage was 27 percent. The same rate of change has occurred for outsiders who were brought in only two or three years before becoming CEO. The message is clear for a career manager with twenty or twenty-five years of service: patience is less likely to be rewarded than it was in the good old days.

Bringing an outsider directly into the position of CEO is still very unusual: only 7.1 percent of new appointments occur in that fashion — usually in an overt crisis. Even in those situations, the new CEO was not always a stranger; of those direct CEO appointments, 16 percent were then serving as an outside member of the board of directors. Hicks Waldron at Avon is one example. Some of the others apparently illustrate Paul Casey's situation described above; when something unexpected happens to a solo CEO, a member of the board will step in for a brief period during the search for a successor.

The cost of bringing in an outsider is organizational disruption, as the board well knows. The story below describes that, and also illustrates how the new CEO and his board deal with the perennial issue of finding the next CEO.

Hicks Waldron at Avon

Hicks B. Waldron became the CEO of Avon in 1983. Then sixty, he spent the first twenty years of his career at GE. He was recruited into Heublein as president in 1973 and appointed CEO two years later. In late 1982, RJR Industries acquired Heublein and Waldron took a high-level job with RJR. The story below, based on our discussions in early 1984, focuses on his first six months at Avon, but also describes how he dealt with the issue of providing for his own succession. I encouraged Waldron to tell his story at some length because he has more accumulated experience in coming in from outside than most CEOs.

> *Dave Mitchell offered me the job in May 1983. I accepted it on August 1, and moved into the office in the middle of that month. The opportunity to once again become CEO of a major consumer marketing company was simply irresistible. Avon's stock price hit its all-time high of $140 a share in the halcyon days of 1973, and was trading just below $20 in mid-August of 1982 before the new*

bull market took off. It rose with that market to $37 in
June of 1983, and then began to drop again, touching its
low for the year in October, at $21.50. Nobody needed to
be convinced that there was something wrong. The world
had passed us by.

Mandate from the Board. Going in, the board
made no attempt to give me an explicit set of marching orders. Nevertheless, I felt that it was very important in that
first meeting with them to calibrate their expectations. I
didn't want them to think that I was arriving with some
magical elixir that would solve our problems immediately.
Avon was in crisis. There was no strategic plan, no sense
of direction. Put those two items together, and it meant
there was a lack of strong leadership. I would have to start
at square one. And Dave Mitchell backed me up on all of
those statements. He was terrific!

I defined my own mandate, in effect, by describing the
process I would follow in trying to come to grips with
these problems. First, I needed a total immersion in the
company, both to understand the business and, more importantly, to understand its people. I allotted nine weeks
for that purpose. Then, I would hole up somewhere and
sort it all out, defining both the strategic direction the
company should be following and the priority actions required to get us there. I would present that to the board in
its December meeting, and with their blessing, would announce it to the organization in early 1984. The board
understood that I could not honestly be more explicit than
that, and they wished me well.

Guidelines for Taking Over. Coming in as a
high-level outsider was not exactly a new experience for
me. I had done it at Heublein in 1973, when I joined that
company as president, and again in 1982 after Heublein
merged into RJR Industries, and I took over the Del Monte
businesses in that corporation. One lesson I learned from
those experiences is that it's very important to understand

the culture of each business that you're dealing with. In Heublein, for example, there was no particular culture at the corporate level, but there was a distinct culture in Kentucky Fried Chicken — and it was very different from the culture of the liquor business. Similarly, Avon had no corporate culture, but there were strong cultures in Avon's beauty business, its direct mail catalog business, Tiffany's jewelry business, and Mallinckrodt's chemical business. The cultures are different because the businesses are different, and if I'm trying to internalize what really makes a business tick, I find it useful to understand the way that people managing it think about it, the rules of thumb they use, and how they work together.

The other lesson I've learned about coming from outside is that it's very important to understand the people, identifying the strong ones, and trying to figure out who has what sort of power. Cleaning house is a messy business, and I've never had to do it. Heublein was growing rapidly when I came in, and Del Monte was very solid. Even Avon was profitable, if moribund, and I decided to use the management cadre that was on board. In fact, I only brought two people in from outside during those first few months: my strategic planning officer from Heublein, Bob Pratt, and my public relations officer from Reynolds, John Cox.

The third lesson I learned is the simplest one: never say, "Well, I spent twenty years at General Electric and the way we used to do it over there was. . . ." The people you say that to are already aware of your credentials, assume that you are adequately smart, and expect that you will provide unique solutions to their particular problems. In a way, it's like getting married for a second or third time. It's almost impossible not to do a certain amount of comparative analysis, but it's not good form to discuss that analysis with your new mate.

The Nine-Week Orientation. Following those simple rules, I then spent nine solid weeks talking —

really, listening—to anybody and everybody who might help me. Dave Mitchell continued as chairman during this period, thus relieving me from any day-to-day business responsibilities. I visited half of our manufacturing operations in the United States, and later made brief visits to Brazil, Mexico, and Great Britain. These trips provided the opportunity for in-depth reviews of each of our businesses. I made the trip alone or with the executive vice president in charge of the operation. In a typical all-day meeting on site, I would be exposed to about one hundred persons in that location, managers as far as three levels down into that organization. I also asked the closest regional sales manager to arrange a meeting with twenty of our Avon ladies who buy the products from us and sell them door to door. At the end of that round of visits, I concluded that our technical functions of manufacturing, distribution, and quality control were in very good shape and managed by competent people. Our problem was on the sales and marketing side, as I had expected.

The larger problem, I discovered, was even more fundamental: everywhere I went, people said to me, "If you do anything for us, please tell us which we are. Are we a direct sales organization, capable of peddling almost anything, or are we in the business of marketing beauty products?" In fact, of course, we were both at that time, but it was clear that we needed to make a strategic choice because continuing that combined strategy was no longer viable.

Filling the chinks in my schedule during those nine weeks, I also arranged to meet privately with each member of the board, and with the full array of professional service providers: commercial bankers, investment bankers, advertising agencies, CPAs, and lawyers. By the time I was through, I thought I had a pretty good grasp of the situation.

Live at Carnegie Hall. Bob Pratt had joined us in October, just as I was finishing my travels, to help put together the new strategic directions for the company. We covered the entire spectrum of issues, but the major problem was the domestic beauty business. I presented my analysis to the board of directors, and they had no trouble accepting my recommendations to make major changes in our core business.

Avon had been built almost like a paramilitary organization, with new recruits signing on at the bottom of that pyramid and rising to the top. Dave Mitchell's career was almost a stereotype of that. All those people were understandably apprehensive, waiting to hear what my conclusions were. To communicate the new priorities and strategies in an effective way, and to introduce myself in a proper forum, I decided to hold a mass meeting for all New York City employees and tape the event for all others. We did it in Carnegie Hall in January 1984.

The basic message was that we're now looking at the consumer rather than at our sales reps as being our customer. This is a major change. In the past we were "campaign-driven," with a new sales campaign every other week, introducing 250 new products a year. Now we are marketing- and product-driven, looking at things like market share, in both absolute and relative terms against our non-direct-selling competitors. Our strategy is that the Avon lady will continue to perform forever, but not enough to provide the growth that we ought to achieve. So, we'll keep that, but we won't try to overgrow it, thus saving money which will be spent improving the productivity of that force.

That message played pretty well in Carnegie Hall, and everyone was enthusiastic. But we all knew that the real question was, How do we get it to play equally well in Peoria? The 2,500 managers in that auditorium cheered, and then went home and began to develop the plans that could support the new strategies.

Changing the Culture. Late in 1983, I persuaded Spencer Stuart to come work with me as a personal consultant. I had known Spencer for many years, and he had retired from the executive recruiting firm he founded, but I managed to persuade him to give me a hand. I needed a confidant, someone I could talk to on a continuous basis, and you really can't use the board of directors for that role. To allow him to become acquainted with the key people at Avon, we agreed that he would conduct a "climate survey," to help identify some of the issues that needed to be dealt with, given the massive change in mindset that would be required of many of our managers. During the next several months he interviewed more than fifty of our key executives, and I promised each of them that their comments would be held in strict confidence by him. I think it was useful for them to have someone that they could talk to safely, voicing some of their concerns about the direction and pace of change at Avon. Subsequently, he issued a feedback report on his generalized findings, and we used it for discussion in our corporate management committee of the nine top executives that report directly to me.

I found that having a confidant like Spencer was extremely useful. We would meet frequently with no particular agenda. He has very good ears, in terms of listening to the people that he was meeting with, and is very insightful. Some part of what he did was to validate my own appraisal of some of the executives, and he was also helpful on the issue of providing for my successor.

Providing for Succession. Dave Mitchell stepped down as chairman in December 1983, leaving me with all three titles. The board had a right to be concerned about the succession issue, particularly because we knew that we could not expect Dave to come back in the event that something happened to me unexpectedly. But the board was even more concerned that I devote my full efforts to saving the company first so that it would have the need for someone to succeed me. I actually got more pressure from the security analysts on Wall Street than I did from my own board about the fact that there was no one standing by to back me up.

One of the first things I did when Mitchell moved out was to move into his office and convert the president's office into a conference room. This physical message to the organization was not misunderstood: There is no uncertainty about who is president of Avon; it's Waldron. The more subtle message was that I was in no hurry to name a president, so everybody ought to keep their nose to the grindstone. In fact, I did need a successor because I had too much work to do.

Spencer and I defined three alternative solutions to that problem. First, we could persuade a retired executive from another company to join Avon as president and chief operating officer, or perhaps as chairman, with me holding the titles of president and CEO. The second alternative was to recruit someone a few years younger than me who could become president immediately and ultimately succeed me for a tenure of his own as CEO of four to six years. The third alternative would be to find some young superstar in his late forties or early fifties to come in as president and take over as CEO when I retired.

We finally chose the second option, believing that it was best for the organization. I did want to develop a lot of the younger managerial talent in Avon, and was reluctant to close off the top for some of our comers that were in their late forties. Spencer Stuart Associates came up with the precise person: Jack Chamberlin, whom I had worked with at GE, agreed to become president of Avon early in 1985. The current plan is for me to retire in 1988, when I turn sixty-five. At that point, or a little before, Chamberlin will be fifty-nine and will become CEO. Also at that time or shortly after, we hope that we will be able to identify an internal candidate who can become president under Chamberlin and eventually the CEO of Avon. The bottom line is that we have resolved our succession problem for the moment, the board is happy about that, and we are working hard to develop a cadre of contenders,

*one of whom will be named president under Chamberlin
and, we hope, become the next CEO of Avon.*

        Commentary. Avon was nearing a crisis, but Waldron's experience gave him the confidence to move fast, presenting his board with a new strategic direction just four months after taking office. Experience aside, he could not have moved quite so fast if he had not been a director for three prior years. He knew the directors well enough to present a detailed agenda at his first board meeting as CEO.

        The three lessons Waldron described near the beginning of his comments are probably applicable in most situations where a new CEO comes in from outside. Beyond that, it is dangerous to generalize from a single experience. Certainly, his pace was too fast for most new outsiders. On the other hand, his initial focus on strategic analysis is consistent with the general hypothesis that an outsider's mandate is to make strategic changes. Only after he knew where he was going could he then unveil his vision of the future of Avon and the actions needed to make it a reality.

        I have seen the videotape of Waldron's performance in Carnegie Hall, and watching it was an emotionally moving experience. He addressed, head-on, the inevitable anxieties of that group of managers, and the only word to describe the impact he had is "leadership." He has turned Avon around now, divesting some businesses and acquiring others, and the future looks bright.

Managing Expectations

The new CEO, insider or outsider, is thrust immediately into the spotlight. There *is* a honeymoon — a period of forbearance — because almost everyone involved is rooting for the new CEO, hoping he can lead the organization to great success. Those early months are crucial ones.

        I think there are some lessons to be learned from the stories told above — simple lessons that may have some value for members of the board, the new CEO, and the group of senior managers that work with him. The focal point, I believe, is cast in terms of expectations. What do the directors and senior officers need and expect from the new CEO? And, reciprocally, what does the new CEO need from them?

Needs of the Board of Directors

First and foremost, the directors need confirmation of their collective wisdom in selecting the new CEO. The mandate from the board is frequently not explicit, particularly for a CEO promoted from inside. The directors, instead, expect the new CEO to define his own agenda, reflecting his leadership, and to present it to the board for validation. How quickly this is done depends on the circumstances, of course, but we see it occurring quite early for Waldron, a new CEO from outside. The intent, under any circumstances, is for the new CEO and his board to have a shared understanding of what will be accomplished during the first year or two. Time-phased milestones and/or near-term projections of financial performance will allow the board to calibrate the ability of the CEO to deliver on what he promises.

Secondarily, but very early, the board needs to have some sort of a plan to deal with the contingency of the disability or death of the new CEO. As discussed earlier, in some situations, such as at General Electric and Ex-Cell-O, a contingency plan is all that is needed. In other situations, there is a real need for the CEO to act more or less quickly to identify an heir apparent. In Bill Schreyer's situation at Merrill Lynch, he moved quite rapidly; Hicks Waldron at Avon had to save the company before finding a new president and heir apparent.

Needs of the Senior Officers

Power—and careers—are at stake among the senior officer group when a new CEO takes over, whether he is from inside or outside. The new CEO is well aware of the inevitable anxiety, and again the issue is one of pace. An insider is able to move faster, as Schreyer did in his first three months, to outline his new team. An outsider will, and should, take more time to get acquainted with his new colleagues. Unless there is an extreme crisis, a new CEO from outside will frequently make it clear that he plans no major organizational changes for a year or so, thus giving everyone a chance to take a deep breath.

Needs of the New CEO

Aware of these needs of his officers and directors, the new CEO needs to manage their expectations about what will evolve. He needs to coalesce his team of senior managers as quickly as he can—but not precipitously. He needs to build trust with the board of directors so that he may increasingly count on its approving his recommendations. His best path for meeting these needs is substantive: He must embrace his role as chief strategist, and within the first year or so, produce a strategic blueprint for his tenure. The entire organization wants to know what the CEO's vision of the future is and how he expects to get there. If he can't provide that, no one else can. When and if he does provide it, everyone can adjust his or her expectations about what lies ahead.

Summing up, almost any CEO must face three critical tasks early in his tenure: (1) managing the expectations of his officers and directors; (2) taking ownership of the strategic thrust of the corporation during his tenure; and (3) building confidence among all parties by achieving an initial, realistic set of performance goals in his first year or two.

3

CEO Tenure: Two Dilemmas

Hey! This is fun! In your first two years as CEO you've taken
hold, strategically and organizationally. There have been
few surprises, and no disasters. This is a *good job*. You could do
it forever. Well . . . you are mortal, but let's not think about that
right now.

But we must think about it now; the chronology of CEO
succession demands it, because the prospective retirement date
of the incumbent CEO is the primary variable pacing the succession process. Having survived the first two years, you will probably continue to serve as CEO until your mandatory retirement
date—if you want to. The benefit of doing some early, private
thinking about your tenure is simply that you have more options
now than you will have later. Now, you can control the pace of
events and, if you handle it well, the remainder of your career.

You realize how seductive your job can be. The operative
word is "power," although you avoid using that word in polite
company. Still, the buck does stop here, and you must admit that
you've come to relish the soul-searching analysis that precedes a
major decision. There are some shots that only you can call. That
responsibility, plus the trappings of power that go with it, means
that you will stay until the end—whenever that occurs.

Focus of this Chapter

The participants at my CEO succession seminars set their own
agenda at the beginning, and inevitably we spent more time talking about CEO tenure than any other topic. In part, this was
because of the composition of the group; nearly all the participants were incumbent CEOs and each of them knew he was facing a decision at some future point. But the tenure issue also
turned out to be an integral part of other topics we tried to discuss
separately, particularly when to name an heir apparent and how
to handle the transition from then until retirement. My overall

assessment of those discussions was that the participants were not concerned about protecting their own tenure as much as they were about trying to discern the right way to handle it.

This chapter addresses three topics related to CEO tenure. Two of them were discussed in the seminars and one was not. The first topic was usually stated as a question: What is the proper length of tenure for a CEO? In each seminar, the incumbents' tenure ranged from less than three years to more than fifteen. The best discussion occurred in April 1985. Don Perkins, then fifty-eight, was three years into his second career as an independent director, having resigned as CEO at Jewel after ten years in office. At the other end of the spectrum we had Dick Gelb, then sixty-one, who had served thirteen years as CEO at Bristol-Myers and was still four years from retirement. (Phil Barach set the record: at fifty-five, he had already been CEO of U. S. Shoe Company for seventeen years, and was still ten years from retirement.) The argument was friendly, but intense. Paul Casey, CEO of Ex-Cell-O Corp., whose own position was somewhere between the two extremes, summed up the issue as follows: "A CEO who has served for ten years and still has, say, seven years to retirement, is faced with a personal dilemma. On the one hand, he has to admit that there is some virtue to the argument for 'fresh eyes.' On the other hand, the only way that fresh eyes can be obtained is for him to step down at great personal cost."

The second topic we discussed zeroed in on those personal costs, trying to identify the various elements involved and ways the costs might be mitigated. This topic is examined in the second section below under the title "Barriers to Exit," and reappears in chapter 7 as part of the discussion relating to the CEO's transition to retirement.

The final topic discussed in this chapter is, I think, the most important one, even though it was never raised during the seminars. Phrased as a question, the issue is: At what point should the tenure of an incumbent CEO be truncated because of poor performance? Not all CEOs are superstars; some of them must be more or less mediocre. The incumbent CEOs at my seminars did not even want to think about mediocrity, much less discuss it in a group. This issue can pose a major dilemma for the board of directors: should you live with the mediocre devil you know, or hire a new devil and hope he turns out to be a superstar? I don't have a pat answer to that question, but I'll discuss the issue in terms of roles and responsibilities for senior officers and directors.

CEO Tenure: The Theory and the Facts

The April 1985 seminar convinced me that I should write a book on the subject, and it then took us eight months to produce the data base on CEO succession. In the interim, I asked Don Perkins and Dick Gelb to write a formal argument defending their position on the question of long-tenured CEOs. Each of them produced a thoughtful, persuasive essay, presented below.

Don Perkins at Jewel: Ten Years is Enough

I decided at the beginning of my tenure as chairman and CEO of Jewel to limit my term to ten years. I had been fortunate to have become president of Jewel at age thirty-seven, and the question of what was right for Jewel and for me was in my thoughts during the six years before I became chairman and CEO. I'll try to recall my thoughts at that time.

My predecessors had set an example. Frank Lunding had voluntarily stepped aside in his late fifties to make way for George Clements and me. George made a similar decision in his early sixties because he felt I was ready to be chairman and Wes Christopherson, president. Their decisions presented me with unusual opportunities. With appreciation for what they had done it seemed natural for me to consider the wisdom of being in the chairman's role for the twenty-two years that remained until age sixty-five.

I could not have made a case for ten years as opposed to eight or twelve . . . the number was not as important as the idea. I have always believed that organizations were stronger when they were periodically revitalized with new and typically younger leadership. It seemed to me that one way to repay Jewel for providing me with extraordinary and early opportunities would be to work diligently on the development of successor management and help them to be in place. I was guessing that that could be done in a decade. As I thought about the subject it wasn't difficult to observe more companies being hurt by CEOs who stayed too long than by those who stayed too short. My personal sense of responsibility to Jewel and to myself required that I never be caught in the "too long" category.

Retailing is a business requiring young people with high energy. Retailing flourishes on innovative ideas. A retail company usually succeeds or fails based upon its ability to attract younger generations of customers to replace the natural loss of older ones. Jewel had had a pattern of young CEOs and COOs taking over in their thirties and forties. While Jewel was becoming a much larger company there was a common feeling among top management that such an approach should be perpetuated. Although I was succeeded by Wes Christopherson who was two years older, we both focused on the development of management talent who would be in their forties or thirties when my ten years were completed. Dick Cline was forty-five when he became president in 1980.

Having personally spent considerable time and effort recruiting and developing young Jewel talent I did not want to contribute to the departure of the very best of them. Subtracting my age from sixty-five would have been discouraging to their chances to hold one of the several top corporate posts.

I had observed in others and expected to find in myself some very human CEO traits from which I hoped Jewel could be spared. There are few people who are as challenged in the tenth year they look at an annual budget as they are the first year. Similarly, old but important questions, the answers to which a long-term CEO thought about early in his tenure, have a tendency to keep coming up. They are more likely to be revisited under new leadership . . . and times do change!

Of course I also knew that it was all too human to feel that the ten-year idea was a great thought at the beginning *of the decade but to expect to have increasing doubts about the wisdom of it as the years passed. From the beginning, I was so convinced of the desirability of turning over the leadership of Jewel after ten years that I told the board and a number of senior managers of my intention. As the decade progressed, I began to make my personal plans to stay busy subsequently. Many who heard me doubted that I would stick to my plan but those who knew me best were not surprised. The Jewel board probably would have questioned the extent of my outside involvements during the last year or two of the decade had they not understood my intentions and my plans to stay busy rather than retire after 1980.*

Now, looking back and drawing on my experiences on several boards, it seems to me that few decisions in corporate life are more subjective than that of a CEO's retirement. He may decide to retire early, or to work to an exact retirement age. Or, he may decide that no one could do a better job, thus requiring continuation beyond an expected retirement age. In my personal experience the principal factor weighing on that subjective judgment often has less to do with the loss of salary and perquisites and more to do with fear connected with the ending of a career and all that that means in terms of personal challenge and satisfaction. For some it may seem like an admission of mortality. Those of us lucky enough to enjoy additional careers (or as Arjay Miller says, be "repotted") have less of a problem in this regard. This reality suggests why a decade or so may be an attractive time frame, most particularly for those who start the ten years at an early enough age.

Dick Gelb at Bristol-Myers: It All Depends

After further reflection on our discussion of CEO tenure, plus a little research, I came away with the strong conviction that there is no simple answer. Any general rules about the optimum time for an individual to be CEO of a large U.S. corporation will be invalid most of the time. The right solution for each company depends on its own distinctive situation, and arriving at that solution takes a high degree of common sense and pragmatism—not rules. Both the facts and my own observations suggest an answer to the CEO tenure issue that is clear but not simple: It all depends.

As I see it, those who argue for numerical limitations on CEO tenure overlook a host of other variables that bear on the decision to change CEOs. Typically, no one of these variables is controlling—it is the combination that determines the decision.

The Complexity and Diversity of the Corporation. Complex corporations have two characteristics quite distinct from those in a single business (such as Jewel Tea). First, the CEO of a complex, multidivision company cannot be as deeply involved in the details of each business—it is a physical and mental impossibility. Thus, the complex-company CEO's central task is to be a leader of leaders, creating and communicating a sense of the mission and values that guide the company, and building and maintaining a culture within which highly talented people will thrive. The CEO is a value leader, a creator of meanings, and a developer and selector of people rather than an operator of the business. The complex-company CEO also has more time to think, to study the internal and external environment, and to adapt and change.

In contrast, the CEO of the large, monolithic company tends to be the hands-on operator, deeply involved in the day-to-day business. In my view, he is more subject to both tunnel vision in the face of industry change, and to burnout in the heat of battle—which could argue for more frequent change.

Second, in the diverse corporation, middle and upper management have many more opportunities for promotion and development experiences, most importantly in general management positions. A large number of executives can be "CEOs" of their individual businesses, and through both structural change and reassignment of key people, new opportunities and new learning experiences can occur throughout a career and stimulate individual executives of high competence without their ever becoming corporate CEOs. In fact, since at most only three or four individuals can become CEO of a company within a generation, companies with many qualified executives should focus on the general management of major businesses as the ultimate career goal, rather than excessively emphasizing the corporate CEO as the only winner in the executive race. I also believe that, in complex companies, division presidents should typically change jobs more frequently than the CEO, for two reasons: to further their development, and to avoid the risk of burnout inherent in operating the same business too long.

Finally, the diverse company is dependent on a team of highly skilled executives if it is to be successful in the long term. No one individual can determine the success of our largest organizations, while one person may have ultimate impact in the single business or monolithic company.

Business Strengths and Competitive Position. If a company is the leader in its field and has an organization with the vitality to retain that position over the years, the need for new CEO leadership is clearly less than in a company which requires shake-up, a turnaround, or a dramatic redirection of its businesses in order to succeed financially or compete effectively. To put it simply, good companies need CEO change less than companies that are mediocre or worse.

Organizational and Human Characteristics, Requirements and Constraints. NUMBER OF QUALIFIED CANDIDATES. Obviously, if a company has no qualified candidates, it should take whatever time is required to develop one or more—assuming the current CEO is competent. In contrast, if there is but a single candidate, and he is likely to leave if not promoted, there may be a good case for accelerating succession to a time prior to the normal retirement of the incumbent CEO. But even in these cases, the board of directors must carefully weigh the decision to promote a new CEO against the loss of his predecessor's talents and possible disruption to the corporate culture.

On the other hand, if there is a large number of qualified candidates, a company could either decide to act within a reasonable time frame to promote one to the CEO position and do the best it can to retain the others, or it might make a particular effort to seek out exciting new opportunities for all of these candidates to contribute as members of the top management team for a much longer period, avoiding the risk of losing many by promoting one. Following the latter course naturally requires that a very strong CEO be in place. Certainly it is an option that a good number of companies have pursued successfully (e.g., Citicorp, General Electric).

THE AGE MIX OF SENIOR MANAGEMENT. If a highly qualified successor CEO of age sixty-one or sixty-two is available at the time the predecessor CEO should be stepping down, and if there are several potentially qualified younger executives also in the company, it is a very rational choice to appoint the older executive for three or four years as a transition CEO. This gives the senior executive time to make an impact on the company and to further develop, test, and train the younger executives before making a selection among them.

In contrast, if an outstanding candidate is available at age forty-five, it makes no sense whatever to preclude the possibility of that individual's continuing to be CEO up to age sixty-five. Many executives do not seek a second career, as did Don Perkins; and many have sustained an outstanding culture for two decades or even more.

THE CULTURE AND STYLE OF THE COMPANY. If a company has established a policy of always promoting from within and of appointing a new CEO every half-decade or so, so that that pattern is built into the expectations of the senior management group, the board of directors might be wise to stay with that policy. In contrast, those that are accustomed to long-term CEO tenures probably do not require rapid CEO turnover—their executives are attuned to more gradual change. Perhaps more important, companies with a culture that puts top emphasis on teamwork and collaboration versus competition and confrontational management will tend to thrive under a highly effective leader for a long period of time, while the latter type of culture may require more frequent change at the CEO level as well as in other key corporate positions.

CEO EFFECTIVENESS. The most important organizational variable of all is the effectiveness of the incumbent CEO. If a CEO is not changing with the times or developing an organization that is able to adapt, innovate, and respond to new technologies, market conditions, and competitive initiatives, he should step down or be eased out over a short time by the board of directors. If he continues to be effective as a leader, and not only gains and maintains the respect of his organization but also motivates them to effort beyond the ordinary, the board should hesitate before encouraging him to leave prior to normal retirement.

Summary. In brief, perhaps the most important variable to consider in deciding on the length of CEO tenure is simply how well the whole thing is working. In the best companies, there is frequently a strong case for long continuity of CEO leadership, but, as earlier noted, relatively shorter continuity of the many leadership jobs below that level. If things are not working well, it is obvious that the board should reevaluate the incumbent CEO regardless of his tenure, since it is essential to provide the major cultural redirection that is required to turn around a mediocre or floundering company.

> *Perhaps I was wrong at the outset. Perhaps there is a*
> *simple answer: It all depends on common sense. I rather*
> *like the way Abe Lincoln put it when giving his answer to*
> *the question of how long a man's legs should be: "They*
> *should be just long enough to reach the ground."*

A Few Facts About Tenure

The comments by Perkins and Gelb are not really in conflict. Perkins is making a personal statement about his successful career, and extrapolating from that to recommend it as a useful model for others. Gelb's statement is a sensitive analysis of the situational variables that should be considered in deciding on the tenure of a CEO. Both statements were written without the benefit of the demographic data I will now use to shed some further light on the issue. I will then discuss the more general issue of establishing a retirement date for an incumbent CEO.

Capping the CEO's Tenure. In the seminar, the argument between Perkins and Gelb was honest and intense, but reduced to its essence, the issue is whether to establish a maximum tenure for a CEO. In all three seminars, a consensus emerged on that issue, although we took no vote. We could not get an agreement on a specific number of years, but most participants agreed "ten years, plus or minus two" was about right. At the other end of the tenure spectrum, there was unanimity that too short a tenure could be an even greater threat to the corporation; the minimum tenure for a new CEO should be at least five years. My own position, during the first two seminars, was on the side of the structuralists: *why not* have a maximum tenure? The prospective benefits are clear, while the prospective costs (losing an effective, mature CEO), are less certain. Subsequently, after analyzing the data on length of tenure, I changed my mind.

The first thing to be said about establishing a maximum term for CEO tenure is that it is simply not necessary for the great majority of companies. For the entire population of newly appointed CEOs, only 12.8 percent have a tenure that lasts more than twelve years, and only 6.5 percent have a tenure that exceeds fifteen years. One way of interpreting the consensus in the seminars was that the participants were comfortable with the idea of limiting tenure to a span of eight to twelve years because their own tenure would fall into that range. My current belief is that the concern for CEOs whose tenure is "too long" is over-blown, fed by the publicity awarded to a few "curmudgeons," such as Bill Paley at CBS or Peter Grace at W. R. Grace. We hear less about CEOs like Dick Gelb and Phil Barach, who have managed their companies for nearly two decades with remark-able effectiveness.

Departure Routes. Taking a more comprehensive look at the history of CEO tenure over the last twenty-five years produces the graph shown in Exhibit 3.1. For the entire popula-tion of CEOs appointed between 1960 and 1984 whose length of

EXHIBIT 3.1

Tenure (in Years) of CEOs Appointed 1960—1984

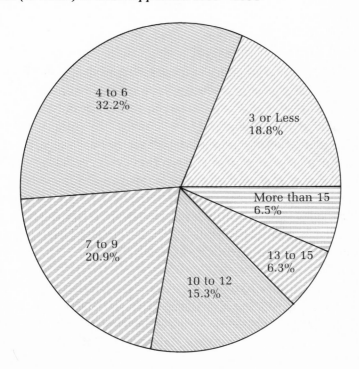

EXHIBIT 3.2

CEO Careers: Departure Routes · Percentage of CEOs
Assigned to Each Route

Departure Route	Percent
1. Mandatory retirement	47.2
2. Early retirement policy	12.4
"Normal" retirements	59.6
3. Replacement CEO	9.0
4. Late-appointment CEO	6.7
"Normal" tenures	75.3
5. Curmudgeon	4.0
"Successful" tenures	79.3
6. Early failure	4.8
7. Two-career CEO	6.2
8. Other departures	9.7
Total	100.0

tenure is known, the graph shows how long they served as CEO before stepping down or retiring. Trying to get behind that macro data, I asked myself: What are the prevailing circumstances at the time that an incumbent CEO relinquishes his title? Pulling on that thread, I defined seven "departure routes," each of which describes the "career" of a CEO in that category. This classification system is not perfect, but as shown in Exhibit 3.2, it does allow me to label 90 percent of the CEOs in our population. Departure Route 8 is a catch-all category. I will first describe each career briefly (for more detail see Appendix A, Exhibit A.3), and then analyze the implications of these data.

1. *Mandatory Retirement.* This is the most common career for a CEO. Stepping down at age sixty-five is mandatory in many companies, and frequently CEOs will relinquish that title two or three years earlier. This career includes

CEOs who relinquish the title between ages sixty-two and sixty-six, regardless of whether they continue to serve as chairman or on the board of directors.

2. *Early Retirement Policy.* Some companies have explicit policies or established traditions that encourage a CEO to step down at age sixty, while permitting him to serve as the chairman of the board or simply as a director. This career includes those CEOs who retire under such conditions between age fifty-six and sixty-one, after serving a tenure of four years or more.

3. *Replacement CEO.* When a CEO resigns completely from the company at age sixty-one or earlier, the planning for an orderly succession may not be far enough along to provide a permanent successor. A common practice under these conditions is to appoint a replacement to serve for a period of three years or less while a permanent successor is selected. CEOs classified under this career are those who serve three years or less, and were appointed at age fifty-eight or more.

4. *Late-Appointment CEO.* Some CEOs are appointed rather late in their careers and may serve a normal tenure even though they stay on past the mandatory retirement date. The criteria for this career are a tenure of four years or more, not to exceed twelve years, and retirement at age sixty-seven or more.

5. *Curmudgeons.* Some CEOs refuse to retire prior to age sixty-seven and may stay on for various lengths of time after that. If their tenure was more than twelve years in length, I classify them as curmudgeons. This career does not include replacements who previously served as CEO and then returned for a short stint until a new successor was named.

6. *Early Failure.* Some newly appointed CEOs don't last very long. I assume that those appointed CEO before age fifty-eight who resign from that position in three years or less failed to meet the expectations of their senior officers and directors and were asked to depart (or to resign for "health" reasons).

7. *Two-Career CEOs.* Don Perkins typifies this career, a CEO who has served in that office for four years or more and retires at age fifty-five or earlier.
8. *Other Departures.* This is a catch-all category comprising CEOs who step down from that post between age fifty-six and sixty-one, and resign completely from the company, serving neither as chairman nor as a director. It also includes CEOs who die in office, and whose tenure and age-at-retirement did *not* qualify them as curmudgeons. Some such CEOs may be embarking on a second career; others may be resigning for health reasons, but it is also possible that some such departures are caused by mediocre performance and are initiated by the board of directors.

Assessment. Defining these seven careers required some apparently arbitrary criteria, but I was guided by the dozens of succession diagrams I have studied. Imprecise as it may be, this classification permits us to focus on specific situations regarding tenure rather than deal simply with generalities. I make no particular claim for the accuracy of the number of CEOs in each career, but as an order of magnitude, the quantification does help us to understand the frequency with which such situations occur.

Looking again at the subtotals in Exhibit 3.2, I find it comforting that 60 percent of the CEOs take normal retirement. Further, I characterize replacement or late-appointment CEOs as having normal tenures because when they were named to the position their boards knew rather precisely when they would retire. Curmudgeons are a special case because I assume that their performance is good, even though they can create a lot of heartbreak in their boards in the later years. I classify them as having a successful tenure, even if some people think it too long.

That leaves us with 20 percent of the CEOs that—at a maximum—could be classified as failures, and we know that some of the two-career CEOs were very successful, twice. We also know that many of the "other departures" are caused by health problems. My guess is that the failure rate for CEOs, defined as being asked to resign from office, is about 10 percent. Whether you think that's good or bad depends on whether you're an optimist or a pessimist. I'm an optimist.

Setting a Retirement Date. The data we gathered in our survey demonstrate that the "right" tenure for a CEO is determined, in practice, by determining the "right" age for the next person to be appointed CEO. My interpretation of the data below is that many companies have an implicit policy designed to ensure that the tenure of a CEO falls in a fairly narrow band, between eight and twelve years.

Exhibit 3.3 depicts the mean tenure for our population of companies, cross-tabulated by the age of the new CEO when he was appointed. The trend line inevitably falls from left to right, because older CEOs simply do not live long enough to stay in office as long as someone twenty years younger. A clearer pattern emerges, however, when we graph data only for the CEOs who did serve their full term, resigning as a mandatory date approached. That group, comprising 47 percent of the population, shows a much clearer picture in Exhibit 3.4. For that group, departure route 1, the median age of a newly appointed CEO was fifty-six, and 50 percent of the new CEOs fell within the range of fifty-four to fifty-eight years. Departure route 2, which reflects a policy of early retirement, yields similar results (not displayed here). The median age of new CEOs in that group was fifty-one, and 38 percent of the new CEOs fell in the range between forty-nine and fifty-three.

Given these data, it appears to me that the prescription offered by the participants in my seminars is, in fact, the reality in current practice. On an after-the-fact basis, I can say that a newly appointed CEO will ultimately depart using one of seven routes, but I can also say that at the date of appointment, the expected route would be to step down at the end of a normal tenure. This means, in fact, there is an expected retirement date for every new CEO when he is appointed.

Such expectations do not always come to pass, of course, and in our population 25 percent of newly appointed CEOs exited via a route other than a normal tenure. Some resigned, sooner or

E X H I B I T 3 . 3

Tenure as CEO by Age at Appointment

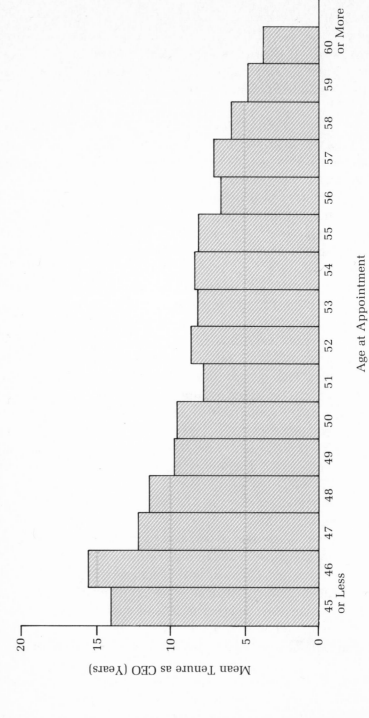

EXHIBIT 3.4

Tenure as CEO by Age at Appointment/Mandatory Retirement CEOs

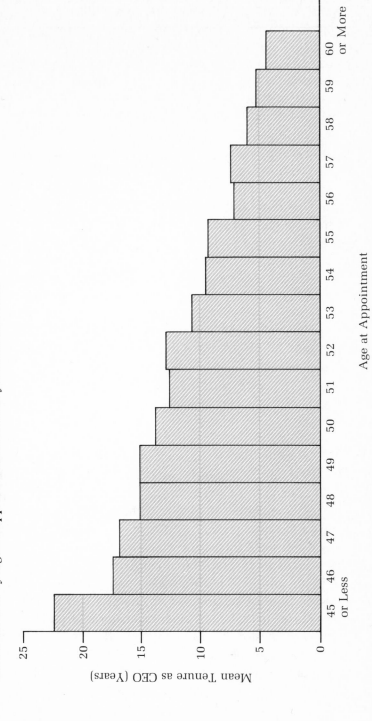

85

later, because of poor performance; some resigned to pursue a second career; some resigned because of ill health or died in office; and some simply refused to resign when the appointed date came around. The message is that succession planning is, inevitably, a contingent exercise.

The final, crucial step in setting a retirement date rests in the hands of the incumbent CEO. Early in his tenure, the expected retirement date is simply "out there," defined by policy or tradition, but never mentioned, because it is so distant. During those early years, as discussed in chapter 2, a committee of the board works with the CEO to develop a contingency plan in the event that something unexpected happens to him. By mid-tenure, however, a sensitive CEO begins to recognize that his officers and directors need a more explicit plan for the succession process. He knows that the implicit question (will he retire as scheduled?) will soon become explicit, particularly from his directors, and a forthcoming CEO retains the initiative by simply announcing that he expects to stay until he retires at age sixty-five. The die has now been cast, and the succession process that follows is likely to be smooth and effective because the CEO has taken charge of managing it.

Miscellaneous Comments. Three other items on the general topic of CEO tenure deserve brief comment. First, the data presented above have an important implication for aspiring CEOs. Many companies appear to manage CEO tenure by selecting a new CEO who is the "right" age. If you are the wrong age, that might not seem fair—and many exceptions *are* made—but you may want to review your own career planning if you are caught in the middle. The "right age" phenomenon is real; as we shall see in the last section of this chapter, Earl Barnes at Dow was "too close" to the age of the incumbent CEO, and was passed over. In the RCA story told in chapter 5, the chairman told Rick Miller he was "the right age" to become the next CEO. Your age is a fact in your life, and you might as well face up to it.

Second, in my conversations with incumbent CEOs, several of them have mentioned the danger of becoming a lame duck if they announce their retirement date too early. The issue is mainly a red herring. In the U.S. political system, a second-term president is not eligible to run for reelection and, near the end of his term, his political power does wane because he cannot repay current support on one issue with future favors on another. A CEO with a mandatory retirement date and an heir apparent in place, is not a lame duck in the same sense—and certainly not in the early years of his heir apparent's tenure. The primary difference is that the board of directors may extend the incumbent CEO beyond his normal retirement, if they think the heir apparent is not suitable. Passing the baton, by transferring responsibilities to the heir apparent, is very desirable, but it does not really affect the CEO's power. His tenure is not over until it's over—or more precisely, it's not over until he publicly announces the name of his successor. Then, there may be an interregnum, analogous to the two-and-a-half-month delay in the U.S. presidential process, when the retiring CEO really is a lame duck.

Finally, a caveat. In this section I've focused quite narrowly on the tenure of the CEO, with special concern for CEOs having a long tenure. A broader, and more appropriate, view would be to look at the CEO's entire career. In our population, the median new CEO has worked for the company for more than twenty years, including a stint as president before becoming CEO and a few years as chairman or as a director after he steps down. But the success of a corporate enterprise rests heavily on the *cadre* of managers who work with the CEO. Bill LaMothe at Kellogg (chapter 5), is a good example: he will end up serving eight or nine years as CEO, but a total of nearly twenty years as a member of the top management organization.

CEO Tenure: Exit Barriers

My analysis concludes that, for the majority of CEOs, actual tenure conformed to expectations when the appointment was made. Even for these normal tenures, however, the precise timing of the incumbent's departure can cause significant, albeit temporary, trauma. For these CEOs, the pervasive dilemma is whether to continue in office until the normal retirement date or to relinquish the CEO title two or three years earlier than expected. That issue might seem rather petty to some readers, but in each of my seminars, it was a topic of lively debate. Second only to the issue of tenure itself, and clearly related, were the questions, "When should a CEO relinquish his title?" and "When should he sever his ties with the company completely?"

Stepping Down; Stepping Out

The two questions are, obviously, related. Stepping down means continuing to serve as chairman of the board (or occasionally, chairman of the executive committee). In our population of CEOs with normal retirements, 44 percent did stay on as chairman for a mean term of 2.3 years. Stepping out means that the incumbent CEO resigned as a full-time employee of the company, although he may have continued to serve as a member of the board. The 56 percent of our CEOs with normal retirement who stepped out usually did so at the expected retirement date. The linkage between the two steps is that CEOs who step down must eventually also step out.

Stepping down is common practice because it is the final step in the process of passing the baton. Taking that step, however, is not without psychic cost to the incumbent CEO. One of the participants in my seminars who had recently relinquished the CEO title but was still chairman described his situation as follows. "Being chairman but not CEO is like being a sprig of parsley on a plate of fish." The new CEO, on the other hand, may also feel some pain. He is ready to get on with his own tenure, and may feel constrained about proposing new initiatives or disposing of past mistakes while his predecessor who was responsible for those sins is still in the room, and, nominally, running the meeting. The pros and cons of stepping down are examined in more detail in chapter 7.

Stepping out, either at the expected retirement date or earlier, is a radical solution to those problems, and it may create a temporary discontinuity at the top. Stepping out early is particularly uncommon in companies using the relay process, and when it occurs, it may signal a personal conflict between the incumbent and his heir apparent. In companies using the team mode of top management organization, the most typical practice is for the chairman/CEO to step down and out as a single event. In that situation, the incumbent may not step out early, because by doing so he loses a few years of peak conpensation that he would have retained if he had only stepped down. I will refer to the costs incurred by the incumbent, who must agree, if not initiate, his own early retirement, as exit barriers — impediments that may delay an earlier transfer of the CEO title.

For an incumbent CEO thinking about the prospects of stepping out early, the nonfinancial barriers are formidable. First, the perquisites that come with the CEO's office are comfortable and seductive; it's more than simply having a limousine or a G2 at your beck and call, it's the pampering in general that creates a matchless ambience. Second, the status of office also entitles the CEO to membership in a select peer group; joining an organization such as the Business Roundtable is not only exhilarating, but also provides a broad set of useful contacts. A third exit barrier, not often discussed, but important in some situations, is that these perquisites and status are shared by the "First Lady," the wife of the CEO. If her husband steps out early, she steps out with him. Fourth, if the CEO has not started to plan for his own retirement, stepping down early simply increases the number of years in which he must find something else to do. The specter of unemployment is a nontrivial exit barrier. The largest barrier to exit, however, is simply the power of the CEO office and the fun and sense of achievement that goes with it. Walking away from all that, voluntarily, is not a natural act. If you take that set of barriers and then add to it the financial dimension, discussed below, it's amazing that any CEO steps out early.

The Money Value of Time

At the seminars, the participants didn't want to discuss the linkage between compensation and tenure. Even though I raised it each time, it was a taboo subject, something to be kept in a closet along with the specter of mediocre CEOs. But in my private interviews with CEOs, a few I knew well admitted that the loss of compensation was an important factor in appraising the pros and cons of voluntary early retirement. Some CEOs do retire early, and others might do it if the financial penalty were reasonable. On the basis of those conversations, I decided to do a rough calculation of the monetary cost of "buying" a few of the best years of the rest of your life.

For this analysis, the primary variables are cash compensation (salary, bonus, and long-term incentive payments) while employed and pension income when retired. For simplicity, I will ignore other fringe benefits, such as payroll savings plans and group life and health insurance coverages. I will also ignore inflation, and the hedge that employment provides if you retire later at a higher salary.

Suppose you are sixty years old and your annual compensation is a salary of $600,000, plus incentive compensation that will average $400,000. If you stay on, your annual pension beginning at age sixty-five will be 60 percent of your salary: $360,000 per year until you die at, say, age seventy-five. If you decide instead to retire at age sixty, your pension will be only 50 percent of your salary because of fewer years of service and fifteen years of receiving a pension of $300,000 a year. The calculations are shown in Exhibit 3.5.

EXHIBIT 3.5

The Money Cost of Early Retirement

Cash Income (000) over Fifteen Years (Age Sixty-Five to Seventy-Five)

Continue as CEO to age sixty-five	Aggregate Cash Flows	Discounted (monthly) at 8 Percent per Annum
$1 million salary and incentives for five years	$5,000	$4,110
$360,000 pension for years six through fifteen	3,600	1,659
	$8,600	$5,769
Retire at age sixty		
$300,000 pension for fifteen years	4,500	2,616
Net cost (pretax)	$4,100	$3,153

I don't claim that $3 million is the right answer, but it is a nontrivial number for most CEOs. Viewed from another perspective, the "golden parachutes" awarded to executives who lose their jobs as a result of a merger or takeover have now been capped by Congress at three times the executives' prior compensation. If a sixty-year-old executive received such a settlement amounting to $3 million (3 years @ $1 million) and could start a reduced pension at that point, he could consider the settlement to be fair. Younger executives would incur a penalty, but as a matter of public policy it is still fair given that the recipient is more likely to be able to find suitable employment.

For an incumbent CEO considering early retirement, the calculus is far more complex. I have discounted the cash flows in my example because we all recognize the time value of money. Voluntary retirement requires an assessment of the money value of time, the benefits of having five "extra" years to use as you please, plus all of the nonfinancial exit barriers mentioned above. Before continuing the analysis, let's look at the policies that Dow Chemical Company has developed to deal with some of these issues.

Paul Oreffice at Dow

I first met Paul F. Oreffice in 1979 when he joined the board of Connecticut General Corporation, now CIGNA. He had been named president and CEO of The Dow Chemical Company a year earlier, after twenty-five years of service with the company.

When I started collecting stories for this book, Paul agreed to participate. I particularly wanted to understand the Dow situation because Dow has the highest percentage of inside directors among large industrial companies in the United States. At the time of our discussions, in January 1986, Dow had eighteen directors; ten were currently full-time executives at Dow, four were retired Dow executives, and four were independents. In fact, although the company was founded in 1897, it did not have more than one outside director until 1979. I asked Oreffice why Dow was structured in this fashion, and how it worked out managerially, particularly with regard to CEO succession. His comments are quoted below.

My colleagues and I know that Dow is an anomaly on the landscape of corporate governance in the United States. The reason we are set up this way, obviously, is that we think it is more effective, both for making critical decisions and for maintaining a cohesive management team. How we make it work is complex—as team management usually is. We do have an explicit set of policies, and some ingrained traditions, that establish some discipline for us. But mainly, it works because we work at making it work. I'll describe the general situation first, and then turn to CEO succession.

Policies and Traditions. Any person who makes a voluntary affiliation with any group or organization had better be sure he or she understands the rules of the club and agrees to be governed by them. So it is with new professional employees coming to work at Dow. They, and we, expect that they will spend their entire career with us, and that they will be successful with us to the extent of their competence. If they rise to the very top of the company, the policies are quite explicit.

The highest managerial title at Dow has always been president, now president and CEO. The CEO must give up that post at age sixty, with the only exception being that if he is appointed CEO after age fifty-five, he shall have a tenure of five years before stepping down. This policy has the effect of putting boundaries on the tenure of a CEO: never less than five years and unlikely to be more than ten years.

An analogous policy applies to all officers who have been successful enough to be elected to the board of directors. We call it "deceleration," and it applies to all officers/directors beginning at age sixty. At that point, an officer/director is supposed to start turning over his duties to younger managers. He is "on deceleration," meaning that he is no longer a member of the active management team. The only exceptions are for officers/directors who receive a significant promotion after age fifty-five. They can stay on the active team for five years.

To remind those officers that deceleration is real, their compensation drops 10 percent each year so that when they turn sixty-five, they are only making 50 percent as much as they were five years earlier. Their pension at that point is based on the average of the three highest-paid years of the last ten years.

Finally, all officers/directors must resign from the board at age sixty-five, even the prior CEO. Our outside directors are permitted to serve until age seventy.

These policies are designed to facilitate the continuation of a set of managerial traditions which have served us well. The first among these is a commitment to developing our own managerial cadre, and finding a new CEO from within the company. Our policies try to generate just the right amount of turnover at the top to accomplish this.

Another tradition is that the CEO will select the members to serve on the operating committee that he chairs. The size of the committee has varied from three to six, including the CEO, and is in effect a subset of the officer/ director group. The purpose of the committee, beyond the advantage of several heads being better than one, is to put a brake on the power of the CEO. We usually operate by consensus, although if someone finally has to break a deadlock, I'm the one to call it. But most of the time, I have to sell my ideas to them just as much as they have to sell their ideas to me.

Finally, our board of directors has traditionally served as a substantive policy-making body, in sharp contrast to many boards around the country. In our board meetings, there are many members who are intimately familiar with the matter being discussed. A free and open discussion is encouraged, and I remember more than one occasion where I voted against the proposal being espoused by the then CEO.

The End of Nepotism. I'm the seventh person to carry the title of president of The Dow Chemical Company. Our founder, Herbert H. Dow, died in 1930 at the age of sixty-four, and was still actively involved in management even in his later years. Mr. Dow's son, Willard, succeeded him and was CEO until 1949, when he died in a plane crash. He was, in turn, replaced by Lee I. Doan, who was married to Willard Dow's sister. Lee Doan served as president until age sixty-eight and then turned the reins over to his son, Herbert D. (Ted) Doan, although Lee Doan continued to serve as a director until age seventy-eight. It was really Ted Doan who killed nepotism at Dow. He became president at age 40, but retired from that post eight years later, naming C. Benson (Ben) Branch as the first nonfamily CEO.

As a practical matter, Dow was run by a troika that coalesced in 1961 and lasted until 1975. The three men were Branch, Carl Gerstacker, and Ted Doan. When Ted Doan decided to step out, the three selected Branch as the new CEO. That troika managed the explosive growth of Dow during the 60s, and also put in place many of the policies I described earlier. Branch was the first CEO to accept the new rules. In 1976, he retired as CEO at age sixty-one, after serving five years, and retired from the board at age sixty-five.

Analysis and Prescription

Stepping out should be a more common event in the process of CEO succession. More specifically, CEOs who are following the normal retirement exit route should be permitted to resign two or three years earlier than the expected retirement date, if they choose to do so. Any employee, of course, can resign at any time, but the financial barriers to exit for an incumbent CEO are awesome, and should be lowered.

My argument is based on the premise that some successful CEOs burn out near the end of their tenure and simply coast to the finish line. Coasting, in fact, is legitimized by the process of passing the baton, stepping down as CEO while continuing to serve as chairman. The term used at Dow is deceleration, but saying the chairman should decelerate begs the question of when he should let go of the baton and retire from the company. As chairman (only) he is in fact a lame duck, and could be viewed as simply serving out his time until normal retirement. I am *not* saying that all such chairmen should retire early; I am saying that taking early retirement in such a situation should be treated as an honorable act — and made as costless as possible.

The prescription to achieve this objective is relatively simple. First, the pension entitlements for a defined group of top officers should be determined as of age sixty, even though the company continues to have a mandatory retirement age of sixty-five. That is the effect of Dow's deceleration policy beginning at age sixty, and an even more explicit policy at IBM was described briefly in chapter 1. Further, it eliminates one part of the voluntary-retirement penalty, discussed above, because the pension is frozen at age sixty. Second, for CEOs only (or a narrowly defined subset of top officers) the differential between current compensation and the pension entitlement should be paid to the retiring CEO as a "consultant's fee" for the years between age sixty and sixty-five. This is the other major cost of the voluntary-retirement penalty and it could amount to a half million dollars or more per year. I do not know of any company that has such an *entitlement* for a retired CEO as a matter of policy. I do know of a number of companies that have been very quick to cut a deal involving compensation of this sort in order to persuade a failing CEO to retire without fanfare. If boards of directors are willing to do this for "bad" guys, why not do it for the good guys as well?

The intent of these policies, obviously, is to eliminate the financial exit barrier from the calculus a CEO performs as he wrestles with the question of whether to retire early. My prediction is that most CEOs would continue to step down two or three years early but would remain as chairman until the mandatory retirement age. If so, then there is no incremental cost to the company of having such policies. On the other hand, I can see two benefits from such policies: (1) the chairman ought to feel better about his role in the company because he knows that he is doing it because he wants to do it, not because he needs the money; and (2) if the time comes that the chairman should be eased out for whatever reason, the board and the chairman will feel better because they will not have to negotiate a de novo compensation contract under traumatic circumstances.

Easing out an incumbent CEO in the prime of his career, on the other hand, is quite a different matter, as discussed in the next section.

Disappointing CEOs

I have been unable to resist the play on words in the title above. If the first word is read as an adjective, it creates an instant dilemma for the board of directors. The solution is to recast the word as a verb and to figure out whether and how to remove the CEO from office.

Earlier, I concluded that the potential problem of a long-tenured CEO is far from pervasive, and that in many such cases the tenure appears to be justified by superior performance. Boards of directors apparently have a high tolerance for success. I have no data regarding the pervasiveness of mediocre CEOs, although I'm confident that it's low. My fear, however, is that boards also have a high tolerance for mediocrity.

Reaching the conclusion that the incumbent CEO should be replaced is an almost impossible task for a board. The judgment itself is harsh—really devastating for the individual involved. And there are structural impediments even to get the ball rolling: some of the directors were invited to join the board by the incumbent, and those already on the board voted for his appointment. Further, it is rare for a board to have a mechanism periodically to assess the *adequacy* of the CEO; the compensation committee's job is to decide how much he should be paid, not whether. The result is a continuation of the status quo, no matter how bad.

At some threshold level of frustration, however, the board of directors will take action and ask the CEO to resign. My interpretation of our data is that roughly 10 percent of the newly appointed CEOs in our population are fired, and half of those firings occur during the first three years of the CEO's tenure. My particular interest in this topic is not *why* a CEO was fired but *how*. Collecting detailed stories on that topic, however, turned out to be almost impossible; the story at Dow, told below, is fascinating but unique. I will discuss the Dow story first, and then offer some general comments under the heading of "Roles and Responsibilities."

Cleaning the Nest at Dow

In my conversation with Paul Oreffice, I asked him to comment on the brief tenure (two years) of his predecessor, Zoltan Merszei. He begged off, but helped me get in touch with Earle Barnes, a former chariman of Dow, now retired and living in Jackson, Wyoming. Barnes and I conversed, by phone and correspondence, and this is what he told me.

> *Earle B. Barnes. You're interested in how Dow is governed, particularly with regard to our preponderance of inside directors, and this is a unique but revealing example of how it works. I submit that it would have been very difficult for a conventional board of directors, all outsiders except two or three, to oust a recently appointed CEO as quickly and quietly as we did. It was a difficult episode, internally, but it did have the benefit of coalescing the entire top management group in terms of how we wanted to run the company . . . but first, some background.*
>
> *When Ted Doan stepped down as CEO in 1971, Ben Branch became the first nonfamily CEO of Dow. The hallmark of Branch's tenure was taking Dow overseas, particularly enhancing our presence in Europe. Zoltan Merszei, an emigrant from Hungary, had started with Dow in Canada but had spent his entire career working for Dow in Europe, and Branch put Merszei in charge of the European operations. At the same time, I was in charge of Dow U.S.A., so Merszei and I were peers — and candidates to succeed Branch. Merszei was not your typical Dow executive; he was a very brassy individual. I had the feeling that he didn't trust me, and the feeling was mutual.*
>
> *In July 1975, my wife and I had just arrived at our summer home in Wyoming for a brief visit when Branch called to say that Zoltan Merszei had been selected as the next CEO of Dow. His call was to inform me of that decision and to tell me that he and the other two members of the troika, Carl Gerstacker and Ted Doan, would arrive the next day to discuss the matter with me. I was disap-*

pointed, of course, and surprised by the timing, because
Branch would not step down as CEO until May 1976. At
that point, Paul Oreffice was not a candidate to succeed
Branch because it was felt he should move up to another
echelon of responsibility — such as head of Dow U.S.A. or
Dow Europe. The troika had not been active in day-to-day
management for nearly four years, but it still was the chief
decision-making body for management succession. The
recommendation to go with Merszei was clearly made by
Branch, and he had won over his colleagues to obtain the
decision. The troika in turn persuaded the rest of the
board to agree.

At that meeting in Wyoming, Branch had talked about
the disadvantage of my age vis-à-vis Merszei — I was fifty-
eight and Merszei fifty-three, and that it would enhance
Dow's image as a truly international company to bring in
a European as CEO. With plenty of time to think it over, I
finally decided that I could not run Dow U.S.A. under
Merszei, and I informed Branch of that decision. When the
succession occurred, I became executive vice president
with responsibility for the technical side of the company
(Manufacturing-Engineering-R&D) and Paul Oreffice succeeded me as the president of Dow U.S.A. When Merszei
took over, as I had surmised, he made Dow U.S.A. a target
for change in the image of Dow Europe. He wanted to be a
dictator, and refused to form an operating committee with
two or three other executives in his cohort. Instead, he set
up his own people, including bringing a few from Europe
to the headquarters in Midland. Merszei's style was one of
intimidation and fear, and he had more than one serious
confrontation with Oreffice. The atmosphere in the company began to sour.

Seven Days in May. After it was all over, we
referred to the episode as "Seven Days in May," after the
title of a melodramatic novel of that time. In fact, the
events occurred during the ten days preceding the board
of directors' meeting in April 1978. A few weeks prior to

that, I had been flying on a plane with Oreffice, and had never seen him so downhearted. The harassment that he was taking from Merszei was almost unbearable, and it sounded to me like he might resign. That was serious, because Oreffice was widely viewed as the next CEO of Dow. I told him, "We've got to do something," and then I realized that he really couldn't do it. So I went to Carl Gerstacker and Ted Doan, telling them how serious the situation had become. Gerstacker then organized a process to deal with the matter, informing Branch, but not including him in the process because Branch was Merszei's original sponsor.

At the March board meeting, Gerstacker suggested that it might be useful for the board to have an opportunity to reaffirm its confidence in Merszei. He proposed that two of the directors who were not standing for reelection the next month conduct a private poll of each director and report back to the board in April. Merszei did not object at all — in fact, he really didn't take it seriously because of his supreme self-confidence. Promptly after the meeting he took off for a two-and-a-half-week trip to the Pacific. While Merszei was away, there was a lot of discussion among the officers/directors, and some of them also talked confidentially with some of the subordinates reporting to them. Shortly after he returned, I'm sure that Merszei must have realized that he might be in trouble.

The first item on the agenda of the April 1978 board meeting was a report on the vote of confidence. The general counsel of the company explained that the private poll had indicated that it would be useful to have a secret ballot taken by the directors in this meeting. No one said anything at that point except Merszei, who spoke briefly about how hard he was trying, and acknowledging his need to be a little more humble. The votes were then cast and collected by the counsel, who then left the room with the two retiring directors. They returned promptly and said that they would not announce the tally but that a majority of the votes indicated that Merszei should step down

*as the CEO. At that point, Merszei got up and left the
room. The next item on the agenda was another vote to
elect a new president and CEO. That also was cast as a
private ballot, and Oreffice was elected.*

*In the aftermath, we all agreed that it would be desir-
able not to hang our dirty linen out to the public. Branch
agreed to step aside as chairman so that Merszei could
take that post. But that didn't work for very long either,
since Merszei was completely ostracized by company management. Merszei finally resigned from the company at the
February 1979 board meeting, after he had obtained an offer from Armand Hammer to join Occidental, and the
board elected me chairman. It was a traumatic event for
all of us, but I think it's also true that we believe that we
did the right thing, and certainly Oreffice's performance
during the last eight years stands as a validation of that.*

Having mulled for several months over what happened at
Dow, I continue to be astonished by it. Searching for analogies
that would help me understand the process, I finally settled on
the House of Commons in the British Parliament. Members of
Parliament (the directors at Dow) elect a prime minister (CEO) to
serve as long as the majority agrees. If the prime minister loses a
vote of confidence, he resigns, and another prime minister is
selected. In fact, that analogy holds true for all U.S. publicly held
corporations, with the important distinction that in most companies a majority of the directors are "independent" outsiders,
not full-time members of management. Dow has consciously decided to be "an anomaly" in terms of corporate governance, and
points to this episode as an example of the effectiveness of its
board. Hence the broader issue deserves at least brief comment.

I am on record as favoring a two-to-one majority of outside
directors, and I will return to this topic in the last chapter. I am
also an advocate of team management, and am particularly intrigued with Dow's system of corporate governance, in which the
CEO serves at the pleasure of his "subordinates." The core issue
in appraising Dow's system against the conventional model is, I
believe, which system is more effective in facilitating change.

Routine oversight by an outside board of directors is a useful discipline, but I believe the primary value of a board of directors today is in bringing in an outsider as CEO, exemplified by the Emhart story told in chapter 6. Dow was seeking to make some change when it appointed a quasi-outsider, Merszei, as CEO, but the attempt failed. Perhaps it should have failed. I can only speculate that an outside board might have made a selection from a broader pool, and provided more support for the new CEO from outside, thereby improving the prospect of successful change.

Disappointments: Roles and Responsibilities

Let me begin to speculate in earnest as I turn to the final topic in this chapter: Who should take the initiative in raising the question of whether the CEO's performance is so poor that he should be asked to resign? Even though I have no stories to tell, I have discussed this topic with more than a dozen CEOs and experienced directors, so my comments are more or less informed. Nevertheless, I make no claim that these comments are a description of current practice about *how* a CEO is deposed. My more modest objective is to define the members of the cast of characters involved and examine the role and responsibilities of each one.

The executives at Dow were willing to tell the Merszei story because it was a *collective* action by the senior officers and directors. In most other situations that I know about, only a subset of that group—a handful or less—were directly involved in the decision. Even at Dow, someone had to take the initiative, and in this case it was Barnes who realized that "we should do something," and then took his insight to the troika, which acted on it. And what was the crucial piece of information that led Barnes to blow the whistle? It was a casual remark by Oreffice that made Barnes think that Oreffice was so fed up that he was considering resigning from the firm. In companies with a more conventional form of governance, there are four potential sources of initiative: outside directors, the prior CEO (still serving as chairman or a member of the board), the heir apparent (usually the president/COO) and other senior officers. For each potential initiator, the first issue is the source and quality of his information, followed by a judgment about how to use that information responsibly. I will discuss these issues for each of the four potential initiators, starting at the bottom of the hierarchy and working up.

Senior Officers. Each member of this group of a dozen or so typically has excellent information on the status of one or more segments of the business, and sufficient contact with the CEO to form judgment about the quality of his leadership. If one such officer concludes that the ship will sink unless the CEO is replaced, there is little that he can do. Sounding the alarm by going directly to one or more members of the board of directors is not likely to be effective. The chairman/CEO and president/COO will stand together, publicly at least, and the senior officer will then resign under the stigma of having been a "troublemaker." Alternatively he can decide simply to wait it out, hoping that someone will take action against the CEO. But the best solution is simply to abandon the ship, with perhaps a minor toot of the whistle in the form of a comment to the prior CEO or other members of the board about why he is leaving. A sufficient number of such straws in the wind may ultimately move the board to take action, but only after a number of the most talented senior officers have been lost.

The Heir Apparent. The president/COO is frequently the best informed executive in the company. He is closer to the action than the CEO, and is in an excellent position to assess the status and momentum of the enterprise as well as the leadership ability of his boss. He is also a member of the board, with easy access to all of the outside directors. If he concludes that the status quo is intolerable, he is then faced with a dilemma of major proportions. The prospective value of his inheritance is declining, and in such a situation he might start looking for greener pastures elsewhere which, once found, would permit him to depart amicably because he was "lured away." On the other hand, he might quite appropriately regard that path as an act of cowardice.

The moral issue for the heir apparent flows from his responsibilities to the shareholders, employees, and other constituencies. If the cost of maintaining the incumbent is too high, he will be the first to know—and he should blow the whistle then. In so doing, he puts his job on the line, knowing that there's a significant likelihood that he will be allowed to "resign." Delaying the whistle until he has found a new job is self-serving, because if the CEO is to be deposed, the heir apparent is expected to be available to take over the company. But blowing the whistle is *overtly* self-serving, because if he is successful he will become the new CEO. If he decides he must take the initiative, his best action is to have a conversation with the prior CEO, if he is still on the board.

The Prior CEO. This member of the board of directors can play a unique role in troubled times. His current information about the status of the corporation may be no greater than that of an outside director, but he is blessed with a deep understanding of the company and its industry, and he has a network of acquaintances that reaches several levels down into the organization. With those assets, the prior CEO himself may decide to take the initiative, admitting that he made a mistake in recommending the incumbent CEO to be his successor. If so, one of the first people he would talk to would probably be the president/COO; the important thing is not which one of the two initiates the topic, but whether they agree on the need for action. The prior CEO, however, is the one to select two or three respected outside directors and initiate a one-on-one discussion with each of them. If there is unanimity among that small group, the prior CEO is the one who has the first conversation with the incumbent, informing him that he is being asked to resign.

Outside Directors. The data available to this group about the status of the company and its prospects are provided by the incumbent CEO. Disappointing performance cannot be hidden forever, and outside directors are not without their own sources of information about the company. Each director has his or her network of friends and associates, and directors are alert to innuendos in casual conversations with officers in financial institutions, customers of the company, or its competitors. Nevertheless, if the prior CEO is no longer a member of the board, it is extremely difficult for a group of outside directors to reach the judgment that the incumbent CEO should be asked to resign. In such situations, the president/COO who takes the initiative by approaching one of the directors to alert him to the seriousness of the situation is at great risk personally, even though there is still some chance that the incumbent will be deposed if the director approached can find two or three other respected members to agree with the president's assessment. Without such an initiative by the prior CEO or the president/COO, it is extremely unlikely that outside directors, on their own initiative, will ask for the CEO's resignation.

Summing up this rather speculative analysis, the CEO can only be asked to resign by his board of directors, but that is not done by formal vote such as occurred at Dow. Rather, a handful or less of respected directors, almost like a junta involved in a political coup, decides that the action is necessary and so informs the incumbent. The rest of the directors may not learn of the resignation until the CEO announces it at his last board meeting. A new insight here, for me, was the realization of the important role a prior CEO can play if he stays on the board. I acknowledge the argument in favor of stepping out in order to clear the decks for the next CEO, but I believe keeping a prior CEO on the board is a relatively cheap insurance policy for the one time out of ten when it is necessary to dis-appoint the incumbent.

Such insurance would not be necessary if the outside directors were better organized. Today, it is all too common for the CEO not only to chair the board but to dominate it. Under such circumstances it is all but impossible for outside directors alone to initiate action to fire the CEO. The solution, for several facets of corporate governance, not just this one, is a more independent board. My prescriptions for achieving that are spelled out in the closing segment of this book.

4

Management Teams

A dmitting to yourself that you're mortal has allowed you to calculate your expected tenure as CEO and you have, privately, established the prospective date of your retirement. That's a watershed event, because from now on you will become increasingly preoccupied with the task of developing a management team that will include your successor and the colleagues the next CEO will need to be successful. Right now, you have such a team, carefully nurtured by the prior CEO, and these people are helping you achieve your strategic objectives. Your personal task is to worry about the next generation of top managers — and you can't start too soon.

You know the ropes, of course, because you were a member of the management team chaired by your predecessor for several years before you became president and heir apparent. As a member of that inner circle, you learned a lot by watching the preceding CEO, including some new dimensions of "the way we do things around here." Your selection, in fact, indicated that you learned those lessons well; there are some important traditions and values in your company that you don't want to change, even if you could. You are a "believer" — but not a clone. Your mandate is not simple continuity, it is evolving change, and a primary tool for making that happen is selecting new members of the management team. You will probably hire a few mid-level managers from outside, if only to help stir the pot.

But the main thing you learned from your predecessor is that an effective management team is not just a good thing — it's everything. Somehow, he managed to select a disparate group of a dozen individuals and mold them into a powerful forum for identifying incipient problems, diagnosing the situation, and taking action. He achieved that, as best you can figure it out, by following three simple rules: (1) he kept the agenda focused on the substantive issues of greatest concern to him; (2) he listened carefully and encouraged discussion by withholding his own opinions; and (3) he squashed any form of individual grandstanding—quite overtly on some occasions—that might be construed as jockeying to become his successor. If you can match that achievement—in your own way, not his—you'll have a productive team, and the succession issue will practically take care of itself.

Focus of this Chapter

Every CEO I know has a management team. If asked to talk about it, he will respond in terms of both structure and process. Referring to an organization chart, he will usually define "his" team as all of the executives reporting directly to him, plus some, but not all, of the managers at the next level. Describing how these managers work together as a team, he will typically talk about one or more committees that he chairs. For each committee, he will identify the members, explain its purpose, scope, and agenda, and describe the frequency and length of its meetings. If asked to specify the size of his team, he immediately becomes vague. "Every manager in the company is a member of the team, but some are more important than others," is his reply.

Formal committees, the overt definition of management teams, are pervasive in large U.S. corporations, and as I have written elsewhere,[1] the variety of ways that committees are used is immense. My focus here, however, is on how management teams affect the process of CEO succession. Stepping back from the bewildering array of situational practices, I find it useful to distinguish between two types of management teams, each of which can be observed in most companies. One type I call operating committees, defining them as formal committees (no matter the actual names used) chaired by the CEO and composed of a subset of his subordinates, at whatever level. Operating committees are focused on substantive issues, but *because* they are chaired by the CEO, they provide arenas for the CEO to observe

1. "How CEOs Use Top Management Committees," *Harvard Business Review*, January–February 1984, 65.

interactions among the members. Most insiders who are selected as heirs apparent have served for several years on one or more operating committees.

The second type of management team I call the top management team, ignoring the companies in our population that use the solo mode. The duo mode of top management organization, using the relay process, was discussed in chapter 1. Here, I focus on top management teams that have three or more executives holding one or more of the five top management titles. CEO succession within such a team can become quite complex in comparison to the more common relay process, and it is useful to discuss it at this point.

The problem remains, however, that there are an infinite number of ways to organize an effective management team. Cummins Engine Company has no operating committees chaired by the CEO, for reasons you will discern, yet it has a committed and effective team of managers and an overt succession process. I'll present that story first, and then return to the topics of operating committees and top management teams in turn.

Passing the Baton at Cummins Engine

At my first seminar on CEO succession, Reg Jones of GE, then age sixty-five, was the star of the show, taking the role of senior citizen and adjunct professor. He came with sheafs of notes, and described in detail the bruising horse race he ran at GE for more than three years. At that point, early in my research, I was enamored with the succession process Reg Jones had designed, a process that yielded Jack Welch as his successor.

In my comments opening the seminar, I aggrandized the important and difficult nature of our topic. The difficulty, I opined, arose because the selection of a successor was a unique decision, different in kind from most of the decisions that arrive at a CEO's desk. Most corporate decisions, capital investments for example, have a repetitive nature. A new CEO may make a few mistakes, but he learns from them, fine-tunes his judgment, and gets progressively better at sorting the wheat from the chaff. For the succession decision, there is no learning curve. Most CEOs have never made such a decision, and they will make it only once. The purpose of our seminar was to identify some of the issues involved and to discuss how they might be dealt with.

Henry B. Schacht, chairman and CEO of Cummins Engine Company, attended that seminar. Then age forty-nine, he was the youngest member of the group, although he had been CEO for ten years, and his company was one of the smallest represented, with roughly 10 percent of GE's revenues. After listening to Jones's story, Schacht, respectfully but persistently, insisted on presenting an alternative process for consideration:

> I strongly feel there is a viable alternate to the idea of a horse race. In this alternate, there is no finish line. There are no winners and losers. I worry a lot about a process that gives too much control to the incumbent. The process should be ever green. We, CEOs, are temporary, not deities. It is the business and the people in it that are the continuity. I didn't realize that yesterday, but Mr. Jones has clarified it for me.
>
> In the alternative that I'm more comfortable with, the process of CEO succession should be just like any other management decision process. Succession is not a unique event, despite what Vancil said at the beginning. It's just part of an ongoing process. There should be no coronation of the new CEO. The deity concept is bad. It's as though the prior CEO had fallen off a cliff. There should not be discontinuity at the top. A relay race is better than a cliff event. The longer the process is drawn out, the better.

Thus did my education on the process of CEO succession begin in earnest! Jones had provided a thesis; Schacht now proposed the antithesis. It took me awhile to work it out, but as the title of this book proclaims, I believe Schacht's model is more appropriate in most situations.

I first met Henry Schacht in the fall of 1960, when he was a first-year student in my classroom. In 1962, he went to work for Irwin Management Company, in Columbus, Indiana. That company managed the financial affairs of J. Irwin Miller and his family, and had been set up to separate those activities from Mr.

Miller's responsibilities as chairman and major stockholder of Cummins Engine Company, a manufacturer of diesel engines. Two years later, Schacht took a position in the financial operations of the engine company, and his career took off from there.

I got acquainted with James A. Henderson, who graduated one year after Schacht, because he stayed at the School as a research assistant for one year and then took a position at Cummins as an assistant to Miller. I was a consultant to Irwin Management Company in the early 60s, and have followed the careers of Schacht and Henderson since then. In April 1986, I spent a day and a half at Cummins, attending the annual stockholders' meeting, and then talking with Miller, Schacht, and Henderson about the process of passing the baton.

J. Irwin Miller

The central figure in this story is J. Irwin MIller, and not simply because his family owned the business and he served as the CEO for forty years. Among his many accomplishments, he majored in Greek, is an amateur violinist, and served as president of the National Council of Churches in the early 60s. Miller is a man of great integrity who sets demanding standards of personal performance for any activity he engages in. His company set the world-class performance standards for heavy-duty diesel engines. For his own community, he used the same criterion. As the largest employer in the little town of Columbus, Indiana, population 35,000, he persuaded the local governing bodies to permit the company foundation to pay architects' fees for public buildings, provided they were designed by internationally famous architects; the governing body picks from a supplied list. The result is that Columbus is an architectural showcase. A director of AT&T, when his company went public in the 1950s Miller put together a stellar group of directors. And, when the time came to assemble a group of managers for the next generation at Cummins, he sought out the best of the brightest. Miller described that process:

> In 1960, when I turned fifty, I realized it was time to
> start thinking about my successor. I didn't want to restrict

myself to the local talent, so I turned to top business schools as the primary source. Drawing from applicants across the country, they were turning out a few thousand MBAs a year—men in their mid-twenties who would have fifteen years to mature before I retired. In those days, Harvard Business School had a practice of identifying the best students after the first year of the two-year program. The top 2.5 percent, called Baker Scholars, became our target, and we hired three or four each year for several years in the early 60s. Most of them were hired into the family management company. This gave them a chance to become familiar with our local community and us a chance to work more closely with them. We ended up with two "keepers" out of that set, Schacht and Henderson, and also added John Hackett, an economist from Ohio State, who is about the same age.

Executive talent may come from anywhere, not only through the universities. Don Tull, then president of Cummins, had only a high school education and began working at Cummins in his teens on the shop floor. He was the wisest business executive I have met. Tull, president and COO, and I had been working together as a team for nearly thirty years at that point, and it had been a very close and effective relationship. Our objective was to find a new pair who could take over from the two of us. One option was an insider, eleven years younger than I, and a seasoned stalwart with many years of service at Cummins. To flesh out that option, in 1966 we brought in an outsider at a high level in the company to see if he and the insider could form a team. The other option was to skip a generation and go directly to Schacht and Henderson, who were twenty-five years younger than I. In all discussions we placed character and wisdom ahead of intelligence, experience, or credentials.

Then, in 1968, Tull's health began to fail and we had to bite the bullet. By then it was clear to us that Schacht had the potential to become a great leader for the company. In making such a decision, however, you can never be sure that you are right on the judgment. The only way you can really find out if a man can do the job is to let him work at it for several years. At thirty-five, Schacht still had a lot to learn, but we decided to make him president while we had enough time left to observe, teach, and counsel.

I am a believer in the "relay race" principle. In the relay race, the runner finishing his lap does not hand over the baton until the runner beginning the next lap is up to speed. That is essentially what we did with Schacht during the next five years. At the same time, however, we agreed that Henderson was the best candidate to be the next COO, and Tull, who had resigned as president when Schacht was appointed, began working with Henderson to pass that baton. As the new president, Schacht was de facto COO, but during those five years, one function at a time, we progressively passed the responsibilities from Schacht to Henderson.

Our outside directors played an important role in the final decision to name Schacht as chairman/CEO and Henderson as president/COO. In public corporations, it does not make sense to me for the outgoing CEO to name his successor, even though this may be a prevailing practice. Those outside directors who will be remaining as directors after the current CEO has retired ought to have the final say, just as they will continue to have the final responsibility.

Don Tull and I always met alone with outside directors at the close of each meeting to give them an opportunity to express any concerns they might have that they would not feel comfortable expressing with insiders present. This custom continues. We also took such occasions to inform the outside directors of the progress of our own thinking on management succession and other matters. Quite often discussion was lively, and the outside directors not only challenged but differed with us. Another regular practice (which continues) is to have each outside director spend the night before the meeting at the home of a *different member of the top management. A purpose in doing this is to make certain that each outside director knows in some depth a rather large group of the company's top management. The process that ties all this together then results in a recommendation for management succession from the outgoing CEO, and a company climate that permits the outside directors to make an informed and unhurried decision.*

I stepped down as CEO in 1974, but continued as a full-time chairman for three more years before retiring to the sidelines. The double hand-off was complete. I still continue as part-time chairman of the Executive Committee, but it has not been too difficult for me to change my working relations with Cummins. I have total confidence in the present management. They tend to keep me over- rather than under-informed. Schacht has developed a practice of calling me every day that he and I are both in town, and I have lunch frequently with him and Henderson. My role is that of counselor — only as needed. On those rare occasions where I do have a serious concern, I know they will listen carefully — but that does not necessarily mean they will choose my solution. That is, I think, as it should be. My problem is always to find the right balance between too much interference and too little availability.

Schacht and Henderson

Schacht, Henderson, and I spent several hours together during my visit to Columbus in April 1986. Both Schacht and Henderson were then fifty-one, and they have worked as a team for twenty-two years. They are obviously compatible; occasionally, one would find himself completing a sentence begun by the other. We decided that the easiest way for them to present their story would be to use plural pronouns and last names when referring to each other. They did occasionally disagree, particularly in terms of emphasis on a topic, but we decided it was not worth sorting that out for this purpose. Here is what they said:

In 1969, when Don Tull's illness made it clear that he would step down soon, the two of us and John Hackett talked together a lot about what might happen. Our assessment was that the insider was the odds-on favorite to become the next president, and if not he, then the outsider who had come in three years earlier would likely get that post. Henderson, then the chief personnel officer, was somewhat conflicted because he was counseling with Miller and Tull about their choice. Once that decision was made, Henderson told Schacht and Hackett that he had recommended Schacht as the proper person to choose from the next generation, if that was the way Miller decided to go. After Schacht was selected, Henderson and Hackett talked together and decided they would stay because they were willing to work with Schacht, and they were both learning a lot.

In more ways than one, we [Schacht and Henderson] were the beneficiaries of Miller's decision to skip a generation. There had been a gentle hores race between the two generations, but it was not a personal sort of thing. Nevertheless, we were glad we had been selected. More important, Miller's and Tull's decision to move us in early provided for a long training period, and we really needed that. The relay process takes a long time — eight years in our case — but we did not chafe under it because we knew we would still have a long tenure of our own and a chance to really do something for the company. We are really proud that three of the four most senior managers stayed on after we were selected, and are still with the company, functioning very effectively; a byproduct of the relay concept, we believe.

The relay race — really, the relay process of passing the baton — is our primary vehicle for management development. The relay process is currently going on in every department of the company. The only real trick in making it work is to make early, deep selection from among the two or three prospects for a higher-level job, doing it be-

*fore armed camps have a chance to coalesce. A relay is
not the opposite of a horse race. The relay follows the
horse race, and what we try to do is to make the horse
race very low key and quick so we can then spend as
much time as necessary to pass the baton smoothly. When
we do it well, most people are not even aware that a decision has been made. They simply observe that, over time,
the responsibilities of one manager are being transferred to
one of his subordinates in increasing amounts.*

Team Management at Cummins

The value of the Cummins story is in the clarity of the succession
process, first between the principals involved and then, increasingly, for the entire organization. It is easier, here, to see how the
relay process worked if only because the company was small
(revenues were $400 million in 1969, when Schacht became pres-
ident) and the cast of characters was only a handful of people.
More important, the process was managed by Irwin Miller, a
thoughtful, articulate owner with a lot at stake. His objective was
explicit: to groom a new world-class management team for the
next generation.

The relay process cannot be separated from the broader context in which it occurs; as Schacht said at the seminar, management succession is an integral part of the regular management
process, and the CEO is just another manager. Several CEOs in
the seminar disagreed with his diminution of the CEO's role, but
he was really trying to explain how team management works at
Cummins.

Today, with Cummins's revenues over $2 billion, the team
embraces several dozen managers working together in a family-
like culture. The trappings of status are minimal: equal-sized
offices with no doors, no reserved parking spaces, relatively
small salary differentials between grade levels, no personal use of
corporate aircraft for any executive, and so forth. The eighteen-
person board of directors includes eight insiders, which helps to
demystify that august body. And, most telling, there is a deep and
continuing respect for the retired senior members of management. The team works together for the good of the company, and

its members "share the pain, share the gain" in their cyclical industry.

In this context, the formal announcement of a promotion appears almost as an afterthought. The person taking a new title has already demonstrated a growing competence for the task over several years, and, more important, that competence is implicitly acknowledged by his or her peers. The fait accompli is then disclosed to the rest of the organization, but with precious little fanfare. So it is, also, in producing a new CEO at Cummins. The stakes are higher, but the process is essentially the same.

One useful way to think about the relay process for a new CEO is to focus on how the incumbent CEO manages the pace of events. The contrast between Miller's timetable at Cummins and Jones's at GE is stark, and the difference between them has two dimensions: the amount of elapsed time and the way that time was used. Jones, using the horse-race model, had his road map, and the succession process began in early 1977 when he identified the contenders. It ended when Jones resigned as chairman and director in March 1981. Miller, using the relay process, spent twice as long, beginning in 1967 or so and ending in 1977, when he stepped down as chairman, although staying on as a director. In both situations there was one significant interim event that I call selection, the date when the incumbent CEO's heir becomes apparent to members of the organization. At GE, that event occurred in August 1979, or maybe several months later; at Cummins it occurred in 1974. The transition period begins then, and ends with the validation of the heir apparent when he becomes CEO, or in Miller's case, when the Henderson half of the new team became president.

Jones, with four years in his timetable, used two-thirds or more of the time for selection and the remainder for validation. Miller, with ten years, spent only 20 percent of the time before selecting Schacht and the remaining eight years for passing the baton. GE and Cummins are totally different situations, and in chapter 6 I will explain in detail why I believe Jones's process was appropriate for GE. Here, my point is that Miller's process was right for Cummins. Miller knew that selecting the right person as his successor was important—you can't make a silk purse out of a sow's ear—but bringing that new, prospective CEO up to speed, permitting a smooth hand-off of the baton, was even more important.

Summary

The Cummins story is important and powerful, but I do not hold it up as a universal model. On the other hand, given my target audience, Cummins is typical of an important subset of that population. Cummins is a small company in the sense that its strategic focus is on a single product, albeit in a worldwide market. More important for our purposes, Cummins is organized functionally. There are no internal profit centers within Cummins. In contrast, Ex-Cell-O Corporation (chapter 2) and Corning Glass Works (later in this chapter) have about the same revenues as Cummins, but both are engaged in a more diversified set of product markets, each one headed by a division general manager.

The extent of a corporation's product-market diversity has a major impact on the process of CEO succession. At one end of the spectrum we have Cummins (or IBM, at least until the early 1980s), with a narrow focus and a centralized organization. At the other end we have, say, General Electric, with enormous diversity and a decentralized organization. At Cummins there are very few "general manager" jobs, which makes it difficult to train and develop people ultimately to become CEO. The business simply does not come together as a business until you find yourself in the CEO's office. In such situations, the Cummins solution has a lot of merit: bring in a very few highly talented people, select the next CEO from that group as early as possible, and then give him a long period of time to grow into the job. That's really what the relay process is all about.

Operating Committees

Let me turn now to the topic of operating committees and the role they can play in CEO succession. Most CEOs chair one or more such committees, each with a defined membership, and meeting with a frequency that ranges from once a week to once a month. The pervasive use of such committees is testimony to their value for a CEO. First, I will describe why such committees are useful, and how the CEO uses them. Then, Jack Hanley, coming into Monsanto as a new CEO from outside, will tell how he used an operating committee to help him address the issues that faced him.

Value Added by Operating Committees

In my earlier article on committees, I used IBM and GE as polar extremes on the diversification spectrum to illustrate that the major differences in the substantive work of an operating committee are dictated by the scope of the corporation's activities and the interdependence among the operating units of the company. Putting that point aside, at a more general level a number of benefits accrue from such committees, and I discuss them below under the headings of corporate governance, cohesion, and efficiency.

Corporate Governance. A CEO and the members of his operating committees need each other to be effective, and they all know it. A new CEO, inheriting one or more such committees, can make radical changes in their number, size, membership, and roles in very short order. He is not likely, however, to abolish all such committees, because their benefits exceed their costs. The primary cost, implicit in his agreement to take counsel from his colleagues as a group rather than one at a time, is a reduction in his ability to call the shots. But the calculus is simple: the prospective benefits may be quite large. So, he changes the modus operandi of the meetings to suit his style, and makes evolutionary changes in the membership.

The primary benefit operating committees provide is to legitimatize the informal information networks that help link the CEO to the broader management cadre — and the communications on those networks flow in both directions. Each committee member, as an individual, can be useful to the CEO because he or she typically has a constituency or a zone of responsibility that reaches several layers down into the organization. The members know how the CEO works and what his concerns are. When a new piece of information bubbles up, they can decide whether it should be passed to the CEO urgently or delayed until the next committee meeting. Their membership on the committee includes the right to deal directly with the CEO on urgent matters. They obtain such information by spending a lot of time in the lower levels of their constituencies. The information channel, of course, works in both directions. Members can explain corporate policies and actions and, in exchange, ask questions — or just listen. Gossip is important.

A ten-member committee adjourns at 11 a.m., and before lunch is over each member has told two or three of his subordinates what of interest happened in the meeting. Each of them, in turn, passes that along to a few of his or her subordinates, and by the end of the day more than a hundred managers are repeating a slightly garbled version of what the CEO said that morning. For the CEO, this informal network provides almost personal communication with many managers, and is very convenient for the informal testing of new initiatives or subtle changes in direction. This network facilitates the implementation that will be required when a decision is made, and perhaps more important, many managers down in the organization have a sense of belonging to the larger team. Each member of the committee provides that by giving them access to the inner counsels of top management.

An operating committee, acting as a group, can also help the CEO on another dimension of corporate governance. There is important, substantive work to be done, and occasionally an issue will arise that is extremely controversial. The CEO, of course, can always call the shot, knowing that it will create winners and losers. Alternatively, faced with a lack of consensus within his committee, he can table the item without appearing indecisive, on grounds that more spadework needs to be done. Sometimes, the corporate world is more predictable and more civilized when the CEO reigns and his operating committee reins.

Cohesion. For most managers, becoming a member of the operating committee is the definition of "making it." Each member knows that he may not be the next CEO, but at least he has the opportunity to play a vital role in corporate management. To gain the full benefit of such a committee, the CEO must bind the members into a cohesive, effective team. He does this, in part, by arranging social activities, such as a corporate retreat, in addition to holding regular meetings. But the meetings themselves create, over time, a large base of shared experiences. As the committee members work together, discussion becomes more efficient, a common data base evolves, a shared jargon develops, and biases become clear. Managers who have been through many wars together can handle a heavy agenda because they need not waste a lot of time trying to understand each other. In times of crisis a well-organized management team can mobilize corporate resources quickly.

This cohesion, to be effective, must be achieved without creating a clone-like homogeneity. Disparate points of view are required if there is to be a thorough thrashing out of the issues involved in a complex decision. If a choice is to be made, some members will have to back away from their initial stance. The CEO's objective here is to have each such member acknowledge that his constituency will be modestly harmed, but to agree that the choice is in the best interests of the corporation as a whole. Obtaining this consent from each member reinforces the cohesion of the group. From consent comes consensus, and concerted action.

Efficiency. Created and chaired by the CEO, an operating committee deals with those items on the CEO's agenda with which he thinks it can help. Each committee has a nominal focal point or agenda, and some of these must be honored. Processes, such as strategic planning and budgeting, create each year a calendar-driven series of meetings involving the CEO and his committees. The schedule itself provides an efficient discipline for these important management tasks. But the CEO's personal agenda cannot be programmed. He must address the relentless questions: What is the situation now? What, if anything, should we do? Asking those questions of his operating committee may bring to the surface a specific topic or news item that needs to be reviewed in a broader context. The CEO's task then becomes one of diagnosis and initiation of action.

An operating committee is often extremely efficient at diagnosing such ill-defined questions as, "Is there a problem?" and

"What is the problem?" Collectively, its members bring to the table a broad range of knowledge and experience that enables them to define the multifaceted character of a complex issue. Early on, their discussions begin to sketch out implications for corporate action—not through formal hypotheses but through such speculation as, "If this is so, then that means . . ."—until a consensus starts to emerge. If a new initiative is required, the committee can help frame the options from which the CEO can choose. If there is a need for action and for deciding who should do what, the "who" is often seated at the table. The committee's task, then, is to help that member and the CEO agree on a course of action with which both are comfortable.

Summary. Operating committees are pervasive because they are flexible, personal tools for strengthening the leadership of the CEO. Committees are easy to form, and they continue to exist only at the pleasure of the CEO. Their agenda is totally in the CEO's hands, and they provide an excellent means of sending signals down into the organization. Operating committees, fostering shared objectives and the commitment to achieve them, are the glue that helps hold a corporation together.

Tucked into a corner of the mind of every member of an operating committee is the realization that the company's next CEO is probably in the room. In selecting a new member for a committee, or promoting someone to a position that carries membership with it, the CEO is choosing the initial set of colleagues who will work with the next CEO. Watching the committee members work together over several years also permits the CEO to judge which members might be most effective as the next leader of the group. CEO succession is not on the agenda of any operating committee, and yet these committees are an important part of the succession process. Lower-level managers know who the committee members are, and the gossip mill grinds out its speculations as to whose star is rising or falling. The operating committee, in one sense, serves as a stage on which the candidates can demonstrate their abilities, thus helping the broader organization calibrate its expectations about who will be the next CEO. Let us turn now to the story of Jack Hanley at Monsanto and how he used his operating committee to produce his successor.

Jack Hanley at Monsanto

John W. Hanley became CEO of Monsanto in 1972 and retired eleven years later at the age of sixty-one. Al McDonald, my collaborator in the seminars, invited him to attend one, but Hanley had a prior commitment. I knew Hanley only by reputation, but I pursued him nevertheless, sensing that he might have a good story. We finally met in his hotel in Boston in January 1986, and this is what he told me:

I'm not the expert on the history of Monsanto prior to my arrival, but I've been told that it was run like a family company. Edgar Monsanto Queeny was the only son of the founder, and he dominated the company until the day he died in 1968 at age seventy-one. The board of directors had always been dominated by insiders, but in 1972 there were four outside directors and they were really strong individuals. They were unhappy with Ed Bock's leadership and with the performance of the company, so they insisted that Ed resign. Charlie Sommer held all the titles for a few months during 1972 while the board figured out what to do next.

At that time, the company was organized into five business groups, each headed by a managing director. I've been told that those five, as a group, went to Sommer and said, "Pick any one of us as the next CEO, but don't bring in an outsider." Nobody, except three of the outside directors, wanted to bring in an outsider—I even advised them not to do so before I accepted the job—but they decided that was the only thing they could do. I was at Procter & Gamble at the time and was responsible for, among other things, the purchasing of chemicals. I knew Monsanto well because I was their biggest customer, and they also knew me quite well. I was ranked number three in the hierarchy at P&G, but not likely to become the next CEO, so I accepted Monsanto's offer. My mandate from the board, essentially, was to change the company from family management to professional management.

Coming in, it didn't take me very long to set some objectives for myself. First, I was appalled at the low quality of their investment analysis. A chemical company is very capital-intensive, but they simply weren't doing their homework. Under Sommer and Bock, one of the managing directors would personally take his proposal to the CEO for approval. That greased the skids for approval by the board and there was really no analysis.

Second, the five businesses were really run as fiefdoms, and were managed very differently. It was clear to me that we needed to have a common culture, something that we ended up calling the "Monsanto management style." And, third, I knew that I needed to find who the good people were in the company—the people who could help me get the ship moving forward again. The people in the organization were depressed, so on the very first day I arrived I announced that I would serve as CEO for ten years and that, if I had anything to say about it, Monsanto would never again hire another CEO from outside.

I had to tackle the people problem first, because I really didn't know much about how to run a big chemical company. I tried to establish a collegial atmosphere among the senior officers, and after a few months formalized that into a Corporate Administrative Committee (CAC) that served as my advisory group on major issues. There were about fifteen members, both line and staff, and we met once a week to hash out common policies and review investment decisions. Prior to my arrival, there had been a very small executive committee of the board, but that was not a vehicle that produced much cohesion among the officer group. The CAC is apparently a permanent fixture; it's still running even though I've been out of the management for two years.

During the first year or so, I spent a lot of time personally getting acquainted with managers three and four levels down into the organization. I ultimately ended up with a list of thirty or forty people who had good potential to help run Monsanto in the future. I only had to go outside to fill two special-purpose jobs, one for our human resources function and another for corporate affairs. Before the first year was over, I retained a solo consultant to work with us on management style, so I started to make some progress on that objective. Then about a year and a half into the job I retained a consulting firm [Bain and Company] to do a strategic analysis and really help us figure out where we should be putting our chips. They did an excellent job — really overfulfilling my desire to develop rigorous standards for our new investments. (After I retired, they [Bain] turned the tables, and I am now serving as a consultant to them.)

In 1975, Charlie Sommer stepped down as chairman, and I held all three titles for a while. It's not a situation I recommend, but at that point it was simply too early to designate an heir apparent by naming a new president and chief operating officer. At that time I had about ten candidates on my short list and seven of them were really good. But none of them was ready yet, so I had to continue the grooming. Mahoney, for example, held five different jobs during the first eight years I was CEO.

My personal objective for the selection of my successor was to have him emerge naturally, so that when the decision was announced, everyone would say, "Of course, he ought to be the next CEO." More than anything else, I wanted to avoid a horse race, with one winner and several losers.

It's natural for people who realize they might be chosen to have some anxiety about their chances. I met with each candidate and told him, "Relax. You know you're doing well, and you're continuing to grow. I have no doubt you'll make the first team, but you can't pick your own position on that team. Someone will be CEO, but it's the team that's important." With that philosophy, we didn't lose any of our best people when Mahoney was named CEO. I think that the way to retain people is to redefine what we mean by success. Success is making the first team. When that works, it is the team members who implicitly pick their leader, and he knows it. As a new CEO, he can't be obviously autocratic: he's just first among equals — but "first" when necessary!

Hanley's comments touch on several issues I discussed in chapters 2 and 3. Hanley's entrance into Monsanto is similar in many ways to Hicks Waldron's taking charge at Avon, although Monsanto is a larger and more complex situation. Both men inherited a demoralized organization, floundering for lack of a strategic focus. And, each man had a clear mandate from his board of directors: take our parochial company and turn it into a successful, professionally managed organization. Given that mandate, both men accepted the same self-imposed constraint: they would not bring in a large number of executives from outside the company. In fact, each brought in only two executives, both for high-level staff positions.

A final similarity between Hanley and Waldron is the way they used consultants. Both retained a solo consultant to work with them on what I would broadly describe as the management process. Such a consultant can be useful to a CEO who is trying to change the mindset of his organization. Waldron needed a vehicle that would allow his managers to express their frustrations and anxieties, and ultimately, allow Avon to evolve from its embedded set of shared values into an ethic that would look toward the future rather than the past. Hanley's need was to tame the barons by changing the modus operandi of decision making at Monsanto. His label for that, style, has an upbeat note, and sounds like something one should be proud of. More broadly, for a CEO trying to professionalize the management in a moribund situation, consultants can serve a very useful role as teachers; they bring in their managerial technology, of whatever stripe, and show the managers in the company how it can be used effectively. Then, most important, they go away and let the managers do it themselves.

Hanley's comments also touched briefly on two issues regarding CEO tenure that I examined in chapter 3. First, Monsanto provides another data point to document that boards of directors do occasionally take the bit in their teeth and request the resignation of an incumbent CEO. I decided not to pursue the why and how of that event because it was nearly fifteen years ago. Second, regarding his own tenure, Hanley announced at the beginning that "ten years is enough." In his case, however, the announcement was much more than a statement of intent. His managerial cadre was in disarray, and his mandate was to professionalize it. He allowed himself ten years to achieve that objective, stating in effect that if his successor was not an insider, he would have failed to achieve his goal. Once the organization realized what he had said, it must have helped greatly to facilitate the changes that he was trying to make.

The new dimension in Hanley's comments has to do with how he organized and used an operating committee to achieve his multiple objectives. Coming in, he did not inherit any existing committees, and he had to delay several months until he sized up the individuals before formally establishing his Corporate Administrative Committee. A primary, substantive objective was to improve the quality of investment decisions, and Hanley did that by using consultants for analysis and using the CAC as a schoolroom for learning the criteria that defined a "good" investment. He also sought to have a "cohesive" team, which I infer to have two dimensions. First, the barons would now be expected to comment on and criticize the proposals from their peers, thus beginning to share the power that had been more unilateral in the past. Second, corporate staff executives, sitting in the same room with the line officers, inevitably had some increase in their power, if only the right to critique in an open forum. Hanley's new rules of the game at Monsanto, embodied in the operations of the CAC and intensified by weekly meetings, required that every member adopt a more corporate perspective. That result is almost the definition of a professional manager.

Hanley served as a "solo CEO" for five years before naming Mahoney president and COO. The CAC was the place where the succession process was acted out, and near the end, half the members were "really good" candidates to be Hanley's successor. Having developed a pool of talent, Hanley wanted to keep it for the benefit of his successor. His master stroke, in my opinion, was "redefining success" as being a member of the "first team." Making that concept an honest reality turns on the behavior of the new CEO, but if Mahoney does want to reign as first among equals, then Hanley can walk away proudly, saying, "mission accomplished!"

Top Management Teams

The distinction I drew in chapter 1 between the duo and team modes of top management is not simply a matter of counting noses. The dynamics of the interactions among a group of three or more near-peers are far more complex than is typical in the more conventional duo situation. Thus far, I have focused most of my attention on the duo mode, and the relay process that goes with it, because it is so pervasive. But the team mode is fascinating because of its complexity, and is worth studying because it appears to be increasingly more widely used. Operating committees are almost universal, without regard to the mode of top management, but at least for issues involving CEO succession, they are less significant for the team mode than they are for the solo and duo modes.

The difference between operating committees and top management teams is structural—and important. An operating committee is a major tool for the CEO. It is flexible, informal, and temporal in the sense that the membership evolves over time. A top management team consists of three or more executives, each holding one or more of the top five titles, and all of them members of the board of directors. Membership is permanent and official; they're expected to stay on the team until they retire. One member carries the CEO title, but that power is inevitably shared if only because he has two or more colleagues to listen to, and consensus is always preferable to conflict. Put another way, the team collectively is responsible for the health and survival of the company, resulting in a shared fate.

As I noted in chapter 1, top management teams are becoming more popular. At the end of 1984, more than 25 percent of large U.S. corporations had a top management team. Not quite accidentally, six of the twenty companies that provided stories for this book use top management teams. Three of these stories appear in this chapter: Chemical Bank, Corning Glass Works, and Dow Chemical. I will comment briefly on each story as it unfolds, and then summarize across that set in the concluding section.

Don Platten at Chemical Bank

Donald C. Platten is what we call a "good friend of the School." A loyal alumnus of our AMP, he came to the campus regularly in the latter stages of his career, addressing groups of students. I met him at cocktail parties after such events, beginning in the late 70s. When I started thinking about this book, he was one of the first persons I contacted to see if it would be possible to collect undisguised stories. He had recently stepped down as chairman of Chemical Bank, having put a new team in place, and he agreed to talk with me. Subsequently, he arranged for me to meet with his successor, Walter V. Shipley; Shipley's story is told in chapter 7.

The CEO succession process at Chemical Bank is the clearest example I have seen of top management teams where the succession from one team to the next is achieved by comtemporaneously promoting several executives from the next generation at the same time that those of the prior generation retire. Here, we can talk about the tenure of a team; the team that preceded Platten's began its tenure in 1960 and ended in 1972. At that point, Platten took over with his new team and its tenure ran from 1972 until 1983. Now, Shipley and his new team are in place, and if that team continues until Shipley's retirement, it will work together for seventeen years. I was intrigued by that approach, and at a meeting with Platten in April 1984 I asked him to tell me how he managed to pull it off. Here is what he said:

> I really didn't start to think about my own successor until mid-1975, when I was doing some international travel. Once, as I was about to leave for Italy, two directors came to me with some concern about the terrorism there at the time, and asked who my successor should be if something happened to me. With some thought, I told them Berkeley was my current choice.
>
> By 1979, I was working seriously on the succession issue. We had a number of good candidates, and the board was very comfortable that we did not need to look outside. At the time, the candidates were Berkeley, aged fifty-eight, Shipley, forty-eight, Callander, fifty-two, Johnson, forty-two, and Lipp, forty-five. Subsequently, Alan Fishman, thirty-seven, also had to be considered. I decided that Shipley and Lipp were the two best candidates of the next generation and, in 1979, we promoted them to a new title called senior executive vice president. They were not

made directors at that time, but I did make sure they had a lot of exposure to the board of directors, in addition to their frequent contact with the Policy Committee: LeBlond, Berkeley, Carson, and me.

In May 1980, we set up a Strategic Planning Committee and retained a consultant to help us. Berkeley asked to run the committee, and I agreed, but he had not included Callander in the set, and I put him in so that all five of the younger generation were a part of it, reporting occasionally to me, LeBlond, and Carson. For a year and a half, that group of five had to ignore their own turf and try to figure out the right strategy for the bank as a whole. They ultimately concluded that the bank really had three main pieces: a retail side, a wholesale side, and the capital markets function.

The Strategic Planning Committee was really an integral part of the succession process. These were the five guys that were going to run the bank. They needed to own the strategy that they would then use to deal with major changes in the environment. In one sense it was a team-building activity. First the Strategic Planning Committee, and then all five of the younger members became members of the Policy Committee after Berkeley left.

Berkeley decided in the spring of 1981 to take early retirement at age sixty. This was disclosed to the directors, but not announced to the organization. It meant that the board finally had to make a choice between the two candidates, and I then visited each director individually, explaining why I thought Shipley was the right guy. The board of directors meeting as a group never had a serious discussion about whether Shipley was better than Lipp. The Nominating Committee did discuss Shipley, and of course all of these directors talk with each other. But my job was to provide succession, and I hoped that the board would accept my recommendation. I don't think I railroaded Shipley into the job, but, obviously, I wanted each director to understand my feelings. In October 1981, the board elected Shipley as the next president of Chemical

Bank, effective January 1, 1982, and in December 1981, we promoted Johnson and Callander to the title of senior executive vice president, joining Lipp, who still held that rank. Fishman was subsequently promoted to senior executive vice president in 1983.

I've talked with Shipley and Lipp, and looking back, each says he thought that the process was fair. It was not any single thing like being on the Policy Committee or Strategic Planning Committee, but simply day-to-day interactions that I had with them and how I listened. I tried to make sure that each man got a chance to show his stuff, and I was just myself.

If you want to hear how Shipley worked out the rest of the succession issues, skip ahead to chapter 7. My purpose in this chapter is to discuss the why and how of top management teams at a more general level. Given that purpose, I call your attention to two or three aspects of Platten's story.

First, commercial banks, more than any other sector in our population, have a long tradition of using top management teams. That practice reflects the nature of their business; high-level relationships with bank officials are important to their large clients. The CEO of a major industrial company wants to meet occasionally with his peer, the CEO of "his" bank. The first thing he discovers is that there may not be a CEO at his bank; instead there are one chairman, several vice chairmen, and perhaps more than one president. If I break the entire population into only two segments, commercial banks and all other large corporations, in 1984 only 70 percent of the commercial banks officially used the title CEO, whereas 96 percent of all the other companies used it. Chemical Bank is one of those that does not use the CEO title, although traditionally, the chairman is the de facto CEO. The importance of top management titles for customer relations in banks leads me to infer that the cohesion in banks' top management teams may be somewhat less than in other corporations that choose this mode of top management. Nevertheless, those are the people who run the bank and the succession issues still have to be dealt with.

Second, faced with those issues and the deregulation of financial institutions begun in the late 70s, Platten made simultaneous progress on both fronts by establishing a strategic planning committee. By the time he set up the committee, Platten's own thinking about his successor must have been pretty far along. Still, the committee provided nearly a year of further testing for Shipley with his colleagues before he emerged as the clear leader in that group.

Finally, Platten's objective from the outset of the succession process was to produce not only a new chairman but also the set of senior officers who would work with him for the next decade or more. The Strategic Planning Committee was substantive and real — the bank did need to reorganize for its new environment — but it was also a powerful force for allowing the emerging team to learn how to work together and make major decisions they could all support. Creating that cohesion among the team helped stabilize the situation, thereby giving Shipley some time to work out how to retain the services of his prospective colleagues.

Jamie Houghton at Corning Glass

Corning Glass Works was founded in 1851 in Cambridge, Massachusetts, and moved its headquarters to Corning, New York, in 1868. The Houghton family has been associated with the company since its founding and for almost the entire period have been major shareholders.

I met Amory Houghton, Jr. (Amo) in 1970. Then CEO and chairman of Corning, he was having a problem with his strategic planning process, and asked for my help. I spent a lot of time in Corning, New York, during the next eighteen months, meeting all of the senior managers, including Amo's younger brother, James R. Houghton (Jamie). During that period, I learned a great deal about the character of a strong family-driven culture and its effect on the management process.

Jamie Houghton became chairman and CEO of Corning in 1983, and I invited him to my seminar in the spring of 1985. That renewed our relationship, and I subsequently asked him to comment on family management of a publicly held company and, more specifically, on the new team he had put into place when he became CEO. Here is what he said:

> My brother Amo and I represent the fifth generation of Houghtons to be active in the management of the corporation. In our recent history we have always tried to balance family and nonfamily membership in the top management of the company. Having a significant family financial and management interest has, we've always felt, allowed us to take the long-term view (we spend more than twice what the average company does on R&D) and not be slaves solely to quarterly earnings reports. On the other hand, to avoid inbreeding, we've always had very strong nonfamily members at the top of the company.
>
> When my father became president of the company in 1930, an outsider was the chairman. Later, when my father became chairman, William Decker, a brilliant and highly professional manager, became president. Decker then succeeded my father as chairman in 1961, and my brother Amo was appointed president and chief operating officer of the company. (My brother had previously held several positions in the company, most recently being the vice president of staffs.)
>
> Decker retired as chairman in 1964 and the title passed to my brother, who was thirty-eight years old at the time. His choice for president was R. Lee Waterman, who had joined the company relatively late in his career but had made a brilliant record. When Waterman retired as president in 1971, Amo chose Thomas C. MacAvoy, then forty-three years old, to become the next president. MacAvoy had joined the company as a research chemist and had moved out of the laboratory into the operating side fairly early in his career. He had successfully run several divisions. At the same time that MacAvoy was appointed president, Amo installed two new vice chairmen. One was William H. Armistead, who for years had been the chief technical officer of the corporation. The other

was me. I was then thirty-five and most of my nine years with the company had been spent on the international side of the business. As vice chairman I continued in that role, as well as having responsibility for several of the corporate staffs.

When Armistead retired, my brother decided on a realignment. He gave MacAvoy responsibility for all of the line operations, both domestic and international, and gave me responsibility for all of the staff or "resource groups" in the company. I was given the additional title of chief strategic officer and was charged with developing a long-range plan for the company.

In 1983 my brother decided to step down after nineteen years as chairman and CEO, and he asked me to take that role. My brother remains active in the company as a member of the board and as chairman of the Executive Committee.

When I was asked to become CEO, I debated whether or not I should appoint a traditional chief operating officer. I decided not to do so for two fundamental reasons. First of all, our businesses were so diverse that I felt no single COO was going to be able to be intimately enough involved with the businesses that he could make as much contribution as I thought was necessary. Second, I frankly wanted to be closer to the businesses myself and I felt that if there was a chief operating officer between me and the businesses, it would be more difficult for me to become involved.

I therefore decided on a structure that had three group presidents and two vice chairmen. One of the vice chairmen is Tom MacAvoy, who relinquished his role as the chief operating officer and became our vice chairman and chief technical officer. With his scientific and technological background he was ideally suited for this. The other vice chairman, Van Campbell, is responsible for all the other staff activities and especially for strategic planning. Van's background had been both line and staff, but his particular strength had been in the financial and strategic

*planning areas. The three group presidents that were ap-
pointed reflected our different business portfolios. The six
of us, as a set, are a fairly young team, ranging in age
from forty-five to fifty-five.*

*Putting together this new team, I also insisted that we
operate as a Management Committee. They are all members of the board of directors and we spend a great deal of
time as a committee of the whole, operating on corporate
problems, issues, and opportunities. We operate in an extremely open and participative manner and the team has
been jelling ever since it was formed. Perhaps at another
time we will change the form of organization, but at the
moment I am extremely satisfied.*

*The team approach fits in very well with a concept
we have been developing in the company called Total
Quality. This is a basic management style that encourages
openness, participation on the part of every employee, and
concern with "meeting the customers' (whether they be the
traditional external customers or internal customers, i.e.,
one's fellow workers) requirements 100 percent of the
time." In this environment, teamwork is very important,
and my goal is to make the Management Committee the
beacon for the entire corporation in terms of a successful
team effort.*

As our stories begin to accumulate, the analysis becomes
richer. Here, I find it very useful to compare Corning with Cummins Engine. There are several similarities, and one important
difference. Irwin Miller at Cummins provided only one generation of family management before turning over the reins to nonfamily executives. Corning Glass is a much older company, but
the Houghton family has provided five generations of family
managers. Because of its maturity, Corning allows us to see more
clearly the path of CEO succession when family managers are
involved.

The pattern of CEO succession at Corning, reflecting an explicit policy adopted by the Houghton family, might be called a
balance of power. Working with only two titles, chairman and

president, since 1930, a member of the Houghton family has held one title but a nonfamily member has held the other. In 1971, when it became time to start providing for Amo's successor, the company adopted the team mode, creating two vice chairmen. But the balance of power was stable, with two Houghtons and two nonfamily members. That team stayed in place for ten years until Armistead retired, and two years later Jamie put his new team in place consisting of six members in total, with only one active Houghton.

The new insight, for me, in thinking about these two companies was the sudden realization that the "deep early selection" at Cummins is not a problem for Corning Glass; it's almost preordained by birth. That, at least, is one way of explaining why both companies use a prolonged relay process. At Corning, a mature, seasoned executive runs alongside the heir apparent or fledgling CEO. Amo had Decker and then Waterman; Jamie had MacAvoy and Armistead, and his own brother. Using nonfamily executives this way achieved two purposes: first, it provided an overt balance of power that protected the company from the criticism of inbreeding, and second, it played a more substantive role by grooming the next CEO to handle his responsibilities.

I think the relay process is very useful for family-controlled companies. The next CEO may be *almost* preordained, but his partner running alongside inevitably plays a role beyond that of a trainer; he also comes to know the candidate well enough to pass judgment on his overall competence for the task. At some point, the next CEO will not be a member of the family, and his partner in the relay process is likely to be the first one to realize that fact.

Paul Oreffice at Dow

In chapter 3, Paul Oreffice told part of his story about how the top management team works at Dow, focusing on the policies and traditions by which Dow manages the tenure of its senior officers. In the same interview, Oreffice also talked about the role of his team in CEO succession:

> *Starting my tenure as CEO, I immediately chose Bob Lundeen and Earle Barnes to work with me as the Operat-*

ing Committee. Barnes, who became chairman when Merszei left, had a background in R&D and manufacturing,
while Lundeen was familiar with our international operations. I wanted a diverse set of talents to help me.

The number of members on the Operating Committee
and its composition have evolved over the years. We have
had as few as three and as many as six members. After
Barnes retired, David Rooke and Bob Keil joined the
group. Lundeen and Rooke later dropped out, although remaining on the board, when they started on their deceleration. They have been excellent directors and very useful to
me. Today, there are six members of the Operating Committee. Two of them are my cohorts, within months of my
own age: Keil and Hunter Henry. The other three are three
to eight years younger than I am, and will be solid members of management after I give up my direct line responsibilities; they are Joseph Temple, Keith McKennon, and
Frank Popoff.

So, the evolution of management rolls along, and I
will step down as CEO before the end of 1987. Obviously,
I've given a lot of thought to who should be my successor,
and I asked Keil and Henry, the two senior members of the
Operating Committee, to work directly with me on that issue. In our first private discussion on this matter, in 1984,
we identified three candidates. We all agreed that the list
was correct, so I then asked them to rank the three. We
had general agreement on the ranking, but with varying
gaps as to which we thought was the most qualified. We've
done that ranking annually since then, and the gap appears to be narrowing in favor of one of the three. When the
decision is finally made in 1987, I don't think that many
people will be surprised. That's the way we like to make it
work at Dow Chemical.

Ever the maverick, Dow Chemical does not satisfy my technical definition for having a top management team. Only two
officers carry any of the five top management titles, and the vice
chairman title is not used at all. So much for definitions. It is

perfectly clear that Dow does have a top management team in every sense of that term. Perversely, they call that the Operating Committee, which should not be confused with my prior definition of an operating committee as one that is chaired by the CEO and reaches two or three levels down in the organization. My primary criterion for defining a top management team, however, is that it plays a major role in CEO succession. Oreffice's team as he described it clearly meets that test.

"Making it" at Dow means being elected to the board of directors. Becoming a director is Dow's equivalent of the "first team" that Hanley talked about at Monsanto, but it is a more formal team, and those who make it stay until they retire. A board meeting at Dow is analogous to meetings of the generic operating committee that is used by other companies; the agenda is substantive, but the meetings also provide data about the next generation of leaders. A subset of that group, Dow's Operating Committee, finally makes a recommendation to the full board as to which person should be selected as the next CEO.

Coming into office, the new CEO selects the members to serve with him on the Operating Committee (or fails to do so at his own peril, as we saw in Merszei's case). If Oreffice's tenure is typical, the membership of the Operating Committee then evolves over time. In 1986, nearing the end of his tenure, Oreffice's committee consisted of two generations, and he describes that as the "evolution of management."

At Dow, CEO succession is analogous to a triple relay process. One younger member will become the new CEO, but the other two contemporaries will surely stay, and all three need to be brought up to speed. When the successor is selected, if he follows Oreffice's model, he will select two older members to serve on his Operating Committee, thereby permitting the relay to continue for another few years. And then the evolutionary process will begin all over again.

Moving now to a more general level, I will conclude this chapter by commenting briefly on three topics: succession patterns in top management teams, the issue of inside directors, and the current status of a recently discovered virus called CEOitis.

Succession Patterns in Top Management Teams

The use of top management teams (except in commercial banks) is a recent phenomenon and is far from pervasive. Those companies that have adopted this mode are still learning how to use it, and there is not enough history to discern patterns. The first thing that can be said is that such teams vary widely in name, size, and membership. For the six companies included in this book, we have a five-person Policy Committee at Chemical Bank, a six-person Management Committee at Corning, a six-person Operating Committee at Dow, a four-person team at Kellogg, a five-person Office of the Chairman at AT&T, and a three-person Corporate Executive Office at GE. In each case, the members hold one or more of the five top management titles and are members of the board of directors.

Using just this small sample, it is possible to discern two ends of a spectrum in terms of the membership of the team. At one end we have teams that are created episodically, put into place as a group, and expected to work together over a number of years. At the other end we have teams that are evolutionary, where the membership changes slowly but continuously over the years. The members of episodic teams, such as at Chemical Bank and Corning Glass, are typically close in age. The members of evolutionary teams, such as at Dow Chemical, Kellogg, and AT&T, may represent two or three generations of management. Somewhere in the middle we have General Electric, where a new team was put in place all at once, but there has already been one change in membership.

The "right" position on that spectrum obviously depends on the situation. And one could argue either side of the issue of which team is likely to be more cohesive. It could be the contemporaries working together to make their mark on the corporation, or it could be the intergenerational team because there is less competition among the members. The spectrum is useful, however, in terms of one issue: Who should pick the members of a new CEO's team? Practice varies on this dimension as well, and I will return to it in chapter 6. My only other comment at this point is that I believe episodic teams are much more difficult to handle in the succession process, and evolutionary teams are more commonly used.

I have examined a number of succession diagrams for companies using the top management team mode in an evolutionary fashion. The most common pattern appears to be one in which the chairman always carries the title of CEO (except in Dow, where the president always carries that title). The other members of the team carry the titles of president or vice chairman, and they may range widely in age. Typically, however, two or more younger members join the team a few years before the chairman is scheduled to retire. Those candidates may carry the title of president or vice chairman. Sometimes the person carrying the title of president is really an heir apparent and goes on to become the next CEO. But it is also not uncommon to see a young vice chairman be made the next CEO. It's hard to tell just from the age and title of the candidates whether or not an heir apparent has been selected.

One last comment on patterns in top management teams. In many situations there are a chairman and a president who operate, in effect, in the duo mode and work out the relay process between them. At the same time, there may be one or two older executives carrying the title of vice chairman as they serve out the time until they obtain their gold watch. In situations where I know the circumstances, I find this practice to be honorable and deserved, but it does raise the issue of the number of inside directors, a topic to which I now turn.

Inside Directors: Pro and Con

A decade ago, I was persuaded by the arguments of Harold M. Williams, then chairman of the SEC, that the governance of large U.S. corporations would be improved if all directors were independent outsiders, with the chairman and president the only officers serving on the board. That seems like a long time ago. Williams was effective, and the typical board in 1984 had a solid two-to-one majority of outsiders. But the trend appears to have peaked, and my opinion is that the status quo is just about right.

This issue is not restricted to companies using top management teams, but it is convenient to discuss it here because such companies, by definition, have three or more inside directors. Across the entire population of large U.S. corporations, the typical company in 1984 had thirteen members on its board of directors, four of whom were current or retired members of management. Across that range of companies, only 2 percent had one inside director, the CEO. At the other end of that spectrum, companies like Dow with a preponderance of inside directors are also rare. Only 13 percent of our population had a majority of more than 50 percent. Practice does vary widely.

I see three primary benefits to having several insiders on the board of directors. First, and most important, both insiders and outsiders receive current, firsthand information about the range of opinions among the members of the other group. This interaction should help produce a better-informed consensus for the board as a whole. More subtly, direct interaction reduces the power of the CEO; he no longer can serve as a gatekeeper, telling his officers what the outside directors think about an issue and vice versa. Put bluntly, a board made up entirely of outsiders can become a captive of the CEO if he is the only source of information. Having other members of management seated at the same table helps keep the CEO honest.

The other two benefits of inside directors relate directly to the process of CEO succession. First, if there are two or three candidates to succeed the incumbent CEO, putting them on the board two or three years ahead of the event is an excellent way for the outside directors to get acquainted with them. This benefit is so desirable that it is not surprising to find that this is fairly common practice. Second, once the selection decision is made, it may be easier to retain the other candidates if they are offered positions as vice chairmen. That decision, itself, is a sticky one, related to the new CEO's "right" to pick his own team. My point is simply that a company that has a policy against vice chairmen forecloses an option that can be quite valuable.

Stacked against these benefits of having inside directors, the arguments for a pure outside board are rather thin. The primary argument is that having insiders in the room may stifle open discussion among the outside directors on sensitive issues. The solution to that, commonly practiced, is for the board to go into executive session including only outside directors, and some-times excluding even the CEO. Another argument is that insiders need not be directors in order to attend board meetings and com-ment when requested. In my view, that misses the point com-pletely; making an insider a member of the board obligates him to decide when he should speak.

Twenty years ago—and less—outside directors could ap-propriately be accused of being too passive. The arguments for a pure outside board were an effective way to remind outside di-rectors of their independence and their responsibility for corpo-rate governance. I think we are past that phase, if only because directors are now very conscious of their legal exposure to liabil-ity suits. Today, the corporate governance issue that concerns me most is the ascendancy of the CEO.

CEOitis: The Deity Syndrome

Coming full circle, I return to Henry Schacht at Cummins Engine. Speaking softly to a dozen CEOs in the room, he said, "We are not deities," and several of them almost choked. One, incredulous at Schacht's comment, said, "If we downplay the appointment of a new CEO as you suggest, people might infer that the job is not very important." Schacht, aware that he was not about to win a convert to his position, simply nodded his head solemnly.

I believe that the CEO title, invented to facilitate the suc-cession process, has had an unintentional backlash. By reducing the ambiguity about whether the chairman or the president is the more powerful, the CEO title seems to lodge all the power in the hands of one person. The relay process does work, trans-ferring power gradually from one to the other, but it is not appar-ent to the man in the street, or to many employees within the company. To them, the CEO sounds like the Almighty.

You can mitigate the deification of your office, if you choose to do so. Sharing the power of the CEO—overtly—is both honest and effective; you can't do it all, and your colleagues are talented. An operating committee with a dozen members, and two or three inside directors in addition to you, are two good structural de-vices that put self-imposed constraints on your freedom of action. The remainder of the prescription to help you ward off CEOitis is more personal, dealing with your personal style and your ego needs.

The objective of most CEOs I have talked with is to build a productive partnership with their colleagues and directors. The five stories in this chapter illustrate that this can be done in a variety of ways. Partnership management will continue to be an important theme as we proceed toward the next phase of CEO succession.

5

Marshalling the Candidates

The clock is inexorable. It's hard to believe that within a couple of years you'll be half way through your expected tenure as CEO. If the chairman conforms to tradition, he will retire two or three years before the mandatory retirement date, and you will become chairman and CEO. At that time, again traditionally, the board of directors will expect you to recommend an executive to be named president/COO and, if everything works out, that heir apparent will someday be your successor as CEO. You do control the timing of this event, to some extent, because the chairman will stay on for a year or so if need be. Still, sooner than you had expected, the time has come to start devoting explicit attention to the succession process.

The good news is that the news is good. A few of your early initiatives have not worked out as well as you had hoped, but a couple of the more important ones now appear to be clear winners. Also, you realize now that you tried to make too many decisions on your own authority during the first couple of years. After all, you *are* the CEO, and CEOs are supposed to be decisive. Since then, you've invested heavily in developing a cohesive management team, and the decision-making process is much more effective. Your primary objective taking over as CEO was to hand off to your successor a stronger corporation than the one you inherited. That prospect now seems virtually assured; the pieces are in place, and the momentum is growing.

Now, it's time to start finding that successor. More than half the members of your operating committee are your own appointments, including a couple of outsiders you brought in, and there's a lot of talent in that group. You know each member well, and feel comfortable ranking them in terms of potential. But you wonder whether even the best of that lot is good enough to meet the challenges of the next fifteen years. That's when you realize that your objective of passing on a healthier corporation cannot be achieved unless the CEO who will run that company is as good as or better than you are. Now that's a challenge!

Focus of this Chapter

The core process of CEO succession, discussed in this chapter and the next two, is analogous to a theatrical production; a drama played out in three acts. Each production has its unique twists, but the basic plot is pure formula: the cast of characters includes the CEO, members of his board of directors, and the candidates to succeed him; the suspense-filled question, answered in the final act, is, "Who will be the next CEO?" Act 1 is prologue, serving to introduce the candidates and describe the context of the corporation in which the drama will unfold. Act 2 ends with the selection of an heir apparent to succeed the current CEO, and Act 3, sometimes anticlimactic, ends with the heir apparent becoming CEO and his predecessor stepping down. The star of the show, in each act, is the incumbent CEO.

This chapter focuses on the prologue. The theory of the case is simple. The CEO must ultimately reconcile two important tasks. First, working with his senior officers and directors, he must conduct a strategic analysis of the prospective competitive environment for his company over the next decade or more. I am not talking about the conventional "strategic planning" most companies perform, using a five-year time span, and I use the word "must" knowing full well that most companies do not follow my prescription. Nevertheless, formally or informally, the CEO and his board must ultimately try to agree on the strategic mandate for the next CEO. What are the larger issues that he will face, and what are the skills and experience he will need to handle them properly?

Second, and a task most CEOs do very well, he must continually seek to hire, identify, and develop a cadre of high-potential younger executives who will become the next generation of top managers in the company. From these executives, if he's lucky, he will be able to marshal two or three candidates who may be qualified to be his successor. Even then, if the competitive environment is changing rapidly, the best internal candidates may ultimately be judged inadequate to handle the prospective environment.

These two tasks are discussed below. In the closing section I focus on a topic that is in one sense unrelated to the CEO's tasks, but is useful to discuss here because it occurs simultaneously. As my research unfolded, I became intensely interested in the perspective of the candidates who are on the receiving end of all this effort by the incumbent CEO. Fortunately, I found two executives who agreed to be collaborators, and their comments may yield useful insights for their counterparts as well as for CEOs conducting the succession process.

Strategy and CEO Succession

The three stories in this section provide a conceptual spectrum of strategic threats and opportunities. I present the CIGNA case first, because it holds the middle ground between the other two companies and because it provides a detailed account of both of the CEOs' tasks. Following that, the Kellogg and Allied Corp. stories are told.

Bob Kilpatrick at CIGNA

I decided to include a CIGNA story in this book, despite my insider status as a board member and the resulting loss of objectivity. The substantive reason (I rationalized) was that there was a good, generic story to tell: many companies, two or three years before the incumbent CEO retires, restructure the top-end organization for one or both of two objectives. CIGNA's reorganization in January 1985 embraced both, seeking to solidify the emerging strategic consensus about the future of the enterprise, and marshalling the CEO candidates for a final period of personal development and demonstrated performance. I also admitted to myself, however, that I wanted to have CIGNA in the book for the same reason that CEOs in other companies had collaborated with me: at CIGNA, we're proud of the way the company is managed, and willing to share our experience.

The decision, of course, was not mine alone to make, but Bob Kilpatrick agreed immediately when I raised the question with him. Robert D. Kilpatrick joined the Connecticut General Life Insurance Company in 1954 and was elected president and CEO in 1976, just before I joined the board of directors. Even though we have known each other for ten years, this new academic collaboration required some explicit ground rules. We agreed that my usual practice of interviewing a CEO and then preparing a draft statement for his review and revision was appropriate here, as well, and would mitigate any tendency I might have toward editorializing, because he would have to sign off on the final statement. He suggested that to enrich my understanding of the situation, I meet with the several individuals who had been involved in planning the reorganization: two senior partners of Booz, Allen & Hamilton and two CIGNA executives, which I did. Below, Kilpatrick talks briefly about the merger between CG and INA, and then describes why and how he reorganized the top management of CIGNA in January 1985.

The creation of CIGNA by merging Connecticut General Insurance Corp. and INA Corp. was negotiated in the fall of 1981 and consummated on March 31, 1982. It was the largest merger of its type at that time. From the outset, the intent was to create a large financial services company, not simply a holding company with two insurance subsidiaries, one primarily in life/employee benefits and the other primarily in property/casualty insurance. The situation was complicated by the fact that the two companies were almost identical in size, and the new company was to be a "merger of equals." There were co-CEOs for the first year, Ralph Saul, former chairman and CEO of INA, and I, and the directors and senior officers were drawn in approximately equal numbers from both companies. The organization structure was designed to cope with the transition, and we spent our first year or so simply trying to consolidate the operations of the two components.

By mid-1983, I felt we had our legs back underneath us so that we could devote some attention to lengthening our time horizon. During the next fifteen months, we conducted a massive strategic analysis of the financial services industry, trying to decide which sectors we should be in and which we should not. Those were exciting times. We set up eight task forces, one each for the major sectors

we were considering. The Finance Committee of the board
met every other month with one or more of those task
forces, and the full board was kept informed of the progress we were making. Finally, we had a one and a half
day meeting of the board in December 1984 to present our
recommendations. Our conclusion was that CIGNA would
concentrate its attention on becoming a worldwide
diversified financial services and health care company. We
would serve primarily commercial customers and continue
to serve the affluent, small-business owner and teacher
segment of the consumer market, and market various personal lines of property/casualty products.

Reassessing our situation in 1984, I could identify several major achievements and one major problem. The consolidation of the two companies was now essentially complete, although not accomplished without a certain
amount of trauma. We had cut our work force in many
areas with minimal loss of top-level talent. For our core
management cadre, about eighty people, many had a different job and/or had made a physical relocation from
Bloomfield, Connecticut, to Philadelphia or vice versa. We
now had the right people in the right jobs, and the organization was beginning to hum. Work to define our longer-
term strategic direction was coming along nicely. In early
1984, reacting to an extraordinary opportunity with great
speed, we were able to acquire AFIA, a major international insurance consortium. The major problem was that
the domestic property/casualty business had continued in
a prolonged down cycle in 1982 and 1983, and it was
clear that we would have major underwriting losses in
1984 and 1985. Finally, there was one new item on my
personal agenda, triggered by the fact that in 1984 I turned
sixty years old. I plan to retire at sixty-five, in 1989, and it
was time to start doing some serious thinking about a process that would produce my successor.

Designing a Visible Process. From time to
time, I take some good-natured ribbing from my senior col-

leagues, who occasionally call me a "process nut." In fact, CIGNA is run by three formal management processes. We have a strategic planning process, to ensure that our longer-run objectives are properly focused; an organization and management continuity review process, to ensure that we are developing our people and organization for the future; and an operational planning and control process, to ensure that our current financial and other performance achieves the objectives we have set for ourselves. These annual processes have served us well, helping every manager understand what his or her role is in the organization and what each one is expected to achieve. CEO succession, obviously, is not an annual topic. Nevertheless, I wanted to design a visible process that would actively involve all of the people who would be most directly affected by the result—a few dozen senior officers plus the board of directors. I knew we had in our management group a number of potential candidates to succeed me. My belief was that if I handled the process right, succession could be achieved with strong support and little disruption.

The first step in that process was to reorganize the senior management group in order to ensure that each strategic sector was receiving the proper attention and was well positioned to work with other sectors where there are important relationships. While doing that, we would also make explicit that the reorganization was the first step in a process that would ultimately provide a successor for me. I asked Jim Farley, former chairman of Booz, Allen & Hamilton, and Hadley Ford, senior vice president, to work with me on this task. I had worked with them previously and knew they were first rate. Two senior CIGNA executives worked with us on the project in coordination and advisory roles. We quickly agreed that we had a complex assignment.

With a single action—reorganization—we sought to achieve three objectives: operational stability, strategic execution, and preparation for management succession. The

first objective was really a constraint: we wanted to minimize the distractions that are caused by a reorganization
because CIGNA was experiencing a period of weak
financial performance and we did not want to make a
tough job even tougher. As a practical matter, this constraint applied primarily to the property/casualty business.
We did not make any organizational changes within that
group, even though strategically some fine-tuning was going on. The second objective was purely substantive: this
was our opportunity to take the various segments in our
several businesses and restructure them in a way that
made good business sense in terms of executing our new
strategic directions. The announcement of the third objective was an end unto itself, telling the organization that
there was a succession dimension to this exercise.

In mid-July, in separate memos to the senior officers
and the directors, I announced that I was beginning a
study of our top management organization. I identified the
three objectives of the study, and described the roles that
would be played by each member of the study team. During the next three months, Booz, Allen interviewed forty-
one senior managers within the company, and they began
a strategic analysis of our key businesses. These one-on-
one meetings provided an opportunity for each person to
identify and comment on the strategic issues relevant to
his or her own situation, and we learned a few things from
that. For example, several people thought that the individual financial services business had more strategic potential than had been credited to it in the sector analysis.
That turned out to have a major effect in realigning some
of our segments. The interviews also gave each person an
opportunity to express his own aspirations and opinions
about some of the obvious candidates to become the next
CEO.

Analyzing the Trade-offs. In September, I began meeting every few weeks with the study team for a
two- or three-hour discussion of what they were learning.

The interviews were invaluable in confirming the tough strategic issues that needed to be addressed and in alerting me to the positions of each individual in terms of his or her aspirations. Armed with that information, I then had to make some tough decisions and feel comfortable with the rationale for each one.

I think it is very important to build a consensus among the managers who are affected by such decisions, and that's what I set out to do. Ultimately, I personally met one-on-one with over thirty of our top executives. Knowing the items on the agenda of each individual, I discussed the options we faced and the tentative choices I had made. In every case, the executives were pleased to be a part of the analysis and enthusiastic about the objective of creating the structure to fit the strategy. By the time we were through, a high percentage of our management group felt a real sense of ownership in the new structure.

Designing the new organizational structure was, nevertheless, a real challenge. Regarding succession, I wanted to be able to work closely with each of my possible successors over the next few years, and that meant I needed them to either report directly to me or be as close as possible, with visible contact. Also, I was keeping in mind succession for key jobs other than CEO. On the strategic side, we had a lot of options in terms of grouping the various parts and segments into operating groups. The trade-off was to design major groups that made strategic sense and could be run by one of the individuals who were obvious candidates to be the next CEO. When we were finally through that exercise, I felt that the trade-off had been roughly 60-40 in favor of strategic issues.

Announcing the Result. Concurrently, during this period, Farley and Ford had been holding one-on-one interviews with each of our sixteen outside directors. One purpose of these interviews was to give the directors the same chance the senior officers had to make their own comments about strategic issues and individual personalities. The second purpose was a little more subtle, in that they used the interviews to raise trial balloons on some of the options that we were discussing, thereby allowing the directors to adjust their own expectations as to what the result might be. Subsequently, I reported to the board on the findings from those interviews as a part of my final presentation about the reorganization. The board appeared to have broad consensus on three important items: (1) succession was a high priority for the board, both short term as a back-up for me and long term when I retire; (2) the board believed we had a number of attractive inside candidates; and (3) the board concurred with me that the succession process should take place over time and that an heir apparent should not be named now.

The next formal event in the reorganization process occurred at the board of directors meeting in mid-October 1984. I have made it a practice to use that meeting each year to discuss executive continuity, providing the board with my current assessment of the performance and potential of all of the executives who report directly to me, plus several others who have high potential. I find that the self-imposed discipline of such a discussion is very useful to me, and the directors are universally enthusiastic about the exercise. This time, with the impending reorganization, the discussion was even more intensive, and I was far enough down the road in my own thinking that I could make some additional comments about how some of the individuals would fit into the new organization. The most important point, which the board appreciated, was that many of the candidates to become my successor would be reporting directly to me in the new organization. Other, dark-horse candidates not reporting to me would be in key jobs of great importance to the company.

The final event, announcing the new organization, occurred on January 23, 1985. Starting with the board of directors in executive session, I delivered a formal presentation. I started by reminding them of the background of this whole exercise, the objectives that we were attempting to

EXHIBIT 5.1

Phase I

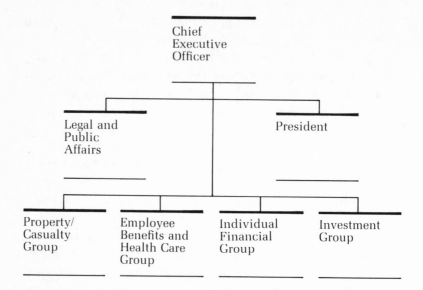

achieve, and the process that we had used in terms of broad participation, and reported on the results from the interviews with directors. Then, I described the approach I thought we should use for CEO succession. Starting that day, the new organization (Exhibit 5.1) would consist of four operating groups reporting directly to me and two staff executives. This structure reduced the number of people reporting directly to me, while at the same time it gave me a direct relationship with some of the better-known candidates to become the next CEO. It also positioned a seasoned executive to replace me on an emergency basis should that become necessary before a long-term successor is identified.

I recommended that we allow this organization to stay in place for about three years, and then select an heir apparent to succeed me, and position him to prepare for the job. Naturally, the final details of the transition structure would be subject to new developments and insights over the next three years. One possibility would be for the heir

EXHIBIT 5.2

Phase II

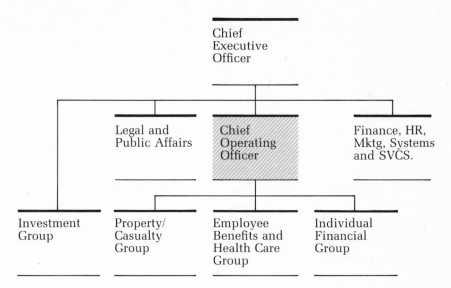

apparent to become chief operating officer (Exhibit 5.2).
About a year later, I would retire and my successor would
take over. The exact organizational design at that point
would have to suit the needs of the new incumbent.

It was clear immediately that the board and the management group felt good about the process and the result.
A year and a half later, I and they still feel good about it.
The new organization is functioning well and we are making good progress in current results and execution of our
longer-term strategies. The CEO succession candidates are
being fully challenged and tested in large, complex jobs
under demanding market conditions. They are experiencing rapid personal growth. I and the board are well positioned to observe and evaluate their strengths, weaknesses,
and accomplishments. I am confident the company's customers, shareholders, and employees will enjoy strong
leadership and success long after I'm gone, and that's
what this is all about.

Commentary. I hope that, now, it is obvious why I wanted Kilpatrick to tell the CIGNA story. I may know it too well, but I view the CIGNA story as a classic, textbook example of the role of the CEO, broadly defined. There are three major substantive variables: strategy, structure, and people, each interacting with the other two. The organization structure should be designed to facilitate the implementation of strategy. But the specific parameters that define each manager's job must be designed to take advantage of the skills and experience of the executive who will fill that post. And strategy, of course, is not God-given; it is invented by people, and the executive charged with implementing a strategy must have a real sense of ownership in it. The perennial task of a CEO is to fine-tune the symbiosis among these three variables. Most of the adjustments he makes are small and incremental, making it hard to see the big picture until something like a major reorganization brings all the trade-offs into stark relief.

Kilpatrick's reorganization dealt with all three variables, and as an avowed "process nut," he created a visible process to identify and resolve the issues, which makes his story particularly useful. In one sense, identifying the issues that concern members of the management cadre is more difficult than resolving them. Using consultants in this first phase of the process was crucial to its success; they provided an unbiased pipeline directly to the CEO, and "everybody" had a chance to be heard before the analysis really began in earnest. Further, everybody knew that a comprehensive agenda had been defined, even though they didn't know all of the items it contained, and this knowledge increased their confidence that all of the right issues would be addressed.

Closing that loop, as the analytical phase was winding up, Kilpatrick engaged in an immense personal effort to build consensus for the interrelated set of decisions that had to be made. Several dozen executives had to "buy in" on both their specific strategic mission and how it related to the broader corporate strategy—and Kilpatrick "sold" it to them, one-on-one. The other result of the process, almost a byproduct, was the identification of a set of candidates to be Kilpatrick's successor. The implications of that need to be discussed in a somewhat broader context.

The most common process for CEO succession — passing the baton — occurs in companies that use the duo mode of top management organization. One of the advantages of the relay process is that it avoids an overt horse race and the trauma that results for several losers. But sometimes, a horse race is the only way to go, as we saw in chapter 2 when Bill Schreyer at Merrill Lynch, newly in office, reorganized to create a horse race because he needed to name an heir apparent within a few months. We will see other examples of solo CEOs reorganizing for the same purpose in the next chapter. Mike Ford at Emhart and Reg Jones at GE were in radically different circumstances, but running a horse race — be it two contenders or seven — was the path they chose.

Kilpatrick at sixty, only two years after a "merger of equals" found himself in the position of being solo CEO in an organization that was not quite finished tearing down walls and building bridges. My assessment is that his highest priority was to ensure that the process that would yield his successor was completely equitable for all conceivable contenders. I believe he is achieving that, and in the process, helping to knit the organization even closer together.

Bill LaMothe at Kellogg

The Kellogg Company is what I call a quiet blue chip, tucked away in a small town in Michigan assiduously minding its own business of breakfast cereals and other packaged foods, with spectacular results. Earnings per share have increased every year since 1951, and return on equity runs at a steady 27 percent. In many ways Kellogg is similar to Dow Chemical: an international company with an insular headquarters, still influenced by the founder (the Kellogg Foundation owns 35 percent of the stock), and committed to lifetime careers and team management.

William E. LaMothe, chairman and CEO of Kellogg, came to my first seminar in April 1984, and I contacted him eighteen months later, knowing that he was more than half way through his tenure and expecting that he was pretty far down the road

toward grooming a set of candidates to succeed him. He acknowledged that and, when we met in New York City in March 1986, he
described what he had been doing:

> I have focused on developing a set of candidates that
> are qualified to be my successor. If you look at the top
> management of our organization, you'll see there are
> thirty-three names, and seventeen of them — more than
> half — are aged forty through forty-nine. There are only six
> people aged fifty-nine or older, including me and four of
> our senior officers. The remarkable thing is that we only
> have four people in the age range from fifty through fifty-
> eight. In effect, we're missing a cohort of people in their
> fifties who ought to be the group from which my successor
> would be chosen. When I became COO in the early
> 70s, I began putting more attention on management devel-
> opment, as well as formalizing our strategic planning pro-
> cess. That effort, I believe, has paid off, and we now have
> several excellent candidates to be my successor.
>
> The next cadre of senior managers at Kellogg will be a
> subset of the large group that is now in its mid-forties. The
> succession will really be a generational change. That
> means the next CEO will have a long tenure, but I don't
> see anything wrong with that at all. I became COO at age
> forty-six, and will have spent nearly twenty years at the
> top by the time I retire. My official tenure as CEO will turn
> out to be only nine or ten years, but continuity over a
> twenty-year time span could be argued to be appropriate
> for our type of company.
>
> I can't claim that there is anything remarkable about
> our management development process. We try to do as
> much job rotation as possible to help develop the capabili-
> ties of our people, and once a year I have a session with
> the board of directors reviewing the top four or five people
> who might be candidates to succeed me. Over time, that
> group changes as some drop out and others are added.
>
> One unique aspect of our succession process concerns
> the role of the Kellogg Foundation. There are four trustees

of the foundation, two of whom are on the board of Kellogg Company. I meet with the trustees with some frequency and they, as well as the board of directors, know what the suggested contingency plan is in the event that something should suddenly happen to me. Our board members are updated at least once a year on these plans and the progress of our succession candidates.

Even though I expect we will make a decision within the next few years, I have tried to avoid politicizing the organization. I have informal, one-on-one meetings with each of the senior officers each year, reviewing their performance. I am making an effort to be careful not to send any strong signals to any of the candidates about their relative standing.

I won't forget my own experience in the mid-60s, when the then CEO told everyone I was the fair-haired boy. Then, suddenly, I was moved to what I thought was an out-of-the-way assignment, and I was crushed. Of course, it turned out to be exactly what I needed. I would have been too inexperienced and immature to have gotten the top job at that time. But, as a result of my own experience, I think there is little to be gained and much to lose by raising expectations prematurely.

So, at the moment, we're working hard but making changes when we feel it's necessary. We have a practice of having a management coffee every Monday morning for the twenty-three senior officers. We test our products and our competitors' products and discuss the current challenges. The chemistry within that group seems to be very healthy. The board meets nine times each year, and we continue the practice of having a number of the next generation attend each meeting. This provides some better exposure for the directors. I believe a consensus is beginning to emerge; and if that does coalesce, the appointment of the next president should come as no surprise to anyone.

As I described above, the CEO is continually fine-tuning the interrelated variables of strategy, structure, and people. Of these, formal organization structure can trace its origins back nearly a century, while the other two are relatively new. Formal strategic planning was a fad in the mid-60s, and I followed it closely for nearly a decade, watching it mature into a cornerstone of professional management. Formal management development, lagging behind a few years, also enjoyed increasing recognition by top managers as they realized that the primary constraint on growth was the availability of competent executives. Bill LaMothe made his mark on Kellogg by embracing both of these new processes. The way he tells it makes it sound easy, and we know that it's not.

Marshalling the candidates in preparation for selecting a new CEO frequently is conflicted by the simultaneous needs for both continuity and change. Across that spectrum, the byword at Kellogg is continuity, and we may rest assured that LaMothe's successor will be an insider. The other end of that spectrum, the need for major change, is typified by John Connor at Allied Chemical.

John Connor at Allied Chemical

A pair of cases at Harvard Business School, designed for classroom discussion, describe how Edward L. Hennessy, Jr., came into Allied Chemical Corp. in 1979 and transformed it from a large, old, sleepy chemical company into the even larger, more dynamic Allied-Signal of today.[1] Looking at the succession history of Allied it is clear that there was a lot of top-level turmoil before Hennessy arrived. John Connor, brought in from outside in 1967 to become CEO, was unable to develop a successor from within. The result was that the board selected Hennessy, another outsider, as the next CEO. Connor accepted my invitation to tell his story.

John T. Connor has had a remarkable career. Trained as a lawyer at Harvard, he joined Merck & Co. in 1947 and was elected president and CEO in 1955 at the age of thirty-nine. He resigned

1. The cases were written under the supervision of Richard R. Elsworth. The (A) case (#383-076) describes the tenure of John T. Connor, the (B) case (#383-078) focuses on Edward L. Hennessy, Jr.

that post ten years later to become Secretary of the U.S. Department of Commerce under President Johnson, serving for two years, and then joined Allied Chemical. After retiring from Allied, he became chairman of the U.S. branch of Schroders Merchant Bank of London, and I met him there in October 1985. He was about to celebrate his seventy-first birthday, but he was clearly a man who was happy with his life, energetic, and thoroughly enjoying a modest amount of wheeling and dealing as an investment banker. His story is fascinating.

I was brought into Allied because the board of directors was worried about the succession issue. Chet Brown was holding all three titles and was approaching age sixty, with no successor yet obvious. They grabbed me as I was coming out of the Department of Commerce, primarily because I had a good track record at Merck in operating management and bottom-line results. Shortly after coming in, I told the board I was shocked that Allied had no management development program and no strategic planning; that, in effect, became my mandate. Also, it was my suggestion that I should start as president and COO, in order to wrap my arms around the operations of the company before taking the CEO title and responsibilities.

Brown had had three executive vice presidents reporting to him, and had been urging the board to accept his recommendation to promote one of them to be president and heir apparent as his successor. I could see that there was a lot to be done, and knew that I would need a COO. I rejected Brown's recommendation, and instead, when I became chairman and CEO, chose Fred Bissinger, who was already on the board of directors when I arrived. The other two executive vice presidents, also board members, resigned shortly after that, realizing that we were not going to get along together. Bissinger was very solid, but he was three years older than I, and was never a candidate to be my successor.

My other early initiative was to get started on strategic planning. Even the first crude pass at it identified the op-

portunity for us in oil and gas. We had an oil and gas operation, but we were treating it as a source of feedstock for
our chemical operations. I decided with the board's approval that we should treat it as a business in its own
right, and we became engaged in aggressive exploration efforts. That turned out to be successful beyond our dreams,
and was a real lifeline for the company, providing 80 percent of our profits in 1979. That and synthetic fibers were
our two important growth areas. With that undertaking
launched, I turned an increasing amount of my time to the
task of identifying and grooming candidates to be my successor.

My initial assessment of the internal pool of candidates was that it was quite thin. On the other hand, I had
plenty of time to bring in one or more outsiders, and in
fact, did hire three such candidates during my tenure. The
first was Dave Bradford, who had been a divisional president with CONOCO. I hired him in 1969, and put him on
the board in 1970 so that we could have a look at him at
that level. For some reason, Bradford acted as if he was in
competition with Bissinger to be my successor, even
though Bradford was eleven years younger. I did promote
Bradford to president in 1974, when Bissinger became vice
chairman before retirement, but I never gave him the COO
title because some activities still reported to Bissinger. I
finally decided that I could not recommend him as the
next CEO, and when I told him that, he resigned. At about
this time, I hired another high-level executive away from
Exxon, but he stayed less than two years. After being in a
high corporate position with Exxon, he saw us as small
potatoes, and he antagonized a lot of people, particularly
those in oil and gas, by telling them so.

The third outsider I brought in was Sandy Trowbridge.
He had succeeded me as Secretary of the Department of
Commerce, and at my invitation had joined the Allied
board in 1968. When he decided to leave public service,
I persuaded him to become a full-time vice chairman of
Allied, suggesting that he might be a candidate to suc-
ceed me.

The best insider I could identify at this time was Bob Mulcahy, a division president who had been with the company for more than twenty years. When Bradford left, I named Mulcahy president and COO, and for a couple of years, in 1977 and 1978, we had a horse race of sorts between Trowbridge and Mulcahy. Then, suddenly, Allied was sued for some illegal payments, and Mulcahy was accused of having known about it. He denied it, but he was named a party in the action. Even though the case was subsequently dropped, the board did not consider him as the next CEO.

Did I fail in my objective to provide a new CEO for Allied? In one sense the answer is no. About one year before my retirement I told the board of directors that Trowbridge should be the next chairman and CEO and that Bill Geitz should become the president and COO. Geitz was then a division president, and a very solid career employee with the company. Trowbridge and Geitz would have made a fine team to run Allied—almost a replica of my teaming with Bissinger in the early part of my tenure—with the CEO more externally focused and supported by a strong operating manager.

With that recommendation on the table, the board named a nominating committee to work with me, looking at the future. We had a huge cash flow starting to come from our oil and gas properties, and that made us vulnerable as a takeover candidate. We also wanted to diversify and get rid of several of our unproductive businesses. It seemed to us that the next CEO should be aggressive, and an expert in mergers, acquisitions, and divestitures. The board committee concluded that Trowbridge did not fit that set of specifications, and I reluctantly agreed. So we decided to go outside once again, and the nominating committee of the board was actively involved in making the selection of Ed Hennessy. As it turned out, Hennessy was a good choice, and he has done wonders for Allied.

The story has a happy ending, even though there's a note of disappointment in Connor's comments. The incumbent CEO has the obligation, almost from his first day in office, to produce a set of qualified candidates to be his successor, and to recommend one of those candidates to his board. There are never too many good candidates, and Connor, at the end, had only one. But in most cases, one fine candidate is all that is required.

At that point, the role played by the board of directors becomes more critical. It is the board, working with the incumbent CEO, that must address the issues raised in the next two chapters. First, is the rate of environmental change likely to be so massive that major new strategic initiatives will be required? If so, even a paragon of an insider may not be adequate for the task at hand. Connor and his directors answered that question in the affirmative, and turned to an outsider. Even when continuity is more likely to be the order of the day, the board still must face the question whether the best internal candidates are equal to the task.

Management Development

Dozens of books have been written on this important topic, and I will restrict my comments here to those aspects of the management development process that are designed to produce qualified candidates from which the next CEO can be selected. Formal management development programs are relatively new, and take a long time to become effective, as we saw in the stories above. John Connor, coming into Allied Chemical in 1968, initiated Allied's first such programs and, despite major efforts both internally and externally, was unable to produce a successor from inside ten years later. Bill LaMothe at Kellogg, promoted to president in 1972, began Kellogg's initial efforts, but it was already too late to save an entire generation of managers. Kellogg's next CEO will be drawn from a cadre of executives now in their mid-forties. Today, the typical CEO in our population regards his executive in charge of human resource management (HRM) as a key member of his management team. The benefits, of course, go beyond grooming a set of candidates to be the next CEO. A well-designed program of management development increases the effectiveness of all of the managers in the corporation.

In terms of marshalling a set of CEO candidates, HRM provides a discipline that includes a formal annual assessment of every manager, identification of high-potential managers, and careful monitoring of their performance as they move up the ladder on a career path that is sometimes called the fast track. Being on the list of high-potential executives is one thing. Staying on it is another. The qualifications required to become a CEO are a moving target — the threshold keeps creeping up — and the result is that, in many companies, the short list of candidates is too short. Knowing this well in advance, most CEOs, early in their tenure, now bring in mid-career outsiders to enrich the pool of candidates.

Another major trend during the past two decades has been the rapid growth of executive recruiting firms. During this same period, the percentage of CEOs recruited from outside has tripled. The two trends are obviously related: as the demand for better qualified CEOs has grown, the recruiters have expanded in order to supply the market. But CEO appointments are only the tip of the iceberg. In our population, there are perhaps one hundred new CEO appointments in a typical year, and 75 percent of those are filled from inside. The lucrative market for the recruiters is at the third and fourth levels of management, where they fill thousands of jobs each year. Many of those people are high-potential executives, lured away by the prospect of an even faster track, and for some of them it works. The 25 percent of new CEO appointments going to outsiders is based on the definition of an outsider as someone with five years or less employment with the company. The typical "career" insider is promoted to CEO after more than twenty years of employment.

Some observers of these trends deplore what they view as the instant-gratification syndrome among younger managers who think they have high potential. I applaud it. In the "good old days," each corporation was, in effect, a local labor market, promoting from within and with a very few rising to the top. Being available for executive employment in those days usually meant that you had been fired by your previous employer. Today, in effect, we have a national market for executive manpower, made reasonably efficient by the executive recruiters. It seems obvious to me that the allocation of scarce executive resources is likely to be much more efficient now than it was then.

The most difficult task for the incumbent CEO, monitoring the development of candidates who might succeed him, is calibration. At Dow, we saw Paul Oreffice and his two colleagues ranking the three leading contenders to be the next CEO, and they agreed on which one was "best." The more difficult question, not only for Dow, but for every company, is, Is the best good enough? CEOs — and their directors — worry a lot about that question, and well they should. They are competing in national or international markets, and can ill afford to have a CEO who is less than world class. A CEO joins other boards for a variety of reasons, but one benefit has to do with calibration. He has a chance to get acquainted with the contenders in another company and inevitably tries to rank his candidates against those, even though the situations are quite different. At the same time, a CEO encourages his candidates to become involved in outside civic and social activities, providing more data on how they perform in other forums. The best path, however, and one that is productive in its own right, is to hire mid-career executives into the company, where the calibration of performance is continuous and fair.

Management development is the task of the CEO, supported by his HRM executive. The board of directors expects the CEO to marshal a set of qualified candidates to succeed him, but, during the years preceding that event, it is the CEO who decides which insiders to promote, whether to hire outsiders, and if so, how many. If he does that job well, the only effect on the process of CEO succession is to produce a more highly qualified set of candidates for the decision that must be made. Even then, the CEO and his officers and directors will still have a choice to make and will regard it as a difficult and important action, but one with a higher probability of success.

The Candidate's Perspective

As 1985 began, my field work was going better than I had expected. On a well-planned day in New York City I could schedule interviews with three or four current or prior CEOs. I worried most about sins of omission, and wondered what I was missing. The news stories in mid-January announcing AT&T's reorganization provided the answer: I should also be talking with prospective CEOs, executives involved in a more or less overt horse race. I worked out the first set of ground rules with Bob Allen, as I describe below, and subsequently made a similar contract with Rick Miller at RCA. I will present their stories in that sequence.

Bob Allen at AT&T

I first met Bob Allen in late 1978. The announcement of his latest promotion in *The Wall Street Journal* on January 17, 1985 made it clear that he was engaged in a horse race to be the next chairman of AT&T. In what was described as "a major reshuffling of top executives," Robert E. Allen, forty-nine years old, succeeded Charles Marshall, fifty-five, as chairman of AT&T Information Systems, and Randall L. Tobias, forty-two, succeeded Morris Tanenbaum, fifty-six, as chairman of AT&T Communications. Charles L. Brown, Chairman and CEO of AT&T, had been interviewed, and the closing paragraph of the article read as follows:

> Mr. Brown, who devised the four appointments, said the slightly younger age of Messrs. Allen and Tobias wasn't the decisive factor—although it didn't hurt. "For some time it's been clear Allen and Tobias are going to be important people in this business for a good many years to come," Mr. Brown said. "I'm interested in moving them into jobs where they will be getting experiences which will be useful to them in the future." As previously announced, Mr. Brown, 63, plans to retire in 18 months.

I sensed an opportunity and called Allen to describe my "unusual proposal." He listened, asked a few questions, seemed intrigued with the idea, and said he would think about it and call me back. When he called, his suggestion was that we have a meeting to work out the ground rules and define our expectations. We met for an hour in late March 1985 in his office at AT&T headquarters in New York City.

Allen understood that my proposal was based on a coincidence of timing: the manuscript for my book was to be completed by August 1986, and AT&T's succession process would end no later than that. If Allen was willing, once the decisions were announced, he would be able to tell me the story of what happened, from a candidate's point of view. His risk, I pointed out, was small because the events would be history, and he would have full control over what, if anything, I could print. From his perspective, he said he felt that "much could be learned from a candid documentation of AT&T's succession process, interpreted in the context of the dramatic change the company is experiencing as a result of the divestiture of its operating companies."

My reason for wanting to meet with him at this point was to sensitize him to the topics of interest to me that could best be described by a candidate who had a good memory. I wanted him to (1) identify "events" and "signals" that he felt were important at the time they occurred; (2) specify when each event occurred (not when it was made public); and (3) interpret how those events affected him and the other key people involved in the process. I asked him if he was willing to keep a diary, but he deflected that amiably, saying that he couldn't accept a position as my research assistant. "We still have massive challenges to resolve," he said, "and I'm responsible for a major piece of the action. Brown and his board have even more challenges, plus the succession issue. During the months ahead, I'll work on my job and let them do theirs." He did say, however, that he would make an occasional note, to jog his memory when we met again, sometime in 1986.

Background. Agreeing on our "contract" took only fifteen minutes or so, and I suggested that we spend the rest of our time on background information prior to 1985. The next two paragraphs present my brief analysis of AT&T's recent succession history, and a synopsis of Allen's career as he described it to me. Then, in his own words, Allen tells the story of how Brown persuaded him to return to AT&T headquarters in late 1983.

The succession history of AT&T is a good example of team management in a very large corporation. Frederick R. Kappel, the de facto CEO in 1961, set up the first vice chairman position, and over the years that has expanded first to two vice chairmen and, now, three. The tenure of the last four CEOs, including Brown, has run five to seven years. AT&T has a tradition of growing its own top managers, and well it might, with a work force of nearly a million people before the divestiture in 1984. AT&T was also one of the early leaders in formal management development programs, using its twenty-three operating subsidiaries as training grounds, with the very best people ending up at headquarters.

Bob Allen's career is typical of the process that AT&T calls "moving through the chairs." Armed with a liberal arts degree from Wabash College, Allen joined Indiana Bell in 1957 and stayed there for seventeen years, topping out as financial vice president. In 1974, he was sent to Bell of Pennsylvania, and he knew then that he was on "the list" of managers being groomed for broader responsibilities. He stayed only twenty months in Philadelphia and in 1976 moved to Illinois Bell, where Jim Olson was president. Allen's job there was operating vice president (OVP), the number two job in that company. Olson had been OVP at Indiana Bell when Allen was there. Olson left Illinois Bell to go to AT&T eight months after Allen arrived, and Chuck Marshall became president of Illinois Bell for the remaining sixteen months that Allen was there. In 1978, Allen moved to AT&T headquarters for three years to take part in the restructuring of the company that was then beginning to emerge. Then, in August 1981, Allen achieved what he had at one time thought was to be the pinnacle of his career, becoming president of one of the operating companies, the four Chesapeake & Potomac Telephone Companies. Allen described what happened after that:

> Being the president of Chesapeake & Potomac Companies (C&P) was a great opportunity. I learned a lot, and contributed substantially. When, only five months after my arrival, the divestiture agreement was reached in January 1982 (to become effective two years later) C&P became a part of Bell Atlantic, one of the seven new regional telephone companies. Tom Bolger, a former boss at AT&T, and a good friend, came from AT&T headquarters to get it organized as the designated CEO, and I later became the designated president of the management services com-

pany. It was clear that I had a reasonable chance — in time — to succeed Bolger as chairman.

In May 1983, Charlie Brown asked me to come to New York to talk. I knew that Bill Cashel, then CFO, was leaving, but I knew that I hadn't the qualifications to take his place. Brown said that both he and DeButts had served as CFO. Brown said, "I want you to start here and then eventually take over the other corporate functions at divestiture. When divestiture occurs on January 1, 1984, I would expect that you'll join the board of directors. The question for you is really this: Do you want one day to be a candidate for my job?" I said that I'd think about it and would respond within a week. Jim Olson called me to encourage my acceptance. Bolger, on the other hand, naturally preferred that I stay in Bell Atlantic, although he applied no undue pressure and, in the final analysis, counseled me as a friend.

I really did think seriously about whether to take Brown's offer or not. There were several reasons for rejecting it. First, I was really excited about what we had been doing to prepare the new company, Bell Atlantic. I had invested a lot of moral capital there, personally. Second, I was worried about the reaction of the managers in C&P if I walked away from them at that point. Third, I felt an obligation to Bolger both as a friend and as a business associate. Fourth, I was reasonably sure that I could be successful in Bell Atlantic which, after all, is a large company in its own right. Finally, my family and I were very happy living in the Washington, D.C. area, and had no burning desire to return to New Jersey or New York. At that time I also had some reservations about whether I could operate effectively at AT&T, as I knew it would be a very different company in the future.

Ironically, it was that challenge — to help shape a totally new company — as much as any other reason, that caused me to accept Brown's offer. I became an executive VP and CFO of AT&T in August 1983 and then took responsibility for all corporate functions and became a

member of the board as of January 1, 1984. Brown had decided not to replace Bill Ellinghaus when he retired as
chief operating officer, and the role of corporate headquarters after the divestiture was quite undefined. I wrote the
first roles and responsibilities statement early during that
turbulent year.

Our time ran out at that point, and as I left we agreed that the
ball was in his court. I, obviously, would collect press clippings,
and he would make notes if he chose to do so, but the next phone
call would be his, not mine.

Recollections of a Candidate. As it turned out, I
violated my half of that agreement by calling Allen's office on
May 22, 1986 to congratulate him on being named president and
chief operating officer of AT&T. The newspaper stories that day
also reported that Olson was named chairman and CEO, succeed-
ing Brown, and that three vice chairmen had been appointed:
Marshall and Tanenbaum would continue in their staff positions,
and Tobias was to be in charge of both AT&T Information Systems and AT&T Communications. Mr. Olson would assume the
CEO title on June 1, and the other changes would take effect on
September 1. The new team was now in place.

Allen returned my call before the end of the day, and we
chatted briefly. Then, answering my unspoken question, he said
that he had made a few notes during the last fourteen months and
thought that it would be fruitful for us to sit down together. We
agreed to meet a couple of weeks later in New York City, and
during that two-hour conversation, this is what he told me:

The first thing to be said is that we couldn't have
picked a worse time in the history of AT&T to go through
the process of selecting a new CEO. For the last sixteen
months, I've been responsible for the Information Systems
(I.S.) business. During this period, this unit had been as-
sembled piece by piece as regulatory walls were lowered
or removed. Unlike other elements of AT&T, the equipment unit had never operated as a business and its man-

agers consisted of a unique blend of marketing "imports" and Bell System operating people.

I have literally been consumed with the task of putting the fundamentals in place that will lead to sound operations and a turnaround in the equipment business. We have all tried to be completely candid with the board about all aspects of this effort. Many directors understand what we've been going through and offer encouragement. It's an extremely difficult task—made worse by a rapidly changing marketplace and by the snarl of regulatory and legal issues that confront every move—and we're still not through with it.

Given that context, the most convenient way to talk about the succession process is chronologically. There were four major events: (1) the reorganization that became effective on February 1, 1985; (2) the appointment of Olson as chief operating officer on May 17, 1985; (3) the meeting (not a publicly visible event) that Charlie Brown called on February 5, 1986 that included Olson, Tobias, and me; and (4) the announcement of the new team on May 22, 1986. I'll talk about each of those in turn, giving you my interpretation of what was going on behind the scenes during the intervals between events.

All during 1984 it became more apparent that our customers were not being well served through a structure that was conceived to satisfy regulatory walls, and we were missing the synergy because of turf problems. One partial solution was to name a COO. In September, Brown accepted my suggestion that we give Randy Tobias a special assignment to look at our organization structure. This work gave Brown a set of organizational options and, as it turned out, a framework for succession planning.

The changes that took place on February 1, 1985 had to deal first with the four of us who were currently on the board of directors. Tanenbaum had special skills in the scientific and strategic areas, so Brown felt he was the best for finance, planning and research, and Chuck Marshall, who had a great track record in political, regulatory, and work-force relationships, took the external affairs and human resources job. Jim Olson, the only one of us with the title of vice chairman, kept what had been Western Electric, Bell Labs, the components and electronics division, and network systems. I took the information systems set of activities, reporting to Olson, and Tobias was assigned the long distance business. It was a major step up for Tobias to become chairman and chief executive officer of AT&T Communications.

Brown talked with me a few weeks earlier about my new position. He said, "Your job is the toughest, but I think you can learn a lot about an important part of our future business." Also, sending me a signal of some sort or another, Brown said, "I don't want to name a chief operating officer now because I want to give the board of directors a choice." What I inferred from that was that Brown was really telling me he wanted to keep his options open; but he also told me he was telling the same thing to Olson.

Despite that signal, my assessment of my own prospects of being Brown's successor never went beyond my being a dark horse. The issue for the board was whether to select Olson or to skip his generation in order to bring on younger talent. I'm not a political animal, in the internal sense of that word, and I keep a rein on my expectations so that I won't be disappointed. I was confident that if I did a good job on the I.S. business problems I would have earned broader responsibility in AT&T. Further, then and now, I thought that Olson had earned the CEO job, and I was looking forward to working with him. I told Betty (my wife) seventeen years ago that Jim Olson would be CEO of AT&T one day.

When Olson was elected president and COO of AT&T in mid-April, I gave a sigh of relief, for two reasons. First, Tobias and I, finally, had a common boss, and this meant that we could more easily begin the process of integrating our two organizations. Second, my interpretation of the event was that Brown and his board had tentatively decided that Olson should be the next CEO, and had taken the action at that time because we really needed a COO to deal with the business problems. Personally, I was pleased to have the issue resolved, and even more pleased for Olson. He had not shown any overt signs of tension, but when I played golf with him a week or so after he learned of the decision, he shot an eighty-three (not bad for a seventeen-handicapper), and was much more relaxed.

During the next nine months, nothing specific happened in terms of the succession process, but I did receive some signals. By then I had naturally developed informal relationships with several of our directors, and had a couple of confirming signals from that group that Olson would be the next chairman but that I was also held in high regard. In the broader business community, I had several friends not employed by AT&T who reported to me on casual conversations with Brown or other directors in which they implied or were explicit about my status in the corporation. Finally, Olson and I were working together well, leading me to infer that he would want me to be president and COO when he became the CEO.

The major event occurred on February 5, 1986, when Brown called a meeting of Olson, Tobias, and me. Without any fanfare, he said that Olson would become chairman and CEO, I would become president and COO, and Tobias would become a vice chairman with responsibility for both the Information Systems and Communications businesses. The announcement, Brown said, would probably be made in May. I was not particularly surprised, because Olson had implied as much a few days earlier, on the basis, I presumed, of an earlier discussion with Brown. Nevertheless it was good to hear it directly from Brown, and I asked him whether that was the recommendation he planned to make to the board or whether he already had its approval. Brown said, "You know me well enough to know the answer to that question."

Brown had called the meeting because he was concerned that delaying the announcement might slow down Tobias's and my ability to integrate our two businesses.

For that reason, most of us agreed that Olson's change should be announced sooner, and that any further delay also unnecessarily cast some doubt on the board's confidence in Olson. But Brown was adamant that the focus of the annual meeting should be on the 1985 results, not on his retirement. He did say that he would retire in August and would not stay on the board.

At a regular board meeting two weeks later, the directors spent forty minutes in executive session discussing the succession. The only issue remaining was the question of timing. Prior to that meeting, Olson apparently made a strong suggestion that Brown should announce the new titles at the annual meeting in April. But Brown really wanted to avoid becoming a lame duck because of several complex legal and regulatory issues that he was in the best position—and was resolved—to settle. I had told Brown in the February 5 meeting that we could wait until May if necessary. (I'm confident the board offered some advice on the timing issue, although in the last analysis, we all agreed that Brown should have control on the timing.) The announcements, as you know, were made on May 22.

Looking back on it all, it now seems clear that Brown had two objectives for his succession process. The first was to help his board select his successor, and the second was to plant the seeds for potential subsequent leadership. That's why he brought me in from C&P. By far the bigger surprise to others, however, was Brown's selection of Tobias to head up the Communications business. (It was not a surprise to me. After all, I hired him in 1964!) Tobias is seven years younger than I, the youngest vice chairman in the history of AT&T, and probably the first executive to become a member of top management without having served as the president of an operating company. All of that became clear, at least to insiders, in the reorganization Brown announced in early 1985. Brown is not trying to dictate the line of succession at AT&T for the next fifteen years—each of the decisions between now and then will have to be taken one at a time — but he did create some options for his immediate successor and the board of directors. More important, for me at least, is that Brown has cleared away most of the divestiture debris and positioned a new team to bring the business together in a manner that makes sense to everyone, especially our customers. The air has cleared. That's really healthy. Now it's up to us to complete the task of turning AT&T into the profitable, competitive company we all want it to be.

Commentary. Allen said it right: AT&T couldn't have picked a worse time to select a new CEO. There are many facets to Allen's story, but I will focus here on two that I think are the most relevant. First, I will indulge in a speculative discussion of the selection decision that was made at AT&T, trying to relate it to our prior discussion of strategic mandate and hiring CEOs from outside. Then, Allen's story provides more clinical detail than most of my stories on the topic of the timing of events (and nonevents) and I will share my insights on that issue.

CEO SELECTION AT AT&T. My speculations on the decision at AT&T are not entirely de novo. During the sixteen months between the reorganization and the final announcement, the impending decision was a popular item in the business press, and my sheaf of clippings grew rapidly. In the "old" AT&T there would have been no discussion; Olson, five years younger than Brown, had moved through the same set of chairs and would be Brown's successor. Indeed, Olson would have been named president and COO in 1984, when Ellinghaus retired, to signify to the organization that he was the heir apparent. By not making that predictable appointment, Brown and his board sent a powerful message to the organization: the "new AT&T" will have to do a lot of things differently.

It is scarcely speculation to assume that the directors of AT&T spent an increasing amount of time on the succession issue, beginning no later than 1983. Given the massive changes that were about to occur, and the immense stakes involved, the first issue the board had to face was whether to bring in an outsider as the new CEO. AT&T had scores of managers, carefully developed over a number of years, but none of them had ever managed a competitive enterprise. AT&T had always found its next CEO in the "local" internal market; shopping for a new CEO on the national market for talented executives would be a major breach of tradition.

Picking two insiders, a new chairman/CEO and a president/ COO, was still a difficult task. Focusing only on Olson and Allen, the issue was a choice between business as usual, or skipping a generation and appointing Allen as the next chairman and CEO. Allen, seven years younger than Olson, was only a dark horse, but he did offer the advantage of a longer time horizon to deal with a set of problems that would take a decade or more to resolve. The final result, after two years or more of intensive soul searching, was strictly "old AT&T." The core argument for that result must be that, given the discontinuity in the marketplace, a simultaneous discontinuity in management would be counterproductive.

THE TIMING OF SUCCESSION EVENTS. From the beginning of my research, I have been intrigued by the importance of timing in the process of CEO succession. Formal events — public announcements of organizational changes — provide demarcations that allow us to define the phases of the succession process, particularly for those companies using the four-phase relay process of succession. I find it useful to classify succession events in two categories: selection events and transition events. Bob Kilpatrick's reorganization, discussed above, was a selection event because he was overtly marshalling the candidates from which a successor would be chosen. Jim Olson's promotion to president and COO of AT&T was a selection event, identifying him as heir apparent to the incumbent CEO. This will be the primary focus of the next chapter. The transition events, the focal topic of chapter 7, have already been discussed briefly in chapter 3 in connection with CEO tenure. There, the events were defined as stepping down and stepping out, as the prior CEO moves toward retirement.

The process of CEO succession can best be defined as the

nonpublic activities that occur before a formal event. Describing those activities, and explaining why they occurred, is the primary objective of this book. For Bob Allen, identifying four important selection events that led to the appointment of Olson as chairman/CEO and himself as president/COO, the most important event was the nonpublic one: the meeting with Charlie Brown on February 5, 1986. At that point, the membership and titles of the new top management team had all been decided; the only issue that remained was the timing of the public announcement. On May 22, Brown announced that he would step down as CEO on June 1, an interregnum of only ten days, but he retained the chairman's title until he retired on September 1. The length of an interregnum, the time lapse between the announcement date and the effective date of an appointment, varies considerably, but it is not very important because the CEO becomes a lame duck on the announcement date.

The more interesting interval at AT&T is the three and a half months between February 5 and May 22, an interval I call "gestation." This is the time lapse between the day the heir apparent is told he will be recommended to become the next CEO and the day that appointment becomes public information. Gestation, in effect, is a secret interregnum, and in the process of CEO succession, it is more important than the formal interregnum. I found it nearly impossible to collect data about the length of gestation periods, because in the relay process, many CEOs claimed that the selection of the heir apparent was no surprise to the organization. My speculation is that most gestation periods are fairly short, because it's hard to keep a secret — surprise or not. But the gestation period can be important in the transition process, as Bob Allen will describe for us in chapter 7.

Rick Miller at RCA

I met Rick Miller in 1971 in connection with the bankruptcy of the Penn Central Railroad. He had graduated from Harvard Business School in 1970 and less than two years later was the chief financial officer of Arvida Corporation, a real estate development company in Boca Raton, Florida. Arvida was a 58 percent-owned subsidiary of The Pennsylvania Company which, in turn, was

wholly owned by the railroad and managed its nonrail investments. Miller was one of the cadre of new managers brought in to
sort out the mess. I joined the board of Arvida as one of the new
outside directors brought in to oversee the clean-up. Ten years
later, the reborn Penn Central Corp. was a large, diversified conglomerate, and Miller was its chief financial officer. In 1982 he
moved to RCA Corp. in the same capacity.

An article in *The Wall Street Journal* on March 28, 1985 had
Rick Miller's name in the headline, and it was clear that he was in
a horse race to become the next president of RCA. The article
announced a reorganization of RCA's top management, but it was
clear that the underlying issue was CEO succession. Thornton F.
Bradshaw, chairman and former CEO, was sixty-seven years old,
and "will remain for at least the next year or two." Robert R.
Frederick, president (fifty-nine) had become CEO in early March,
and would become chairman when Bradshaw retired. My reading
of the article was that there were now four candidates who might
succeed Frederick as president: Richard W. Miller (forty-four),
and three others who were five to thirteen years older than he.

I put in a call to Miller in early May, and he returned it the
next day. I made the pitch to him about my trying to follow the
horse race from his perspective over the months ahead, and he
immediately agreed to work with me. I explained my publication
deadline, which meant that his story might be too late if the
decision were delayed. Given that, we decided not to meet until
the issue was resolved, but, in response to my request, he agreed
to make a few notes to himself during the months ahead. As it
worked out, GE solved that problem, announcing on December
12, 1985, that it would merge with RCA. The horse race was over,
and nobody had won. Nevertheless, Miller had a story worth
telling, and we spent two hours together in early March 1986,
shortly before the merger was consummated. This is what he told
me:

> I'm at a strange point in my career—almost like a
> vacuum, because RCA will soon disappear and GE will
> probably not need most of RCA's corporate-level person-
> nel. So, I don't know what I'll be doing six months from

now, and I'm actually enjoying the uncertainty of that. Now that the RCA horse race is over, I see no harm in telling you how the process looked through my eyes. Let me start at the beginning.

Coming into RCA. I had done well at Penn Central, and in 1981 the rather politicized board was in the process of finding a new CEO to replace Mr. Dicker. In January 1982, the board voted that Dick Voell should become the CEO effective April 1, but that ultimately didn't work out. I'm not sure that I could have worked under him if I had stayed.

But coincidentally, in January 1982 I started talking to RCA. Thornton Bradshaw went to a meeting where he had breakfast with John McArthur [the current Dean at HBS] and lunch with Larry Fouraker [the prior Dean]. He explained to each of them that he was looking for a chief financial officer at RCA, and both of them recommended me strongly. Bradshaw subsequently called me to have lunch, and we talked until 5 p.m. that day. Following that, he arranged for me to meet individually with some of the directors, and we struck a deal on March 1, 1982. It was an ideal job for me.

Bradshaw and I saw eye to eye on what needed to be done. The finance function in RCA had never had any power or responsibility. The task was to build the finance function, and develop the capability to handle divestments and restructurings. I told Bradshaw I needed control of the investment banking relationship, responsibility for acquisitions and divestments, and eventually responsibility for the strategic planning function. Further, I said that, given that there were four executive vice presidents sitting on the board of directors, I would also need to be a director or those four should resign from the board. Bradshaw had already decided to ask them to resign.

I knew that my new job had upside potential. In fact, some of the directors that I interviewed said I might become RCA's CEO at some point. Bradshaw was not as specific as that.

Relations with Robert Frederick. Frederick had spent his entire career at GE before joining RCA on September 1, 1982 as president and chief operating officer. The line executives reported directly to him, and he also wanted me to report to him. My employment contract, however, said that for the first three years I would report directly to Bradshaw. Apparently, Frederick did not know this and he thought I simply didn't want to work with him. In one sense that may have been the beginning of an early tension between us.

Frederick also wanted to set up a new strategic planning function reporting directly to him, but again that was a part of my employment contract with Bradshaw. Frederick told me he might not have taken the job if he had known he would not have strategic planning reporting to him. Instead, Bradshaw set up a new strategic planning function that reported to him, with Frederick and me on a Strategic Management Committee for oversight.

As CFO, I had a lot of visibility in the press as well as with the board of directors. When Frederick arrived, in order to mitigate the tension, I tried to lower my profile.

Frederick is warm socially, but in business he is cold. No one feels close to him. But he is very savvy on issues of organizational subtlety.

I'm most comfortable operating as a member of the top management team. I like to be a partner in whatever is going on, and began to worry that I might not be able to achieve that with Frederick. I even considered leaving, briefly, but decided that he was treating me just like everybody else. He is a good judge of managers, even if he's not very personal in his contacts with people.

The Reorganization. In May 1984, Bradshaw announced to the world that Frederick would become CEO within twelve months. At that point, Frederick's behavior began to change and he started playing with organization charts. He had very few confidants, and only discussed the matter with a small number of people, of which I was not one. However, I did receive information from people who were privy to Frederick's evolving thinking, and so I knew more about what was going on than I should have. The early word was that I would continue to be CFO with some additional responsibilities.

Then, my relationship with Frederick began to improve. It was still professional, but more one-on-one. We began to get more comfortable with each other.

Frederick was talking with Bradshaw, of course, and Bradshaw in turn had a couple of talks with me during the fall of 1984. He said, "Your age is right to become CEO after Frederick. What role do you want to play in the new organization?" I told him I liked the job I had but I'd also like to have a line job. Bradshaw replied that I might need to remain as CFO, at least for a while.

By this time it was clear within the top management group that a major reorganization was brewing and that, given Frederick's age, the stakes were really to determine who his successor would be. A couple of the candidates had stated their expectations in the new organization, perhaps to their detriment, but I had not done so. Bradshaw solicited my opinion so that he could support me.

His second conversation with me in early December was very precise. "The reorganization will be Frederick's organization but you could go one of two ways. You could either be chief of staff, something broader than CFO, with good visibility with the board of directors, or you could take an important line job." I told him that the major gap in my RCA experience was that I had never had a major line management job. If I was to become CEO of RCA some day, I wanted the organization to think that I had earned it. Bradshaw agreed that I should take the line job, although he pointed out that there was a risk that, beyond my control, operating performance might be down more than up, and this might hurt my chances of success. I told him that I understood the risks.

Up to this point, I had not had a meeting with Frederick concerning the reorganization. He's really not comfortable in having discussions of this sort one-on-one. At a more trivial level, he and Bradshaw had seen to it that my bonus for 1984 was symbolically better, but Frederick was uneasy in talking to me about it and he depended on Bradshaw to inform me. Finally, the week after my December meeting with Bradshaw, Frederick asked for a formal meeting with me. He said, "I know your goal is to be CEO. I want you as a key member of my management team. What kind of job do you want in the reorganization?" I then gave him the response I had given in my first meeting with Bradshaw, saying I would essentially do whatever Frederick wanted, but my preference was for a line job. The meeting lasted less than twenty minutes.

By January, Frederick was creating a new organization chart almost every day, and I was generally aware of the process. Frederick had not really heard what I had told him in our meeting, but Bradshaw and Ed Scanlon, head of employee relations, made sure he got the message. Frederick then had another meeting with me in mid-February, and showed me a chart that had me in an important line management job. A few weeks later I was named executive vice president of RCA's consumer products and entertainment businesses.

Looking Back; Looking Ahead. I've run consumer products for nearly a year now, although we've been in limbo since the merger was announced three months ago. The first nine months were the steepest learning curve I've ever experienced—hard work, and fun. The magnitude of my responsibilities was almost scary; 35,000 employees operating in twenty countries serving a brutally competitive worldwide market. My businesses were not performing well, and I had a major fixed-overhead problem to worry about. My strategy was to play to win (GE had decided to drop out), rather than run a defensive strategy of just letting them bump along. I adopted a two-year time horizon, and spent money as though my businesses would be winners. I think we had a good chance to do it, but now we'll never know.

One surprise, a pleasant one, was the support I received from my people. They knew I was being tested in a new role, and they really wanted me to succeed. Another surprise, less pleasant, was the hidden costs of a horse race. For example, I do not think that [one of the candidates] realized he was a leading candidate to become the next president. Once it was shoved under his nose, he began to behave differently toward me. I really didn't want to be in a competition with him. We needed to work together in terms of the interfaces between our two areas of responsibility, and it's a pity that we had some problems doing that. It was a blessing in one sense that I was traveling so much—all over the world—that I didn't see my competitors very often.

Overall, however, I was pleased with those nine months, and both Frederick and Bradshaw were sending positive signals. My style in dealing with Frederick was different from those my competitors were using. I became more formal with him, because he likes that. At the same time, I took the initiative more, in calling him to arrange a breakfast or lunch together. Bradshaw was also helping me broaden my external exposure in New York City business and social circles.

As to my future, I won't speculate for your record; that's another story, yet to unfold. I like my life. I've had a great career, I'm still learning, and I think I'm qualified to be the CEO of a major company. But I've got some time, and there are a lot of companies out there. At the moment, I need and want more time in a job like my current one, because I'm still coming down a steep learning curve. This sense of personal growth enhances my confidence in my potential as a future CEO.

Miller's comments in March 1986 turned out to be prophetic. On July 1, the business press reported that Miller had been named senior vice president, consumer electronics, at General Electric, and that he would report directly to John F. Welch, GE's chairman and CEO. Working at that level in GE, even if he doesn't become CEO there, puts him in the big leagues. GE is a training ground for CEOs, and Miller's new assignment will give him the experience he needs before becoming a CEO in a very large company. We have not heard the last of Rick Miller.

Signaling the Candidates: Pros and Cons

Finally, I will comment briefly on the pros and cons of signaling the candidates. The first thing to be said on this topic is that the best signal is a good promotion, or perhaps more accurately, a good promotion is the best signal about future success. At AT&T, Brown's initial offer to Allen in May 1983 was much more than a nice promotion. Allen, then aged forty-seven, knew that becoming a member of the board, given AT&T's traditions, meant he would have more than fifteen years as a member of the top management team. He might never become CEO, but he would be a member of the inner circle. In early 1986, Brown replicated that event, promoting Tobias, then aged forty-three, and electing him to the AT&T board. Brown, like Irwin Miller at Cummins, engineered a prolonged relay process for Tobias, putting him on the track to run alongside Olson and Allen, even though he may not receive the baton for a dozen years. Brown had made a "deep, early selection" that is admittedly tentative and nonbinding, but if it works out, the continuity of management at AT&T will set a new record.

Another overt and formal source of signals derives from the human resource management procedures that are widely used in large corporations. Typically these involve a one-on-one discussion between the superior and the subordinate, once or twice a year. One session usually is for setting specific performance goals for the subordinate, another then reviews that performance after the year has ended, and incentive compensation awards are announced at that time. Rick Miller at RCA received a clear signal when Bradshaw told him that his bonus was intentionally a little higher than he should have expected.

The issue, if there is one here, focuses on informal signals: a casual, pregnant, and unexpected comment by the incumbent CEO that allows a candidate to infer that he is likely to be the next successor. Bill LaMothe at Kellogg was "crushed" when he apparently misread a signal. His advice is, "There is little to be gained and much to lose by raising expectations prematurely." Reg Jones at GE, as we shall see in the next chapter, took enormous pains to create a level playing field, trying to ensure equity among candidates who were running in the horse race he devised.

The problem is that, given the prolonged process of CEO succession and the frequent contact between the incumbent CEO and the candidates, it is almost impossible not to send informal signals. And the candidates, if they're as smart as they ought to be, become expert at reading them. My inference from Bob Allen's comments at AT&T was that he felt comfortably informed all during the succession process, as a result of comments by Olson, members of the board of directors, and friends outside AT&T. My advice to you is a little more equivocal than Bill LaMothe's: If you decide to send a signal, it should be done casually but not accidentally. The candidate will be listening for what you do *not* say as well as what you do say, so even a brief comment should be rehearsed. Careful signals can be useful and humane in helping a candidate recalibrate his own expectations.

6

Selecting the Likely Successor

T he moment of decision is at hand — and it's probably the most important decision you'll make as CEO. You've thrown the dice for big stakes on several occasions, but the selection of your likely successor is almost like betting the company. You'll still be around for several years, and as chairman/CEO you can make sure that the new president/COO doesn't make any foolish mistakes. But if he doesn't make it, that will be a blot on your record — and the company will have missed an opportunity for you to provide the final grooming of the next CEO.

Your board wants and expects you to provide leadership on this decision, although the directors have also made it clear that they want to be involved and to help you as best they can. In the last eighteen months, you've had two or three executive sessions of the board (excluding candidates who are also directors) to discuss the long-term challenges and opportunities for your company and assess the qualifications of the inside candidates. The result is a general consensus that two or three are qualified, and there is no need to bring in an outsider. The remaining issues are which candidate to select, and when.

The timing of the "short strokes" from now until the decision is made can be quite tricky. You'll need someone to talk it through with — several people, in fact, to get different perspectives. The chairman of the executive compensation committee of your board is one candidate, one or two other directors whose judgment you admire will also help if asked, and your HRM executive can be useful as a barometer within the organization. You can sense that tensions are already starting to grow; the candidates are watching the clock as closely as you are. At some point you'll decide, if the deed must be done, "then 'twere well it were done quickly."

Focus of this Chapter

This is the most important chapter for me, as well as for you. Selection is the main event, no matter how you do it. My interest, as you know, is riveted on the "how," the *process* of selection. *How* a successor is selected is very situational, but I think I have nailed down both ends of the spectrum. At one end we see Irwin Miller at Cummins creating a relay process in which selection is a nonevent. At the other end we have Reg Jones at GE, managing an avowed meritocracy and organizing a seven-person horse race to decide who will be the next CEO. These two extreme cases are useful because of their clarity of purpose; most companies fall somewhere in the middle. For those companies, the selection process is designed by defining the role to be played by the members of the cast: the incumbent CEO, members of the board of directors, and senior officers.

This chapter has two main sections. First, I present two detailed data points on the spectrum mentioned above, exploring the role of the incumbent CEO. Reg Jones is finally permitted to tell his story, and I analyze it. Then, I present a more typical situation—Dick Munro at Time Inc.—with richly detailed data about the short strokes involved in timing the selection event. I believe that the Time Inc. story will be the most useful one in this book for most readers, almost as archetype, because of the size of the company, the interplay between the CEO and his directors, and the issues that are grappled with.

The final section examines the role of the board of directors explicitly, again setting up a spectrum of practice that ranges from total responsibility for the decision at one end (Jewel Companies) to an almost perfunctory ratification of the incumbent CEO's recommendations (Xerox) at the other. The final story describes how Mike Ford, chairman and CEO at Emhart Corp., formed an effective partnership with his board in the selection process, producing a result that he calls, "the best of both worlds."

The Role of the CEO

Conceptually, the first step in the selection process is an agreement by the incumbent CEO and his board of directors that the successor should be chosen from among candidates already employed by the company. That pool may include one or more outsiders who have been hired during the last few years, but it is rare for the board to decide to bring in an unknown outsider to be the heir apparent. Once the board has agreed, the CEO takes command, designing a more or less overt process for selecting his successor, as we shall see in the two stories told below.

Reg Jones at General Electric

I was fascinated by the process Reg Jones designed to select his successor. The process was designed to produce melodrama, and the cast of characters was large: seven "competitors" (Jones's term for the candidates), two retiring vice chairmen, at least five outside directors (members of the Management Development Compensation Committee of the board), and several dozen senior GE executives, not candidates but vitally interested in the result. My objective in this section is to identify and dissect the formal steps in the process that Jones designed and managed. If there is a simple lesson to be learned here, it is that the succession process can be extremely complex, as suggested by the chronology in Exhibit 6.1. If there is a useful caveat, it is that a complex process does not necessarily mean that the incumbent CEO as the designer will control the selection decision.

Background. I first met John F. Welch, Jr., in the summer of 1978. Through a friend at GE, I discovered that Welch and I had a common need. Welch was then a sector executive, about a year into the job, and had just been given the extracurricular task of managing GE's efforts to recruit students graduating from our MBA program. I was teaching an elective course in the second year of the program, and wanted an executive from GE who could come to my class each semester and talk candidly with my students about the informal processes of management in a large organization. My classroom would give Welch another forum during his visits to the School, and he agreed to work with me. He came that fall, and was a great hit with the students. Fortunately, we videotaped his question-and-answer session

EXHIBIT 6.1

Chronology of Succession Events at GE • 1977–1981

Early in 1977: Jones announces a reorganization, creating a new level of management and appointing six sector executives reporting directly to the Corporate Executive Office.

Early 1978 to mid-1979: Jones conducts a series of four "airplane interviews" with each of seven or eight "competitors" to become the next CEO.

August, 1979: GE announces that three executives (Welch, Burlingame, and Hood) have been elected vice chairmen and members of the board. (The two existing vice chairmen retired at the end of the year.)

The next few months: three of the competitors resign from GE and take high-level jobs in other companies.

December, 1980: GE announces that Welch will become chairman and CEO on April 1, 1981.

with them, and during the next four semesters (1979 and 1980), he "attended" class either live or on videotape.

Welch's youth, extremely high energy level, candor in responding to tough questions, and obvious leadership qualities combined to captivate my students. Welch was engaged in a horse race, and I told my students that. In the class following each of Welch's appearances, I asked the students whether they thought he would be the next chairman of GE, winning out over six other candidates. Knowing nothing about the other six candidates, my students, each time, concluded that Welch did not fit their stereotype of GE's CEO, and the job would probably go to someone more conventional. Welch *was* a maverick, he let the students know it, and they loved him for it, but that's what happens to mavericks. I didn't know the other candidates either, but I shared my students' view, and was astonished at the announcement in December 1980 that Welch had won the race. In January, I went to GE headquarters on other business and managed to spend fifteen congratulatory minutes with Welch. I invited him to come "one more time" to be videotaped with my students, and he agreed. That videotape, cut in late March when he had been in office for only three weeks, was a masterpiece. He was jubilant, almost like a kid who had just been given the keys to the candy store, and it was clear that GE had a strong new leader.

In the fall of 1981, I brought my Welch videotapes into the Advanced Management Program (AMP). The participants, executives in their mid-forties, were also surprised at this uncommon man, and one of them suggested that it might be useful to have Reg Jones on videotape so they could compare the two individuals. I didn't know Jones, so I called Welch first to make sure he had no objections to what I proposed to do. Jones's first reaction to my call was that he doubted it was worth the effort, because we would not see much difference between the two of them. I suggested that he view the Welch tapes before making a final decision. He called me back a couple of weeks later saying that he now understood what I was trying to do and he came to my classroom in mid-March 1982. Jones, reserved and patrician, did fulfill the stereotype of a GE chairman, and the AMPs did see a common characteristic: both Jones and Welch are hands-on managers. I videotaped the wide-ranging Q&A session with Jones, but the high point was clearly his comments about the succession process. In a slightly edited version of that transcript, Jones's comments are quoted below.[1]

> The Airplane Interviews. *One technique that I used is what may be called the airplane interview. My predecessor, Fred Borch, used this technique in a somewhat similar situation, but it had impressed me as most helpful, and I had learned much from his effective use of this approach.*
>
> *I sat down for a couple of hours, unannounced, with each of these seven or eight candidates. They didn't know the purpose of the meeting, and I made sure they didn't tell the others, so that everybody came in surprised. (And they wouldn't tell, once they went through the experience,*

---

1. The videotapes of Welch and Jones are available for educational purposes through Harvard Business School Case Services.

because they wouldn't want the other guy to have the advantage of knowing what this was all about.)

You call a fellow in, close the door, get out your pipe, and try to get him relaxed. Then you say to him, "Well, look now, Bill, you and I are flying in one of the company planes, and this plane crashes. (Pause) Who should be the chairman of the General Electric Company?"

Well, some of them try to climb out of the wreckage, but you say, "No, no, you and I are killed. (Pause) Who should be the chairman of General Electric Company?" And boy, this really catches them cold. They fumble around for awhile and fumble around, and you have a two-hour conversation. And you learn a great deal from that meeting.

When you've done that seven or eight times, once with each of the leading competitors to replace you, it's amazing what you learn about the chemistry among that group—who will work with whom, who just despises the other guy—and things come out, because this is a totally confidential session you're having with them, totally confidential. Because they've not had any warning that this was going to strike, they blurt things out that you damned well better remember, because sometimes those are more important than the studied comments that you get at a later date.

Now, having done that across the field of candidates, the next thing I did was to call them back three months later, and do it all over again. This time they knew it was coming, and they had been through the experience. Now they came in with sheaves of notes, studied comments; there were statesmen developing, you see, in this process. And we went through the whole thing again—it took a couple of hours.

While I was holding these interviews, I also did the same thing with those senior officers with whom I could talk. These were the ones who were not contenders, the ones who were going to retire before me or with me, whose opinions I valued. They were generally senior staff people.

And you get their reactions as to who should be running the company, what teams will work together, what individuals don't fit, and so on. I shared all this with the five members of the Management Development and Compensation Committee of the board, in depth, and of course with the senior vice president of executive manpower, who was intimately familiar with all these people.

Now, in the next series of interviews (again two in number and again the first one unannounced), you call the fellow in and say, "Remember our airplane conversations . . . ?" "Oh, yeah . . . ," and he starts to sweat a little bit. "Now," you say, "this time, we're out there together, we're flying in a plane and the plane crashes. I'm done, but you live. Now who should be the chairman of General Electric?"

And again, you get a very interesting set of responses. Some don't want any part of it: "Here's the guy you should pick." Others: "I'm your man." And you say, "Okay, if you're the man, what do you see ahead as the major challenges facing GE, what sort of environment do you visualize, what programs would you mount, and who should be the other members of the Corporate Executive Office?" Now you're getting very specific about the chemistry, about interpersonal relationships. And then you do that again on an announced basis, just as you did the first time; the second time they come in, they're really ready for you. They've got all their notes and you have a very informed discussion.

Now, that was the way that we developed the information, which we shared again with the Management Development and Compensation Committee of the board and, finally, the full board. And the full board, having known these people intimately and been very much involved in the entire succession process, arrived at a set of conclusions as to the three candidates that we should move up to vice chairmen.

We then ran with a Corporate Executive Office of myself and these three new vice chairmen for a period of *about fifteen months, during which the board could look at these three in greater depth. Remember, they were attending every board meeting and they were seeing board members in social as well as business situations. Only after that period of time did the board make the final selection as to the chairman.*

Analysis and Assessment. What follows is my speculative analysis of the events at GE. I make no claim that this is the "truth," but it is a believable scenario of what happened. The traditions at GE, described by Jones in chapter 2, are an important backdrop. An overt horse race, given the company's meritocracy, was the best way to determine who should be the next CEO. The seven contenders were not too many; they had earned the right to be in the race, and no one would be surprised when several of the losers left. To ensure that each contender had a fair chance, Jones reorganized to create a level playing field, and then played musical chairs with the contenders, putting each of them in a new job to see how he could perform. The reorganization not only brought fresh eyes to old problems, but also froze the field of contenders during the length of the race; none of the seven departed from GE until a decision was made. The race was on.

Jones's next step, the first round of the airplane interviews, might be called a peer review process. It is not uncommon for an incumbent CEO to conduct such a set of interviews among the candidates to succeed him, although usually it is done in a less traumatic fashion. The second, more formal round of interviews is quite unusual, but it served to show that Jones was serious, and to some extent, mitigated the trauma of the first interview. In most situations where peer reviews are used as part of the succession process, the purpose is, in effect, to allow the next CEO to be selected by the members of his peer group. A new CEO who cannot retain a cadre of his contemporaries is probably a poor selection. At GE, Jones's objective was analogous. He needed the data from the first two rounds of interviews to permit him to forecast how many of the losers would depart—or put another way—to determine which candidates could marshal a team to support them if they were selected. That forecast was probably particularly important with regard to Welch, the maverick.

I don't know whether Jones planned from the beginning to have four rounds of interviews, but his schedule provided time for them if needed. I assume that he held them because the data from the first two interviews were inadequate. In any event, Jones made a midstream change in the ground rules under which the horse race was being run. Now there would be three winners to share the jackpot, not one, and the new teams were to be formed in real time while the race continued. I was surprised, initially, when some of the contenders said in the third and fourth interviews that they did not want to be the next CEO, but the contenders themselves were not surprised — at least not for very long. From their perspective it was quickly apparent that Jones was asking them to define the feasible teams. And so, the contenders began talking to each other, and some of them decided they would rather be a vice chairman on a winning team than simply another loser. The effect must have been severe politicization of the organization.

By mid-summer 1979, the lid was ready to blow, if an article in *Fortune* serves as a barometer, and the August board meeting must have indeed been a most exciting one. My best guess is that, at that point, three or four of the contenders had made it clear to Jones that they would depart if not selected as the next CEO. At the same time, the process of building coalitions had been somewhat effective and there were two, or perhaps three, defined teams available. The choice facing Jones and his board was whether to select one of the teams, thereby effectively ending the race, or pick the three top contenders to be CEO and let them run a last lap.

The latter alternative was almost unthinkable: if three candidates to become the next CEO were promoted to vice chairman, so that the board could have one final look at them, the other two would probably depart once the decision was made, but in the interim, two or three or perhaps four of the other contenders might depart rather than wait around to see how the situation finally was resolved. The compromise was to elect Welch and two of the other contenders who had agreed to work with him to be vice chairmen, but to maintain the race for another period of time while the board became comfortable with Welch as the next CEO. The rationale for the compromise was that Welch was a risky maverick, but he also might be a great new leader for GE. Giving him a chance to prove his spurs was not very risky. If he failed, the board could always select one of the other two vice chairmen to be the next CEO. The logic of that approach was irresistible, and the board bought it.

That gamble produced a winner, as we now know. During the next fourteen months Welch was not an heir apparent, at least in the sense of public expectations, but the time did give him an interval analogous to the transition I will discuss in the next chapter. Welch used that interval to build the broad support within GE that he needed if he were to become the new CEO, particularly, to build bridges to the supporters of those who had departed. The interval also permitted Welch to overtly display the cohesion developing in his new team, and to lengthen his own time horizon as he began to plan the actions he would take when he assumed office. If nothing else, the interval served to make the succession from Jones to Welch both orderly and civilized.

My assessment of the succession process at GE is to deplore the trauma and to admire the outcome. Here, I am not passing judgment on Welch's effectiveness as a CEO. The outcome that I admire is that somehow the officers and directors of GE were able to select a new CEO who was more likely to make difficult changes than some of the other contenders for the job. The core issue in CEO selection is the tension between continuity and change. In this case, GE was able to select an "outsider" from inside. As to the role played by Reg Jones in this process, I have been intentionally ambiguous because it is not clear to me what his personal recommendation to the board was. I do give him credit for designing a process that produced an effective result. Now, let us look at another CEO involved in selection: Dick Munro at Time Inc.

Dick Munro at Time Inc.

On October 22, 1985, J. Richard Munro, president and CEO of Time Inc., attended my seminar on CEO succession. On July 17,

1986, Time Inc. announced that N. J. Nicholas, Jr., forty-six, had been named president and COO, effective September 1. Ralph P. Davidson, fifty-nine, the current chairman, would become chairman of the Executive Committee on the same date. Munro, fifty-five, formerly president and CEO, would become chairman and continue as CEO.

During the nine months between those two dates, Dick Munro and I talked several times. I told him I wanted to work in real time with a CEO in the selection phase of the succession process, and he agreed. We both viewed it as a speculative but low-risk venture. He would have another person to talk to, and I would learn a lot, even though I might not have a story for my book if the decision was not made before the book went to press. It turned out, obviously, to be a win-win game. He and I tell the story jointly below, recounting what was said each time we talked.

October 22, 1985. I had not met Munro until he showed up at the seminar. I knew that he had graduated from Colgate in 1957, and joined Time Inc. that year. I also knew that he had been named president and CEO in 1980, at age forty-nine. On paper, he was a candidate to be a long-tenured CEO. I also had some knowledge about Time Inc. The first case I wrote as a member of the faculty in 1978 was on TIME Magazine, and I had done some work with the company in the early 60s.

During part of the seminar the group served as a sounding board, allowing a member to describe his situation briefly and then solicit reactions from his peers. When Munro's turn came, he said:

> We bought a forest products company several years ago, but finally shed it in 1984 because it didn't make sense for us to be in that business. We think that we are a very special place to work; we do exciting, innovative things, and believe that we provide the definition today of world-class journalism, cable television system management, pay television programming, and book marketing. More important, we like each other — even though that means that it's difficult for us to absorb outsiders. You

*need to understand that, because it does affect the process
of CEO succession.*

*I've been the CEO for five years, and have about five
years to go before I retire at age sixty. We have an explicit
policy that I created when I became CEO that both the
chairman and the CEO would retire at age sixty. At this
point, I have three excellent candidates to be my successor. They are all the same age, forty-six (eight years younger than I) and I put all three of them on the board in
early 1983. Everything is working fine at the moment, and
they really are a great team, but my problem is this: What
do I do two years from now when our chairman retires?*

*If I step up to become chairman and CEO at that
point, I would want to promote one of them to be president and COO. The risk is that by doing that, we might
lose one or both of the other two. Obviously, I've discussed
this privately with my outside directors, and at their
urging have indicated which one of the three I think is the
likely choice. I guess the issue really is one of timing, triggered by the retirement of the chairman, and so we'll probably play musical chairs in mid-1987. What do you think?*

Munro's peer group wasted no time getting to the core of his
problem. The first person to speak was quite blunt: "Do it now.
The tensions will only grow, the longer you delay. And if you do
it now, you will have most of the power for the next few years,
and can make it work out as well as possible." Several others
chimed in with brief comments supporting that position. The last
person to speak asked Munro a simple question: "Since you've
known all three for more than fifteen years, what more will you
know in two years?" Munro did not respond to that question
except by his silence. Then, he thanked the group for giving him
so much food for thought, and we turned our attention to another
member. My assessment of the interchange was that Munro had
been quite surprised by the unanimity among his colleagues.

January 22, 1986. I wrote to Munro in late Decem-
ber, asking if he would be willing to collaborate in my research.
He agreed to discuss the matter, and we met in his office in New

York City in late January. I started by laying down the ground rules for our collaboration, and he did most of the talking from then on. Forty-five minutes later, he agreed that it would be useful to continue our discussions by meeting again in a month or so. At this first orientation meeting, I asked him to tell me how he became CEO. More than half of the time, however, was devoted to his description and assessment of the three candidates and responses to my questions about how they worked together as a team. His comments on the first topic were as follows:

> My predecessor, Andrew Heiskell, picked me to be the next CEO, but he didn't stop at that. Ralph Davidson was also a candidate and Heiskell thought that we would make a great team so he promoted us together. In practice, Ralph and I have worked things out well between us, with him being "Mr. Outside," and me being "Mr. Inside." Nevertheless, it seemed to me at the time that a new CEO ought to be able to pick the members of his own team, and that bothered me for awhile. Now, looking toward my own successor, I have the same dilemma that Heiskell faced. We have a very effective team of three executive vice presidents. Nick Nicholas, responsible for Home Box Office and ATC, our cable television company, has a first-class track record in key staff and line assignments and a very sophisticated financial mind. Kelso Sutton, with nearly twenty-five years in the magazine business, is currently leading a surge of acquisitions and internal development in our traditional core business. Jerry Levin played a key role in the growth of our pay TV and cable businesses and is now responsible for both our Books and Information Services operations and our Corporate Strategy and Development staff.

> I want to keep them all. On the other hand, I am more convinced than ever that a new CEO should have the opportunity to pick his team.

March 4, 1986. As our January meeting was breaking up, I asked Munro to give some thought to feasible alternatives. He could, of course, wait until Davidson's retirement was imminent, but if he wanted to move faster, what actions should be taken and when? I told him that I would think about it too. When we met in early March, he had much to report:

> Several things have happened since our last meeting. First, I had my annual private session with the outside members of the board of directors to establish my non-financial goals for 1986. We find this a very useful exercise because it gives the board a chance to understand and approve the important items on my personal agenda. This time they were more forthcoming than in the past, saying that I was overworked and that I really should appoint a chief operating officer to share the load. In fact, we do have a lot of balls in the air in our evolving restructuring, and part of their concern was couched in terms of a concern for my health. But then they got into the issue of timing, and asked me when I planned to appoint a COO. I said I thought I would wait a couple of years until Ralph retired, but their question back was, "Why?" The upshot of it was that my nonfinancial objectives for this year include preparing a specific plan for naming a COO.
>
> Second, since we met, two of the candidates have come to me to have a brief private meeting. One of them said, essentially, "Let's get on with it," and made it clear that he wanted the job. The other stopped by briefly to say essentially the same thing—and we agreed to meet again soon. So, the pressure is beginning to mount internally as well as in the board of directors.
>
> Third, as you've noticed, we've been taking a real pounding in the business press during the last month or so. None of that is directly related to the succession issue, but it does take an enormous amount of my time. I've been carrying water on both shoulders, and that enhances the argument for appointing a COO sooner rather than later.

Having been brought up to date, I told Munro that I'd been giving his problem some thought and would like to ask a couple of questions. First, are you really prepared to retire as CEO at age sixty? I know that you've said that is your plan, but looking back at your predecessors, none of them retired that early. You are aware that you could probably stay on longer if you wished, but this is the time to look that issue right in the eye. Munro's response was brief and unequivocal:

> I set that date almost immediately after becoming CEO on the grounds that ten years is long enough to be CEO. I meant it then and I mean it now—I will leave at sixty. I know Davidson would prefer not to retire at sixty, but I believe he understands the policy. One unanswered question is: What compensation arrangements will support the new policy of stepping down at sixty?

Second, from what you told me about the candidates, it sounds like Nicholas and Levin are potentially an effective, complementary corporate management team. Sutton, with his mix of skills and long experience in magazine publishing, seems best suited to continue his leadership of that business. You've likened Nicholas to yourself as an operating type and described Levin as one who could help with the "outside" functions plus provide his unusual vision. Sutton should have his hands full with the growth and changes in the magazine business so, with some luck, you'll have preserved your team. You have the power to make that happen, just as Heiskell did when he named you as his successor. Yet, you've also told me that you think a new CEO should be permitted to select his own team. My question is: Are you prepared to name a new COO without any conditions concerning his willingness to retain and work with the other candidates? Munro's response to that question was not quite as fast as to the first one, but he finally said, "Yes, I really think that that is the way it must be done."

Finally, for the last year or so you have been telling your outside directors that Nicholas is the best candidate for COO. Are you absolutely sure he is the best person to be your successor? Munro's response was prompt again: "Yes, he'll make a great COO and has the potential to become an excellent CEO." Well, I said, then you should promote Nicholas now. There is simply no reason to delay, given your answers to those three questions. My advice is that you should talk with him first and soon, telling him of your decision. I would also suggest that you ask for his help in dealing with his other two colleagues because, if they stay, it will be because of Nicholas's establishing a relationship with them, more than your relationship with them. Our meeting ended cordially, with Munro thanking me for my comments and agreeing that we should meet again in a few weeks.

April 21, 1986. When we met six weeks later, Munro had a lot of news. As a prefatory comment, he said, "Your seminar certainly expedited my timetable." Then, he proceeded to brief me, as follows:

In mid-March, I told Nicholas. Our meeting had been set up several weeks earlier; it was our annual goal-setting meeting, like the one I'd had with the board in February. As Nick sat down I said, "Before you say anything, let me tell you that I'm going to ask the board to name you president and COO."

I told him that I planned to do it at the July board meeting, getting final approval from the outside directors at one of my private semiannual dinner meetings, and that we would announce it in October or November, to be effective at year-end. Nick was obviously pleased and we talked briefly about the implications for Jerry, Kelso, and Ralph Davidson.

As of today, the only people other than Nick and I who know are Don Perkins (an outside director), Bruce Hiland, our chief administrative officer and human resources guru—and you. I know that I must talk with Ralph, Jerry, and Kelso, and I'll do that right after the July board meeting. If I do it before then, I will present the board with a fait accompli and I don't want to do that. What I'll do next is to go to Chicago to meet with Don Perkins and Jim Beré, the chairman of the Personnel and Compensation Committee of the board.

I congratulated Munro on his expeditious handling of the matter, and he thanked me again for my help. We agreed that we need not meet again, and he said he would keep me informed as the remaining events unfolded.

June 26, 1986. I called Munro in late June to discuss how much of his story (if any) I could use. He had a bundle of good news, and by now I had learned to listen carefully to his first comment; he instinctively started with a headline, and then proceeded to elaborate.

I talked one-on-one with each of our fourteen outside directors, and they are all pleased. We will announce the changes after the board meeting on July 17, effective September 1. That's earlier than I'd been planning, but Perkins and Beré changed my mind when I met with them in Chicago in May. They persuaded me that sooner is better—particularly from the point of view of the other two candidates—and the way to expedite it was to get an OK from each director before the July meeting.

Nick and I talk a lot now. He obviously wants very much to keep both of his contemporaries, but each of them will have to decide for himself. During the week beginning July 7 I will tell each of them of the decision, and then Nick will also have a private conversation. Also, I'll talk to Ralph about shifting his role in order to facilitate Nick's promotion.

My last contact with Munro was a call I made on July 18 to congratulate him on the stories appearing in the newspapers that morning. I told him I particularly appreciated his accelerating the process so that his story could meet my publisher's deadline, and we chuckled over our mutual good fortune.

Commentary. I can't claim that Munro's story is typical, but I do believe that the issues he faced in the latter phase of the selection process are common for most companies that use the relay process of CEO succession. Four topics deserve at least brief comment: the conflicts in timing, the involvement of the board of directors, the gestation period, and choosing the team to work with the next CEO. Munro's solutions on these issues are not necessarily right for you, but may provide a starting point for an analysis of your own situation.

Timing the selection of an heir apparent in a company using the duo mode of management forces the incumbent CEO to address an inherent conflict; promoting the heir apparent to president means stripping the chairman of his title. When Munro arrived at the seminar in October 1985, he was quite content to let the selection decision float until a few months before the scheduled retirement of Davidson, the chairman, two years later. Participants at the seminar were the first to advise him to "get on with it," and during the next five months he consistently received the same advice. The board of directors insisted that he prepare a plan for appointing a new president and COO, two of the candidates dropped by to leave the same message, and my advice in early March simply reinforced all that he had been hearing. The net result was to expedite the selection decision by at least one year, but it was not an easy decision for Munro. In effect, he was caught in the middle of a generational gap, and finally had to agree with all of his advisors who counseled him to worry more about the next generation than the prior one.

At first glance, it might appear that Munro ran roughshod over his board of directors, telling Nicholas first that he would be recommended to be the next president, and only then worrying about how to avoid presenting the board with a fait accompli. The context of Munro's action, however, had been carefully structured by the board. The first issue in CEO succession, establishing the tenure of the incumbent CEO, had been resolved early: Munro would retire at sixty. The second issue, selecting the heir apparent, had also been resolved: in early 1985, the board had finally cajoled Munro into naming his choice, and had agreed with his conclusion. In early 1986, the board "requested" that Munro develop a plan for naming a president. Those three actions, in effect, amounted to a mandate for Munro to present the board with a fait accompli, and that is what he did. My assessment is that the board acted impeccably in this situation, display-ing some impatience, but leaving the final choices on timing in Munro's hands.

In mid-March, Munro made the decision to promote Nich-olas, thus beginning the gestation interval that would continue until the decision was announced publicly. Gestation is not an important substantive matter; it is "only" a matter of timing, because the decision has already been made. The selection deci-sion is important, however, and a number of people must be notified before they read about it in the newspaper. Here, the issues for the CEO are the length of the gestation period, and within that period, the schedule for the sequence of notifications and the timing of each one. Secrecy during the gestation interval is desirable because it is humane; a score or more of individuals deserve to hear of the decision directly from the CEO, so that he can explain the rationale for it and the implications it carries for each individual. The secrecy, of course, is fleeting—eventually everyone will know—and one implication of that is that it has been almost impossible for me to gather data about what happens during this interval. Asking a CEO, two or three years after the event, how he handled this issue usually results in a response such as, "And then I talked to everyone who needed to be in-formed, one-on-one." I will briefly dissect Munro's gestation pe-riod, and then return to the topic in the next chapter.

In mid-March, telling Nicholas of his decision, Munro said that the announcement would be made in October or November, thus establishing a prospective gestation period of seven or eight months. Sometime during the next few weeks, Munro notified Don Perkins of his decision, and in May he met with Perkins and Beré together in Chicago. They persuaded him that the announce-ment date could be moved up to July 17 if he would poll each director before that meeting, assuring him, no doubt, that the board would not view his action as a fait accompli, given the con-text described earlier. Munro agreed, thereby shortening the ges-tation period to four months, and polled all the directors by the end of June. At that point there were only three more people to be informed: Levin, Sutton, and Davidson, and Munro delayed those meetings until a few days before the board meeting. By then, the secret was known to more than a dozen people, but there were no leaks. The decision that Munro presented to them *was* a fait accompli, approved by the board and to be announced shortly. The virtue of that approach was that when Munro and then Nicholas met with each of those three men, the discussions could focus on the future role for each of them. The die had been cast.

Those future roles, particularly for Levin and Sutton, were the most difficult issue Munro faced in the entire selection process. Stated more broadly, the issue is who should pick the team to work with the next CEO. As we have seen, that issue can be very complex for companies using the team mode of top management organization. At Time Inc., using the more common duo mode of management, Munro compares his situation with that faced by Andrew Heiskell, his predecessor as CEO. But Heiskell was simply providing Munro with a chairman, four years older, who could handle some of the external chores; Munro chose the three younger executives to help him run the business.

The dilemma for Munro was that *he* wanted to keep Levin and Sutton as members of his team—Munro would continue to be the CEO—but he was not sure that *Nicholas* wanted to keep them. If Munro wanted to perpetuate that trio, he *might* be able to pull it off by promoting the other two to the position of vice chairman—thereby adopting the team mode in a formal fashion. Choosing not to do that, Munro really has no power to decide who Nicholas will choose to work with him. One or both of his contemporaries may decide to stay, but that outcome will be determined by the style and chemistry among the three individuals and the personal ambitions of the two who know they are unlikely to ever become CEO at Time Inc. The generational nature of the relay process of CEO succession is inexorable; a horse race does produce losers, and career choices must be made.

Role of the Board of Directors

Thus far in this chronology, I have devoted relatively little specific attention to the board of directors. In chapter 1 I discussed the relationship between the board and the CEO in broad terms, concluding that a partnership was the best analogy. In chapter 3

I defined the role and the responsibilities of the board in helping the CEO define his tenure and in dealing with "disappointing" CEOs. Most of the action thus far however—molding an effective management team and marshalling the successor candidates—has been initiated and executed by the incumbent CEO. Now, the time has come for the board to perform its single most important duty: selecting the next CEO. The role played by Time Inc.'s board provides a starting point for the analysis. In this section I first provide three other data points describing the role of the board, and then define the three major roles played by directors in the selection process.

The Jewel Companies

Don Perkins has had two remarkable careers: first as successful chairman and CEO of the Jewel Companies, and then as an outside director of blue-ribbon companies including, from our set, AT&T, Corning Glass, Cummins Engine, and Time Inc. As the end of his tenure grew near, he decided, in effect, to write the textbook case on the role of the board in selecting a successor, and took Lawrence E. Fouraker as his handmaiden. Larry Fouraker has had three careers: first, as a widely respected academic, second, as Dean of Harvard Business School for ten years, and then, as an outside director of blue-chip companies including, from our set, Jewel and General Electric. Perkins's and Fouraker's collaboration, as they tell it below, breaks neatly into two pieces: the why and how of board involvement.

> Don Perkins: Why Involve the Board? *Most corporate observers would agree that the selection of a CEO is a board's most important role. Most corporate observers would agree that CEOs are generally selected by the incumbent. Discussions occur but the voice of the incumbent invariably prevails. Succession at Jewel in 1980 seemed obvious, as Wes Christopherson had been a highly successful president and COO for ten years. Yet, neither he nor I was happy simply to let the obvious happen without thoughtful consideration over time by our board. Whether or not they chose to change dramatically or even*

slightly what was evolving, we felt it was important for the outside board members to carefully review their options and to come to a well-considered decision. In addition to the board feeling that they had fulfilled their role, such a process had the obvious advantage of giving my successor the unqualified support of that board. It would have picked him.

Because I had told the board early and occasionally during my decade as CEO that I expected to turn over that responsibility after ten years, discussions about the wisdom of that plan were less important than designing and implementing the process of board involvement with succession. I asked Larry Fouraker to chair a committee of the ten nonmanagement directors (out of twelve and later thirteen total board members). The mission of the committee was to consider any and all alternatives, have private sessions with the three or four most likely possible successors, and in general seek whatever counsel was desired. From the beginning everyone felt that we had ample talent internally and would not be going outside for succession. Time was set aside in connection with the six board meetings prior to the end of the decade so that the work of the ad hoc committee would be facilitated. My objective was for the ten Jewel nonmanagement directors to come away from the Jewel succession process knowing that they had done their job and were fully responsible for their decision.

Larry Fouraker: How to Involve the Board. Don initially asked me to chair the nominations committee, nominally to find, evaluate, and recommend candidates as outside directors for Jewel. I told Don this was a nonfunction, for I would recommend a candidate only if he or she had the respect and confidence of the CEO, and was someone whose respect and confidence the CEO desired to maintain and augment. In my experience, this effort to maintain mutual esteem is the most effective constraint on the CEO and management. If this is accepted, the implication is that, while all directors may initiate proposals, the CEO makes the final choice.

Don then proposed that our committee be the core group to consider management succession, which is a different matter. We agreed immediately that all the outside directors should be invited to participate. Never encourage divisions among the outside directors unless you find civil war stimulating.

I think this process started in 1978, and we met each quarter. We had a long lead time, for Don had shared with the board and other senior managers his decision to leave after ten years. I had even more lead time, since he and I discussed this issue early in 1970 when I became Dean and came to a similar decision, which I shared with senior faculty and our visiting committee, of which Don was a member.

The question of who would succeed Don took no more than five minutes of the first meeting. We had all seen Wes Christopherson resolve a wide variety of management problems, fashion strategic approaches for the long term, and care for and develop people to work in a cooperative process — a strong Jewel tradition. In all of this he was outstanding and had been for nearly a decade as president. We respected his judgment, his commitment, and his personal values. Further, his relationship with Don was much more that of a partner than as a subordinate — a necessary model at the top if the cooperative objective was to be realized at other levels. The question before the committee was not who would succeed Don, but what signal should be sent regarding Wes's succession, which, if Wes followed precedent, would be determined before he was sixty-five.

The specific question was an organizational one: Should a president be named when Wes was chairman, or should Walter Elisha and Dick Cline become vice chairmen? At Jewel, presidents traditionally replaced chairmen; the one not chosen as president would be likely to leave, for both men were superb professionals, ensconced in search firms' lists of future CEOs.

How to organize the business is not a question in which outside directors should take the initiative. But succession and retaining outstanding managers are issues closely related to organization, so extensive discussions with senior management regarding those relationships were in order. The central tendency of those discussions could be summarized.

1) Since intellectual capital is the most difficult resource to develop or acquire, we should try to retain the services of as many of the senior executives as possible during the period of transition.
2) Specifically, it was thought that the two-vice-chairmen alternative was more likely to keep both Dick and Walter than any other.
3) Further, if a choice had to be made at that time, a comfortable consensus would be difficult to achieve.

I had shared an MBA classroom with Walter Elisha and knew that the admissions committee had been successful in the application of its most important screen: Walter had an almost compelling need to be responsible for an organized endeavor. Size, mission, reward were all secondary to the need to lead. I asked the committee if I could talk with Walter and Arlene before the announced vice chairmen appointments, and if another member would do the same with Dick Cline. I had dinner with Walt and Arlene at their house before the board meeting, spent the night with them, and came to work with Walter the next morning. I tried to explain what I have summarized here. I failed to convince Walter, who became CEO of Springs Industries shortly thereafter, and Dick Cline was appointed president.

Several years later Jewel was acquired by American Stores. I told Don I felt as if my alma mater had been acquired by her closest competitor.

Commentary. The situation at Jewel was remarkably similar to that at Time Inc., although it happened several years earlier. The major difference between Time Inc. and Jewel is that Munro's board had accepted one of the three candidates, Nicholas, and the main issue was simply one of timing. At Jewel, with two candidates, the board of directors tried to waffle by offering to make both of them vice chairmen—a path Munro eschewed in his situation. Elisha was unwilling to prolong the horse race, knowing there could only be one successor to Christopherson, and he departed. I assume that Elisha would have stayed if he had been named president and heir apparent, so the issue is: Who picked Cline over Elisha? That question is rhetorical, because there is only one answer: Christopherson. The opinions of the directors, individually or collectively, on which candidate was the better choice, were simply not relevant. If Christopherson was to be the new CEO, no director, even Perkins, would wish to saddle him with a president that he did not want. The directors at Time Inc. achieved the same results in a much simpler fashion: they simply asked Munro to recommend the candidate he preferred.

Having said that, I quickly acknowledge that the directors in both companies—in all companies—have to have some data about the candidates to validate the recommendation that comes from the CEO. Selecting the right person is important, but in companies operating in the duo mode of top management, the decision is not to select a new CEO, but only an heir apparent. In such situations, it is the CEO who has the most at stake in picking the right person, because he will live with him every day for several years.

The process used at Jewel, on the other hand, does offer some modest benefits. First, the candidates themselves are more likely to believe they have been treated equitably in the selection process. Second, the board of directors no doubt "felt good" about its involvement, and the simple task of organizing the outside directors to work on a substantive matter can help improve the cohesion among that group. And, of course, no harm was done by the board's involvement, in the sense that Christopherson made the final choice. If I had been a director at Jewel, I would have participated in the undertaking with great enthusiasm, but I do not endorse it as a universally applicable model.

Peter McColough at Xerox

C. Peter McColough was invited to one of my seminars, but had already scheduled a three-week hiking trip in Nepal. I decided to pursue him, nevertheless, because the history of Xerox is inherently fascinating. The company was a skyrocket for fifteen years beginning in the late 1950s. The apogee, measured by investor excitement, occurred in 1972 when the stock price was forty-seven times earnings and the total market value of the stock was $13.5 billion, more than ten times the book value of $1.3 billion.

McColough's career spanned the entire cycle, including the inevitable return to more sustainable heights. He joined the company shortly after finishing Harvard Business School in 1954, became CEO fourteen years later, and served in that post for fourteen years before stepping down at age sixty. He agreed to collaborate with me, and we met in New York City on February 18, 1986.

> Joe Wilson was the founder of Xerox, although it is a fact that the Haloid Company was founded in 1908 by his father. But it was Joe who recognized the potential of xerography, and he literally bet his company that he could make it a commercial success.
>
> Joe ran the company the way a founder has a right to do; he was the boss, assisted by several of his contemporaries who had joined Haloid in the 1930s. The important exception was Sol Linowitz, a talented lawyer, who handled the protection of our patent positions. But Sol was more than a lawyer, he was a close friend and confidant of Joe's. In recognition of that, Joe asked Linowitz to become chairman in 1961, while Joe continued as president and CEO.
>
> I joined Xerox in 1954, and was one of the first professional managers of the next generation. Joe was my mentor, and I grew up in the hard-driving atmosphere that he had created. When Joe decided in 1966 that he needed a

chief operating officer, I was really the only candidate. By then we were bringing in dozens of talented executives every year, but Joe viewed me as a "younger founder" and so did I. Two years later, Joe decided that things were going well enough that he could begin to back off a little. He passed the CEO title to me, staying on as chairman, but our agreement was that he would pass that title to me when the time came that I needed to appoint a new president as chief operating officer. The primary candidate for that job at that time was Archie McCardell, who had come to us from the financial group at Ford a couple of years earlier. We made him executive vice president (the only one at the time), and a member of the board when I became CEO. In effect, he was serving as the COO and he was perfect for the job. Costs can get out of control in a hi-tech, fast-growing company, but McCardell helped keep the lid on.

We did have a lot of talent around at that time, and I decided that I could afford to spend two or three years picking the next president. In 1969, I selected Joe Flavin and Ray Hay as highly qualified contenders, promoting both of them to executive vice president and membership on the board. Flavin had come to us in 1967 from IBM, and Hay had joined us in 1961 from Monroe Calculating. As it turned out, all three of those candidates ended up being CEOs of other large companies: McCardell at International Harvester, Flavin at Singer, and Hay at LTV.

I let that horse race run for a couple of years, but by 1971 it was time to tie it off. I discussed the selection with Joe Wilson, and McCardell won. That decision was made just a few weeks before Joe died, rather suddenly.

So there we were, McCardell and I, running the darling of Wall Street. I told McCardell that he was clearly a candidate to be my successor as CEO, but that I was making no promises at that time. To the board of directors, I was really derelict. The board during these years consisted of about fifteen people, nine of them insiders. Following in Joe's footsteps, I did not even discuss the issue of succession with the outside directors — and I couldn't discuss it with the insiders. We did not even have a catastrophe plan identifying who would step in if something happened to me. I assumed, and I guess the outside directors did likewise, that Archie would become CEO in that event, and that worried me a bit because I still was not sure. Nevertheless, we were all healthy and reasonably young, and we just didn't worry about succession for a while.

In 1978, McCardell came to me saying that he had accepted an offer from International Harvester to become president and ultimately CEO of that troubled company. It was a big challenge, and right down his alley in terms of what needed to be done. That loss was a temporary shock. Then, mulling it over, I realized that McCardell had been the right guy for us during the 60s and 70s, when our major problem was to improve our operating performance and efficiency. But our primary challenge in the 80s was going to be marketing in an increasingly competitive environment. I needed a new president and COO, and my choice seemed obvious: David Kearns, who had joined us from IBM in 1971 and really had good marketing skills. Having decided that, I held a board meeting, told them that I had talked to Kearns about his becoming president, and asked them to ratify my choice.

As to my own tenure as chairman and CEO, I felt bound by the policy that we had adopted beginning in the early 60s to require that all senior executives retire at age sixty. Joe Wilson, not for that reason really, had set a model by stepping down as CEO at age fifty-nine, and I decided to maintain the tradition. Kearns and I had four years together in tandem, and I stepped down as CEO on schedule in 1982.

Let's remember that this event occurred nearly ten years ago, and that's a long time ago in terms of the role of directors as partners with the CEO. Still, the contrast between Perkins and McColough is stark, and the spectrum of involvement by directors in selection is very broad. If Dick Munro wants to know how to present a fait accompli, he should have a chat with Peter McColough. More seriously, times have changed, and I think we can write off this anachronism as a footnote to history.

An Effective Board at Emhart

I first started to track this story when I read the announcement in the "Who's News" column of *The Wall Street Journal* on February 24, 1984:

> *Farmington, Conn. Emhart Corp. said William C. Lichtenfels, 56 years old, was elected to the new posts of president and chief operating officer.*
>
> *Stephen J. Ruffi, 56, was elected to the new posts of vice chairman and chief administrative officer. Both men were formerly executive vice presidents.*
>
> *T. Mitchell Ford, 62, chairman and chief executive officer, said he plans to continue to hold the posts until his retirement in 1986. Mr. Ford said a decision hasn't been made on his successor.*
>
> *Emhart makes machinery, hardware and chemical products, fasteners and industrial and electronic parts.*

I knew practically nothing about Emhart, but I was interested in horse races (at that time) so I opened a new file in my research cabinet and waited. The next announcement, on November 22, 1985, was worth a brief paragraph on the front page of *The Wall Street Journal:* "Emhart Corp. named Peter L. Scott chairman and chief executive in a surprise move. Mr. Scott, head of a venture capital firm, once was in line for United Technologies' top job." It was clear that there was a story there.

I knew three of the nine outside directors on the Emhart board. James F. English, Jr., and I met in Hartford in the late 50s, when I was stationed there in the U.S. Army, and he was beginning his career at Connecticut Bank and Trust Company. A two-career executive, he became president of the bank in 1965 at thirty-eight, became CEO three years later, and then resigned in 1977 to work for Trinity College, becoming its president in 1981. He joined the Emhart board in 1964 and the CIGNA board in

1967. Since I joined the CIGNA board in 1976, we have seen each other almost every month. Michael S. Scott Morton, a professor of management at MIT, was also an old acquaintance. He had joined the Emhart board in 1976 at the age of thirty-eight. Finally, Marion S. Kellogg, a retired vice president from General Electric, had joined the INA board in 1980, and we got acquainted after the merger with Connecticut General in 1982. She joined the Emhart board in 1983. I called Jim English in late December 1985 to learn more about the situation.

English told me that the sudden turn of events had been triggered by the board of directors. A search committee had been formed consisting of three people: himself, Charles H. Kaman, CEO of Kaman Corporation and a director of Emhart since 1978, and Michael Scott Morton, as chairman of the committee. He said that currently it looked as if the two inside candidates would stay on, and that within a few months I might be able to get a release on what had happened. As a first step, he suggested that I have a conversation with Scott Morton, "academic to academic," and then we could figure out what to do next. Scott Morton and I spent two hours together in late March, and this is what he told me:

> Michael S. Scott Morton. *To understand the recent succession process, you've really got to understand how the board works at Emhart. I joined the board in 1976 and found that I liked all the outside directors. However, I got on particularly well with Jim English, who now is the only other director left from that era. Then, in 1978, Ford brought in three new directors: Kaman, Wilson Wilde, the CEO of Hartford Steam Boiler (an insurance company), and Hershner Cross, a retired senior vice president from General Electric with a great deal of manufacturing operations experience. Cross lived in the Boston area, and we adopted the practice of driving down to Hartford together and having dinner on the evening before a board meeting. Initially, Ford and English would join us, but all of the outside directors were invited and eventually all of them came. Ford then legitimatized that group, calling it the*

Committee on Directors and making me chairman of it. Lichtenfels and Ruffi, the two senior officers, were not officially members of the committee but they were invited on most occasions. The dinners ran from 6 to 9 p.m. in a private dining room, and 90 percent of the conversation was strictly business.

Initially, the agenda was purely strategic. Emhart had been successful in a hostile takeover of the United Shoe Machinery Company in 1976, but two years later we were still in the process of digesting it; it was twice our size and operated all over the world. Without much urging from us, Ford set up a strategic planning group to staff our discussions. We also had the nice problem of a huge cash flow, so there were a lot of investment proposals for us to review, primarily acquisitions. Ford would raise an opportunity for us to discuss when it was still a gleam in his eye, and one of our roles was the constructive killing of most such proposals. Ford is very good at identifying talented directors and then making use of their talent. Ford is an absorbing listener and makes real use of the ideas raised. However, many times it was hard for us to know where he stood on an issue. Viewed from one perspective, he appeared indecisive; from another, he could be seen as trying to stimulate ideas and build consensus within the group. In any event, Mike's style did create a very active board of directors. He let us have our head. We did not involve ourselves in operations, but we were very dedicated to trying to help him reposition the whole company.

By 1980 things were pretty well in hand and we started to devote some of our attention to the issue of succession. We knew we had two good inside candidates. We had only a brief discussion about bringing in an outsider; we all wanted to avoid the disruption that would cause. Another option was to make an acquisition that would produce someone who could be the CEO of Emhart. Peter Scott's name did come up in 1983 when he resigned from the succession rat race then under way at United Technologies. We discovered, however, that in raising money

for his new venture capital firm he had made commitments to investors and could not leave the company for
ten years. So, in February 1984 Mike Ford suggested that
we put the horse race into play, even though we knew it
would politicize the organization to some extent.

By December 1984, we were all becoming quite frustrated. The committee on directors had been seriously discussing succession at six-month intervals for nearly five
years — discussions in which we agreed to continue to disagree. We knew that if we were to bring in an outsider we
were going to have to move promptly, and we started looking around informally, although we decided not to retain a
headhunter. I think it is fair to say, however, that if Ford
had strongly pushed his choice between the two and recommended one of them to the board at that point, we
would have all agreed with a sigh of relief. Instead, he
continued to listen, and the tenor of our discussions began
to change.

Cross and I were perhaps the first to express our views
explicitly, and other directors joined with us, arguing that
the future would be one of rapid change and that what we
needed was vision and leadership from someone who
could operate from a global perspective, with particular
emphasis on the importance of new technologies. That
struck a responsive chord with everyone, and it was captured best by Ford's comment at the press conference in
which he introduced Peter Scott as our next CEO, saying,
"Once we dealt primarily with hydraulics, mechanical
linkages, electricity. Today, it's computers, microelectron-
ics, robotics." It was becoming increasingly clear to all of
us that our two insiders hadn't had the experience we
were going to require.

Finally, in September we decided that we must go outside for a new CEO and prepared a short list of two or
three. The three-person search committee, chaired by me,
was set up in October, and Ford was asked to sit in on all
of our meetings after the first one. It was English who
raised the name of Peter Scott again, and this time Kaman,

*who knew him the best, met with Scott and sounded him
out about the job. After considerable discussion Scott said
he was interested, but there was no way he could renege
on his commitments. That was all we needed, and we began to vigorously explore ways to make it work. We ended
up buying out his investors for about $5 million—which
is a fairly high price to pay for a CEO—but the other way
of looking at it is that we acquired a venture capital firm
and had a first-class CEO thrown in for free.*

T. Mitchell Ford. After my conversation with Scott
Morton, it was clear to me that the only other person I needed to
talk to was Mike Ford. He had succeeded, somehow, in forming a
partnership with his board of directors that was more productive
and effective than any other I know of. When I called him to set a
date for our meeting, I told him that his board was my primary
agenda, but I also sent him a copy of the Emhart succession
diagram as a starting point for our discussion. Our meeting in late
April 1986, in his office in Farmington, lasted a couple of hours,
and here is what he told me:

*I was trained as a lawyer, and joined the legal depart-
ment of American Hardware Company in 1958. We got involved in a messy proxy fight in 1961, and finally resolved
it by buying out the raiders and then merging with Emhart
Manufacturing Company. As your diagram shows, the
management after the merger was a little messy, and we
had two presidents in the space of two years. Dave Muir-
head looked around for an outsider to help him out and
finally turned to me as the next president and COO. I'd
never managed anything in my life up to that point.*

*I'm pleased that you think our board is effective, and I
certainly agree with you. There are several factors, I think,
that help to explain why our board has worked so well.
First, the size and composition of the board are extremely
important. Emhart's board has ranged from nine to fourteen, normally numbering twelve, with only two or three
insiders. That's a small enough group that you can still*

have a real conversation. The acquisition of United Shoe Machinery was extremely important because, among other things, it put us in a whole new league in our ability to attract talented directors. Since 1976, I've recommended seven new directors, each for a very special reason. We are a company with mature products and a major need for cost control. Most of our directors need to understand manufacturing, and I don't have any lawyers or bankers on my board. I have also tried to find young directors (two of them were under forty when appointed), and especially directors who are comfortable with high technology, which is the future for us. Without a talented and diverse set of directors, it's hard to have a good board.

Second, the style of the CEO is the primary variable that will affect the way a board operates. My style is to be informal. The Committee on Directors was set up to provide a forum for informal discussion. It's a lot easier to have a candid conversation on a serious topic around a dinner table than in a board room. And, as Scott Morton said above, I did intentionally delay expressing my own opinions on some topics to facilitate an open discussion by the directors. It's also important to provide unscheduled time for directors to get acquainted with each other; that's one of the primary purposes for making a visit to a plant or, more ambitiously, to the Pacific Basin.

A third factor is one that I don't know how to describe without using the word ego. Let me give you an example. It must have been about 1979, when the Committee on Directors was really getting its legs under it. One time, Scott Morton and Cross, driving home together after a board meeting, constructed a whole new set of strategic issues, including some specific recommendations that they thought should be acted upon. They were so enamored with their analysis that Scott Morton wrote it up and drove back to Farmington the next day to deliver it to me. Some CEOs would feel threatened to receive such a document from outside directors, but I didn't take it as such. We were groping with a messy set of problems, and they *were trying to be helpful. I accepted the document with thanks, but I didn't even respond to it — nor did they ask or expect that I would. On the other hand, there were several good ideas in the document and whenever I decided to use one, I'd throw a one-line bouquet of thanks to Cross or Scott Morton during the board meeting. I really believe that I need all the help I can get, but to encourage that, I have trained myself to be a good listener.*

You've asked me what advice I would give to other CEOs who would like to make their own boards more productive and effective. First, I'd say take a chance on being candid with your board — it goes a long way toward building your credibility with the directors, even though it does run the risk of sometimes appearing to be indecisive. Share your current concerns with the board before you have resolved them, and bring up potential acquisitions or new investments very early in your thinking. Second, the real secret to building bonds among your directors is to spend time outside the board room, visiting plants and socializing with out-of-towners by having dinner with them the night before a meeting. Third, don't confuse substance with process. Our Committee on Directors was purely for process purposes; the substance of our restructuring came from rigorous strategic planning and analysis. And, I quickly qualify all that I have just said by reminding you that what has worked for me will not necessarily work for other people.

One thing is certain: we all agree that the successor produced by our board was better than any result I could have engineered on my own. It now appears that we will have the best of both worlds because both of our inside candidates have said they will stay, and Peter Scott will be a superlative CEO for us.

Commentary. I will comment later, at a more general level, about the role of the board of directors in the selection process. Here, I want to underscore an important insight, for me at least, that emerges from the Emhart story. The Emhart board could be effective in the selection decision *because,* for more than five years before the event, it had been thoroughly involved with Ford on substantive, strategic issues. The group of individuals came to know and respect each other; they had been through the wars, and had psychic ownership of the progress of the company. Selecting a new CEO was just another important issue to resolve, and they could do it. A board that restricts its active involvement to the episodic issue of selection is unlikely to function as well. Esprit de corps among a group of directors is an elusive asset; it cannot be pulled out of a closet once every few years when a selection must be made, and then put back into mothballs.

Mike Ford, in my view, deserves all the credit for the board he created. His advice to his counterparts across the country is honest and sound—and almost impossible to implement. The constraining characteristic *is* ego, and many CEOs, victims of CEOitis, cringe at the thought of being viewed as indecisive. I think it takes a lot more intestinal fortitude for a CEO to solicit advice and then have to make a judgment than it does simply to call every shot.

The Role of Directors in Selection

I find it useful to distinguish between the role of the board as an institution and the role of individual directors. The value added by a board of directors derives first from the diversity of its members, and second from the building of a cohesion within the group that makes the whole greater than the sum of the parts. The board as an independent entity finally casts a vote, usually unanimous, but the quality of that decision is determined by the months or years of discussions that preceded it. The decision itself has two phases. First, two or three years ahead of the target date for a decision, the board must determine whether the selection will be made from among a group of insiders or on the basis of a search for someone from outside the company. Then, the board must select the best candidate from whichever pool it has chosen to examine.

The decision to recruit a new CEO or heir apparent from outside brings us back to the topic of continuity and change, a topic I explore more systematically in chapter 8. The crucial task here — and one in which each individual director brings something unique to the table — is forecasting the broad climate the company will face during the next decade or more. Despite his or her formal training and experience, each director must become an analyst, seeking to predict the challenges and opportunities that lie ahead. The usual consensus is that the expected rate of change is not sufficient to interrupt the continuity provided by selecting an insider. But, as we have seen at Allied Chemical (twice), Monsanto, and Emhart, on some occasions the board will decide that an outsider is required. In such situations, the institutional role of the board becomes more significant, in part because the incumbent CEO has failed to groom candidates to deal with the forthcoming changes and the board must now take matters into its own hands. This is usually done by forming a small committee of directors to screen candidates, but the whole board is kept closely informed.

When the board has agreed that the selection should be made from a group of inside candidates, its role in the process depends on the nature of the decision to be made. For companies using the duo mode of top management organization, the decision is to select an heir apparent who may someday succeed the incumbent CEO, as exemplified above at Time Inc. and Jewel. The selection decision is important, because it is the first step in the relay process. Extending that analogy, the role of the board of directors is analogous to that of the officials at a track meet: their job is to ensure that the agreed-upon rules for the relay process are honored. But the action is on the track: nobody watches the officials, and the credit for a smooth handoff belongs to the runners. The board of directors at Time Inc. did an excellent job of specifying those rules, and then letting Munro deal with the specifics of timing.

In companies using the team mode of top management organization, the situation is much more complex, and individual directors again have a personal role to play. In these situations, the decision to be made is also much more important: the board must select a new chairman/CEO to replace the one who is retiring. At both AT&T and General Electric, my analysis allowed me to infer that at some point in the selection process the board of directors was quite actively involved. At AT&T, the board delayed Olson's promotion to heir apparent as they wrestled with the insider versus outsider issue. At GE, politicized almost to the point of trauma, I think it a safe bet that each director had to declare his or her choice of the best person to be the next CEO. In cases like this, it is the responsibility of each director to search his or her soul, trying to decide the best choice for the company, and then to enunciate that persuasively before the full group. This may result in the temporary politicization of the board itself, but that does not disturb me if the argument is as substantive as selecting the next CEO.

The role of individual directors in selection starts with the premise that the process must be managed by the incumbent CEO. In almost all situations, there is no inherent conflict of objectives between the CEO and each of his directors: both want ultimately to produce a fine successor. But reasonable people, sharing a common objective, can still disagree — productively. When that occasion arises, each director must speak his or her piece forthrightly. That, finally, is what the personal responsibility of a director is all about.

7

Transition: Last Act, First Act

F ulfillment is the only word for it. These last three years as chairman/CEO have been the happiest period of your career as you've watched some of the early seeds you planted grow to fruition. The company's performance is strong, and that helps; more important, the new president/COO you appointed three years ago has already proven his mettle. He'll make a fine successor. But there's another dimension to your contentment: you've mellowed, and you're conscious of it. You're no longer on the make, you're a better listener than you used to be, and you like being referred to as "the old man" or some other term of endearment. You haven't suddenly become avuncular, that's not your style, but your pronouns have changed: more "we's" and fewer "I's." You didn't plan that, it just happened.

Now comes the hard part. Two or three years from now you'll have to pass the baton, stepping down as CEO and, probably, retaining the post of chairman. For more than thirty years, every time your job changed it was a promotion up the ladder. Now, perversely, you're about to be demoted! It hardly seems fair; nobody else around here is publicly demoted before he retires. On an occasional "down" day, the prospect is disheartening; it's hard even to think about it in your usual analytical fashion.

Your internal options, now, are few, and they boil down to severing your ties with the company sooner rather than later. At the moment, you still control the pace of events, but you must retain that initiative if you are to fulfill your objective of retiring with dignity. Again, you need a few people to talk to, but the confidants of three years ago, helpful on a corporate issue, can't help much on your personal problem. Your wife, and retired CEOs of other companies, may help. One thing is clear: at age sixty-two and in good health, you're going to have to find something else to do—probably a combination of golf, fishing, and community service. I'm sure you'll work it out.

Focus of this Chapter

The participants in our Advanced Management Program were very interested in my study, thinking it might help them in their careers, but I explained that the book I was writing would not help them—yet. The book they wanted would be entitled "How to Become a CEO"; my book starts with the appointment of a new CEO and focuses on how he is able to get out of that job. This chapter, finally, addresses that issue, focusing on the incumbent CEO's last major act: relinquishing his title to his successor. As a secondary theme, I also discuss the role of the heir apparent. This chronology began with the appointment of the president and heir apparent to the post of CEO; I intentionally ignored his activities before that event. I will now remedy that gap, discussing his first major act as the incipient CEO: building a partnership with the incumbent CEO.

For companies using the relay process of CEO succession, the transition from one CEO to the next begins when the heir apparent is named, and ends when the transfer of the title to the successor is announced. That public event is called validation. During the final stage of transition, an important, nonpublic event occurs. The decision by the CEO and his board that the heir apparent should become the next CEO marks the beginning of the interval I call gestation. That interval ends when the public announcement is made, but the weeks or months that elapse are worth discussing. After the public announcement has been made, there may be another brief interval—an interregnum—that lasts until the effective date on which the new CEO assumes office. The first section of this chapter is devoted to transition as the final step in passing the baton.

For companies using the team mode of top management organization, the transition from one CEO to the next does not follow any common pattern. In particular, it is not always clear when the transition process has begun, although even then, there will be a gestation period before the public announcement of the new CEO. These issues are discussed in the second section of this chapter. Then, the final section is devoted to the phasing out of the prior CEO, covering the period that begins with the announcement of the new CEO and ending when the prior CEO leaves the board of directors.

Passing the Baton

I keep looking for different ways to describe the relay process of CEO succession. Maybe the simple diagram in Exhibit 7.1 will help. It might be titled, "The Roller Coaster Ride of a CEO." The horizontal issue is time, and it is easy to define the four chronological phases of a CEO's career, although the intervals are not necessarily of the same length. There are two actors in each phase: in the first two phases the president *cum* CEO is teamed with his predecessor; in the last two phases he is teamed with his successor.

EXHIBIT 7.1

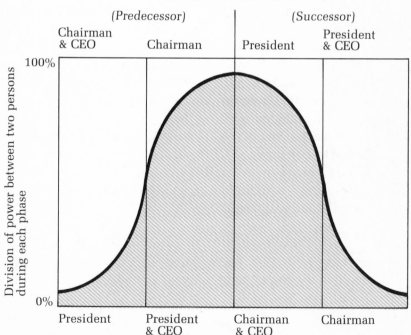

The CEO's Power Curve

The Four-Phase Career of a CEO

The vertical dimension in the diagram is more elusive. I call it the CEO's power curve, but power, theoretically at least, is binary; an individual is either the CEO or he's not, and the CEO has all the power. In practice, the *process* of CEO succession is designed to provide a gradual shift in status over time. The curve, as I view it, reflects the way two executives share the responsibility for important decisions. By that definition, one message in the way the curve is drawn is that the CEO's power is never absolute.

For a real company, there is no way to calibrate the vertical dimension in the diagram. The shape of the curve will vary, however, in each situation, depending on the personal characteristics of each executive and the chemistry between successive pairs of actors. For members of the organization, watching a duo at work, the lack of definition of the vertical axis creates a useful ambiguity about the way that the responsibility is shared. As I have written elsewhere,[1] a certain amount of ambiguity can be a very useful lubricant for many aspects of the management process, broadly defined. Twenty-five years ago, before the use of the CEO title became common, the process of CEO succession was more ambiguous than it is today. Then, there were only two phases in the career of a top manager: a stint as president and then a stint as chairman. It is probably useful in most situations to reduce the ambiguity by telling the organization at the end of phase one that the president is not just doing well, he's made it.

One last glance at the diagram will remind us that we are now near the end of the third phase in the CEO's career, and he is about to step down as CEO and continue for a while as chairman. Here are two stories that illuminate some aspects of the transition process; this section then concludes with a more general analysis of roles and responsibilities.

Walter Shipley at Chemical Bank

In chapter 4, Don Platten described the process by which he molded a team of candidates to provide the next generation of

---

1. Richard F. Vancil, *Decentralization: Managerial Ambiguity by Design*, Dow Jones-Irwin, 1979.

management. Midway through that process, Walter V. Shipley was named president, and became the heir apparent to succeed Platten. I asked Platten to describe how he and Shipley had handled the transition, but he demurred, saying that I ought to get that story from Shipley because he was calling all the shots. With Platten as liaison, Shipley agreed to talk with me, and we met in early May 1984. At that point, Shipley had been chairman for only eight months, and he was still enjoying his honeymoon. Here is what he told me:

> I'll never forget the moment. It was the Friday before Labor Day weekend in early September 1981. Don Platten called me into his office and told me I'd be the next president of Chemical Bank. I was dumbstruck. Maybe I was naive, but it had honestly not occurred to me that I would be his successor as the next chairman of the bank.
>
> Berkeley was the president at the time, a few years younger than Platten, and was presumed by everyone to be Platten's successor as chairman. I knew that I was doing well, and that when Berkeley moved up, I might become president and, if all went well, might succeed him as chairman. Moving faster than that had simply not crossed my mind, except that thinking back on it, Don did send me a couple of signals which I didn't really pick up at that time.
>
> From that day on, Don and I were partners, and he really opened up. He was due to retire in September of 1983, and that gave us two years to really think through the rest of the succession issues.
>
> The very first issue we faced was what to do about the upcoming seminar on managing resources, scheduled for the week of September 20, 1981. That was a group of seventeen executive VPs, and Lipp and me as the senior executive VPs. The question was whether or not I should attend that meeting, since my promotion was still very secret. Learning of it a few weeks later, as the group did on October 8, 1981, might give them the sense that I had betrayed them by attending the meeting as an equal,

knowing that I was to become the boss. We decided that I should attend.

The Transition. Bob Lipp and I at that time were the only senior executive VPs, promoted together in 1979. We had never worked together until we were brought together at headquarters. Then we worked to build a relationship. As the two senior executive VPs, we were allowed to attend one meeting per month with the officer/directors. We called it the "kids' meeting."

An important part of the transition relates to the Strategic Planning Committee that Don set up in 1980. Berkeley was the chairman, and Johnson, Callander, and Fishman joined Lipp and me as the other members. In hindsight, we are implementing the plan we created. But then, we were just the young Turks, free to go at it. We came out united and positive. Berkeley did a great job of running it. He remained opaque on the major issues — he was really the coach.

One evening in late 1980 or early 1981, Berkeley and I had to stay in New York City overnight, and he asked me, "What do you really think of Lipp, Johnson, and Callander?" I started talking about each of them, and ended up telling him that I respected each of them and that if any one of them was named chairman, I would be happy to work for him, and I assumed that the reverse was also true.

After the announcement in October 1981, Don and I sat down to review the talent. At that point, the Policy Committee of the bank consisted of nineteen officers. We cut that back to nine, the four officer/directors, and the five of us in the next generation, with the idea to shrink it down to five as the other four retired. I also said that we should immediately promote Callander and Johnson to senior executive VP, so that they would be on the same par as Lipp, and we did that in December 1981.

In the Policy Committee we then figured out the next layer of management — a lot of tough decisions that involved organization restructuring, such as merging the International Division and the Corporate Division.

With three candidates for the number two position, the strain on my relationship with Bob Callander was severe. Our families have been close friends for twenty-five years. I told him that I would have to bend over backward not to let the decision be influenced by our long friendship, and I also told Lipp and Johnson that. Each of the three of them said that he would stay on my team. There was a lot of loyalty, really morality, here. Very little politicking.

By the summer of 1982, it was getting time to make that decision. One director talked to me, saying, "Don't do anything until Platten retires and you're in complete control."

By the fall, the two critical elements from my point of view were my personal style and the structure required to run the bank that we envisioned. I had grown up in a partnership environment — my father was a partner at Brown Brothers Harriman. I understood the power of a group that had common interests. I personally work well in a small group; I click there. I am able to get people to stretch for me — if they want to do it. If it's their idea. I like to operate on a consensus basis, and I wanted to have that.

Also, I needed to position myself so I could think managerially as the head of a financial services company, not a bank. I didn't want to have a number two who had a bias toward a particular historical part of the institution. Lipp was a natural for retail, Callander for wholesale, and Johnson in the capital markets. And I didn't need anybody between me and them. Finally, I didn't want to name a number two as though I were picking a successor when I was only forty-eight myself.

So, one Monday morning I went to Platten and said, "Why not three presidents?" I argued that industrial companies do it all the time but a bank doesn't. And I didn't want to have a president-Capital Markets or anything like that. I wanted to be able to say to each of them, "You're

230

PASSING THE BATON

the president of Chemical Bank. This is a partnership: all of you will be paid the same." What I was working toward was something like you see at the top of Salomon Brothers or Goldman Sachs.

Don and I then met with the Nominating Committee and Compensation Committee of the board at a joint informal dinner to discuss the idea of three presidents. At the outset there were many questions because it was such an unusual arrangement. After a fair amount of discussion, however, there was general agreement that this structure might, indeed, be most appropriate for us as an institution. We then presented it to the board in January of 1983, and it was approved. The plan was to bring all three onto the board at the April meeting and then to announce the titles in June. The next step was to talk with the people involved.

I was crippled up with a bad back at the time, so we set aside a week for individual visits with all six members of the Policy Committee and then with the group as a whole. Don insisted that they come to my house rather than move into a hotel in New York. As we explained it to each of them, they all thought it was brilliant. Johnson said it best: "This way there are no losers. I didn't really need to win, but I sure did not want to lose."

Building the Partnership. Now we are learning to be a partnership. At this moment, the president of Chemical Bank is in three different places. Each of them is running a major business. We're spending a lot of time together, and the partnership is beginning to jell.

We have a competitive advantage in our new partnership. To make it work, each of us must change his behavior to some extent. We need to learn how to give advice without appearing critical, and how to listen to advice without becoming defensive.

We're really breeding owner/manager attitudes into performance. We did a good job on executive compensation beginning about six years ago by putting in place a

*very meaningful long-term performance plan based on
how the bank as a whole does competitively. Awards
under this plan are paid in Chemical stock and each of us
on the Policy Committee now has between $500,000 and
$1 million worth. The top one hundred people in the bank
are in that plan and are also building significant ownership. Most of our financial advisors suggest that we
should diversify some of our wealth because too much of
it is tied up in Chemical stock, the Chemical pension plan,
etc. I don't buy that argument. I believe people make better decisions when their own net worth is involved.*

Before discussing the transition, let me step back in time and
comment on the role that Platten played in the selection of Shipley, because we have some new data. Shipley was "dumbstruck"
because he had not expected that Berkeley would decide to retire
early. Platten was clearly in charge of the succession process, and
knew that he would have to retire in September 1983. My inference, based on the outcome Platten engineered, is that his objective was to provide the bank with a new CEO *and* a group of
contemporaries who would work with him. Berkeley was caught
between two generations: the youngest of the older group and the
oldest of the younger group. Berkeley's early retirement thus
cleared the way for Shipley to become the next CEO. The timing
of that action, the spring of 1981, was two and a half years before
Platten's retirement, thus leaving plenty of time for an orderly
transition. Platten was then quite forthcoming in achieving his
objective, meeting with each of his directors one-on-one because,
"I wanted each director to understand my feelings," and then
announcing the result to Shipley in early September. I give Platten high marks for his leadership in the succession process.

Chemical Bank uses the team mode of top management organization, but the transition from Platten to Shipley is in the
best traditions of passing the baton, and that's why I have put
their story in this section. The transition interval began in October 1981, when Shipley was announced as the new president and
heir apparent, and ended in June 1983, with the announcement
that Shipley would become chairman. There was a brief interreg-

232

PASSING THE BATON

num, not important in this situation, and Shipley's appointment was effective in September 1983, when Platten retired. During the first few months, Shipley and Platten, working together as partners, made two important decisions. The first was to shrink the size of the policy committee and the second, more important, was to promote the two other candidates to equal status with Lipp. At that point, the situation looked like the three-person horse race that occurs frequently in duo mode companies that are picking a new president to be heir apparent. Shipley would have none of that. His solution, reflecting his personal style of management, was both innovative and effective: he created a partnership.

Nineteen eighty-two was an important year in Shipley's transition. His complex task was made easier because he did not have to appoint a president who would be his successor—and he certainly didn't want to do so. The important nonpublic event occurred in January 1983, when the board approved the idea of naming three presidents. De facto in that decision was the validation of Shipley as the next CEO, and the gestation period began at that point. A careful reader of the corporate tea leaves could probably infer the outcome by the signal implicit in the election of the three candidates to the board of directors in April 1983, but the final announcement did not come until June.

Ron Cape at Cetus

Ronald E. Cape and I were classmates at Harvard Business School, but we never met until our thirtieth reunion in October 1985. By then, the biotechnology partnership he cofounded in 1971 had become a publicly held corporation with a market valuation of $1 billion, and he was about to step down as CEO at age fifty-three.

My original plan for this book was to collect stories from mature companies with at least a twenty-five-year history of CEO succession. In particular, I intended to avoid the first succession from a founder, because such situations are frequently messy and disruptive. A brief discussion with Cape suggested that I had stumbled into a healthy situation—he said that his objective was a "seamless transition"—and when we met again in February 1986, he elaborated as follows.

I first started thinking about management succession in 1981, when we floated our initial public offering and raised $108 million of equity capital. Suddenly we were in the big leagues. One obligation that came with all that money was the responsibility for providing continuity of management, and we really hadn't thought much about that before.

At that point, our board of directors had nine members. Of the original five founders, three were still on board: myself as chairman and CEO, Pete Farley, who was serving as president and chief operating officer, and Nobel laureate Don Glaser, a professor of physics and microbiology at the University of California at Berkeley, who had never been full-time in the company. A fourth member was a professor of chemistry at Stanford who had been an advisor to us from the beginning. The other five seats on the board were filled by representatives of three major corporations that had made significant purchases of our stock in earlier years: two were from Amoco Corp., two from Chevron Corp., and one from National Distillers and Chemical Corporation. Those three companies owned 49 percent of the company just before the public offering, but they had never pushed us around—they had really invested in order to obtain a window on our technology. Today, total large-company ownership is about 25 percent, and another 10 percent is owned by other employees of the company. So, today, we really are a public company with more than 50 percent of our shares owned by passive investors.

After we went public, Farley agreed that we should look for a new president. A little over two years later, several months after Bob Fildes joined Cetus, Pete left the company both as an officer and as a board member. And with a new president in harness who I hoped would eventually succeed me as CEO, I had to rethink what I wanted to do with the rest of my life.

After business school, I had returned to Montreal to run the cosmetics company owned by my family. Then, at the 1962 Seattle World's Fair, I saw an exhibit that explained how DNA replicates, and it greatly excited me. I continued to run the family business, but during the next four years I also earned a PhD in biochemistry at McGill University. That worked out so well that I was awarded a fellowship to do postdoctoral work in molecular biology at the University of California at Berkeley. My wife and I sized up our options, said goodbye to the family business, and moved to the Bay Area. And, as they say, the rest is history.

Creating Cetus was perpetually exciting. During the decade that began in 1971, my job was to assemble the assets—people and money—that would allow the company to survive and grow. Then, the hot stock market in 1981 permitted us to build a capital base that could see us through the final stages of the development of our new products. It was a watershed event, in that the nature of the CEO's job would change dramatically as a result.

Thinking all that through, I came to two conclusions. First, I could not walk away from the company, not only because I was proud of what I had created, but also because I had made a lot of implicit as well as explicit contracts with the investors who had helped us through the first decade and with our employees, too. It's tough for a founder to know when he should get out, but I decided that the answer for me was, not yet. Second, assessing my own capabilities I realized that I am not really a scientist in the academic sense and I'm not really a manager in the administrative sense. I'm a businessman. The new CEO could not possibly duplicate what my role had been, because he would not be a founder. My role as businessman/founder was secure and useful. What we needed in the next CEO was a professional manager who could guide the company through an exciting era of explosive growth.

Having come to that conclusion, I then had two main tasks: to find the right person, and to work carefully with the board of directors so that they were comfortable during the transition. On the first item, I just plain got lucky. I had known Bob Fildes since 1972. The industry is very international, and all of us do a lot of traveling around and socializing, so I kept running into him. He had been a division manager at Bristol-Myers, so he had solid experience in a large corporation, and in 1981 he was serving as president of Biogen Inc., a U.S. subsidiary of a Swiss biotech company. But for some reason, it never occurred to me that he might be the solution to my problem. Instead, I hired a headhunter, they combed through dozens of candidates, and we had serious discussions with a half a dozen or so of those. Then, in the first week of October 1982, Fildes and I ran into each other in Amsterdam, and while we were having a leisurely conversation, the idea suddenly hit me. He mulled over my proposal, and joined us in December as president and COO and board member, and a few months later Farley left. He's turned out to be exactly what we needed, describing himself as a "workaholic" and putting in the sixteen-hour days on administrative details that I really don't want to have anything to do with.

The board of directors was a more delicate matter. I had no trouble selling them on the need to hire a president and COO, but I also could sense that they were not eager for me to step down as CEO. They have great confidence in me, and I didn't want them to think I was planning to walk away from the company. They did agree, however, that we should try to select a president who had the capability of serving as CEO in the event that something happened to me, and who would, if everything worked out, eventually succeed to that title. I told Fildes that, coming in, he should act as though he were CEO from day one; I told the board of directors that, "some day," Fildes would succeed me as CEO. I did not have an explicit date with Fildes, because I really couldn't predict how long it would take the board to be comfortable with a change. Dealing with a board is sometimes like fishing; if you jerk up the rod at the first nibble, the fish will get away. I had to be patient with the board, giving them enough time to become comfortable with the idea.

From time to time during 1984 and 1985, at my initia-

> tion, Bob and I talked about the timing of his assuming
> the CEO title. There was never any sense of urgency about
> it, but I wanted us to control the flow of events and neither
> do it too soon nor wait too long. Finally, in late 1985, Bob
> indicated that he would like to talk some more about the
> timetable, and I realized that everything was coming to
> fruition at just the right time. He was coming up on his
> third anniversary with the company, his stamp on its new
> character was clear, internally and externally, and one
> reflection was that our stock was selling at a new high. So
> I said, "Let's do it." I then contacted each board member
> individually to say that I thought the time had come. They
> knew him well, and their only concern was whether I
> planned to stay on as chairman, and I said yes. A couple
> of them asked why we should promote him now, and I
> simply said that that's what I wanted. The headline on the
> January 10, 1986 issue of the San Francisco Chronicle read,
> "Change of Command at Cetus Corp. No Surprise." My
> objective was a seamless transition, and I think we did it.

I like Cape's story because it is simple and crisp, reinforcing several themes that run through this book and introducing one new element: ownership. I will comment briefly on four items.

First, this is a vivid example of the dichotomy that I refer to as continuity and change. The initial public offering was a watershed event, Cape realized that the strategic mandate for the CEO had changed, and a new type of leadership was required. That was achieved by bringing in an experienced executive from outside. Second, continuity could not be ignored. Cape would continue to play a role, in part because he was the founder, but also because of all those explicit and implicit contracts he had made. Continuity was increased by the deal that Cape struck with Fildes: both expected Fildes to become CEO at some point, but the date was not specified. When it did happen, three years later, Fildes was more of an insider than an outsider.

Third, Cape was careful and thoughtful in dealing with his board of directors during the transition. Here, the ownership issue first arises, because there was a large block of stock in the hands of just a few corporations. Cape was a patient "fisherman," and the board of directors finally got comfortable with the idea of a new CEO. Finally, Cape's personal decision to step down as CEO did not apparently cause him any trauma; there was no generational conflict of the type that I will discuss in a moment. Rather, Cape's analysis was that the company would be better off if there were a professional manager at the helm, and, given his ownership—both psychic and financial—stepping down was the best way to protect that investment. Cape's situation is totally different from that of Walter Shipley at Chemical Bank, but they would agree on one thing: it's useful if the senior officers have a substantial portion of their net worth invested in the company.

Roles and Responsibilities in Transition

The relay process of CEO succession is widely used, even though it has an awkward, structural flaw: in the fourth phase of an executive career in top management, the chairman (no longer CEO) is a lame duck. The rationale for phase 4 is sound. It is useful to have two full-time executives at the top, and it is too soon to select the heir apparent to succeed the current CEO. As the diagram in Exhibit 7.1 illustrates, the same two executives are working together in phase 3 and phase 4, but the sharing of responsibility for major decisions is shifting. Shared responsibility is not a zero-sum game that implies, "You make that decision and I'll make this one." Shared responsibility is intended to produce better decisions by involving two or more executives in the analysis. An operating committee can be an excellent vehicle for such analysis, but in phase 4, the president/CEO chairs that committee and the chairman may not even attend the meetings. The chairman, every bit as talented on his first day in phase 4 as he was on his last day in phase 3, will continue to contribute to the analysis, but progressively, his voice is only one of many that are heard by the president/CEO. The shift in power from one generation to the other is almost as simple as this: as chairman/CEO he was referred to, affectionately, as "the old man"; now he's referred to as "the chairman."

The transition from one generation to the next occurs in phase 3. The incumbent CEO is not a lame duck until he validates the selection of his heir apparent by passing the CEO title to him. Transition begins when the CEO recommends to his board of directors that an heir apparent should be appointed as the new president. The CEO controls the timing of that event, and the action may not be irrevocable—the new president may fail. But, if all goes as expected, the announcement of a new president is really an announcement by the CEO of the beginning of the end of his tenure. During the next five years (more or less), a gradual transition occurs, and I will now comment briefly on the roles and responsibilities of the three main parties: the incumbent CEO, the heir apparent, and the board of directors.

The Heir Apparent. Given the opportunity to become the next CEO, the new president must prove he deserves it. My first piece of advice is: continue to be yourself—it's gotten you this far, and it will probably carry you the rest of the way. These transition years are precious, however, giving you an opportunity to groom yourself to fill the CEO's shoes. You've been selected because you were the best-qualified insider capable of dealing with the challenges the company will face over the next decade or two. During the next few years, if you handle it right, you can affect the strategic mandate for your prospective tenure, and can also work to fill some of the gaps in your own experience so that you'll be qualified to execute that agenda.

More immediately, however, your first tasks fall into the category called building relationships. You won the horse race, and now, like Shipley at Chemical Bank or Nicholas at Time Inc., you must move quickly if you are to retain your contemporaries to serve as members of your emerging team. Your relationship with the incumbent CEO will also change dramatically, if all goes well. You are now engaged in a ritual called passing the baton, and you should be able to learn a great deal from a man who is smart enough to recommend you as his successor. Finally, you'll become a member of the board and this will give you the opportunity over time to get better acquainted with the outside directors. You—and they—know that they have one more important decision to make concerning your career. Ignore that, as best you can, and simply deal with each one as an individual.

Mainly, you've got time—fifteen years or more until normal retirement—so don't try to move too fast. Your roller coaster is just pulling away from the loading platform, and the ride is going to be long. Meanwhile, the chairman/CEO is at the peak of his career, and unconsciously, he believes there is a long flat spot at the top. There will be a few rough spots for him on that downward slope, and your role is to cushion the shocks and provide him with a soft landing and a dignified exit. You'll be in a similar situation a few years from now, and it's worth thinking about how you hope your successor will handle you when that time comes.

The Incumbent CEO. The incumbent CEO scarcely needs to read the three preceding paragraphs—he's more likely to claim that he wrote them. He understands all that and, at the conscious level, knows that his dual role in transition is that of advisor and advisee. The CEO controls the pace of the transition, within the constraint of his own retirement date. Platten and Shipley at Chemical Bank had only two years, and moved rapidly on reorganizing the bank to execute the new strategy. Munro and Nicholas at Time Inc. have five years, and the pace will be more leisurely. Cape and Fildes at Cetus had an indeterminate period that turned out to be three years. As mentor to the heir apparent, the CEO believes the right person has been selected. The CEO's task is to ensure that his protégé is a success, and he uses the time available to progressively broaden the range of the heir apparent's responsibilities. Near the end, the CEO's role is that of a trusted advisor as the two men work toward a common goal of passing the baton.

Simultaneously—and conflictingly—the mentor must also serve as the evaluator. It is the incumbent CEO who must finally decide whether and when to recommend to his board of directors that the CEO title be passed to the president. The nominal criteria, competence and demonstrated performance, are usually not in doubt; the real issue is the breadth of the consensus supporting the leadership of the prospective CEO. The incumbent CEO knows how to read the signals of support within the organization, and he does not explicitly seek advice, but he listens carefully.

The support of outside directors is also important, and the CEO solicits their opinions explicitly, usually one-on-one.

Finally, as to the precise timing of the validation event, the CEO is acutely aware that he is in less of a rush than the heir apparent is. Most CEOs in the relay process step down a few years before their normal retirement date. To retain the initiative on this important personal event, the CEO is well advised to solicit the private council of two or three respected directors.

The Board of Directors. If all is going well, the transition from one CEO to the next that occurs in the relay process is filled with "no surprises" for the board of directors. Individually, and as an institution, the directors were actively involved in the selection process. That careful choice has now been proven, and the validation of it is almost a nonevent, except for the timing. During the transition interval, each director individually should be sensitized to signals about the performance and character of the heir apparent, particularly comments from friends outside the corporation. But, it is not a dereliction of duty to recognize that an effective process is in place and is producing a desirable outcome.

Transition in Top Management Teams

For companies using the team mode of top management organization, the process of CEO succession is not as predictable as it is in the relay process. I have presented three such stories: Chemical Bank, AT&T, and General Electric. The only common thread, even in a set as small as this, is that the CEO title is always carried by the chairman. In contrast to the four-phase career of an executive in the relay process, the three to five members of a top management team have only one or two phases: either they are a member of the team, with the title of vice chairman or president, or they are running the team, with the title of chairman and CEO. Obviously, not all members of the team become the CEO. And when the CEO steps down, he also steps out of full-time management, although he may continue to serve on the board of directors. Even these common elements across these three companies would not necessarily hold for a broader universe of top management teams.

Each of the three situations is different, but a careful analysis of each one and a comparative analysis across the set may reveal an insight or two. In my analysis of Chemical Bank, I found that the transition from Platten to Shipley was very similar to what would be found in companies using the relay process of CEO succession. The only difference was that when Shipley became chairman/CEO, no heir apparent was selected because the members of the four-person team are contemporaries. I will now present some additional data on AT&T and General Electric, and then proceed with my analysis.

Bob Allen at AT&T

The story Bob Allen told in chapter 5 focused on the major reorganization in January 1985 that put in place the new management team to succeed Charlie Brown. Taking a different cut across that same set of events yields some insights about transition from the point of view of the incoming team. This was a topic that Allen particularly wanted to talk about, once the drama was ended. But first, let me complete the chronology of events.

My current speculation is that Brown and his board made their final decisions on the composition of the new team in December 1985, but did not decide when the appointments would be announced and when they would become effective. Sometime between then and early February, Brown talked with each of the five members of the new team, explaining the decisions while leaving the timing issue unresolved. Then, on February 5, he held a meeting with the team and let the other shoe drop: the announcement would be made in May, and he would retire in August. The board ratified that timetable at a subsequent meeting. The announcement that the CEO title would pass to Mr. Olson on June 1 and that all other changes would be effective September 1, 1986 finally appeared in the business press on May 22.

During those intervening three months, the press continued to speculate. On February 25, *The Wall Street Journal* ran a story quoting Mr. Brown as saying that his successor will be named "in the summer sometime." On March 9, in its Sunday Business Section, the *New York Times* ran a feature story on the topic: "Today, James E. Olson is by all accounts the front-runner to become chairman of AT&T . . . with only five months left to the transfer of power, the company has given no public indication that Mr. Olson will take over for Mr. Brown, or that the succession issue has even been decided . . . 'It's like watching the Kremlin' said one analyst . . . Leading the field of dark horses is Robert E. Allen, 51, chairman and chief executive of AT&T's Information Systems Group." Then, on March 24, *The Wall Street Journal* ran an article quoting undisclosed sources saying that: "AT&T Chairman Charles L. Brown is recommending James E. Olson, president and chief operating officer, as his successor, and Robert E. Allen, chairman of the Information Systems Unit, as the company's new president. . . . Although the sources said that Mr. Allen is Mr. Brown's current candidate as president, some thought Mr. Brown might reexamine the decision in the light of last year's poor profit from the Information Systems Unit." One of my undisclosed sources (not Bob Allen) told me that this story in the *Journal* was an "official leak" by AT&T, intended to end some of the speculation. If so, it was effective, and there were no further news stories until the official announcement on May 22.

When Allen and I met in June, one of the questions I asked him was, given the comment in the *Sunday Times* in March, whether in the period between February 5 and May 21 he had ever had any qualms about his being appointed the next president and COO. "Not at all," he said, "I've been operating in a new mode since early February, knowing that Charlie Brown is a man of his word." Allen also said that he had learned a lot about the transition process over the last few months, and here is what he told me:

> I've learned some important lessons during the last few months about that transition phase of the succession process. There has to be a transition period, and it can have some very important benefits, but it can also cause a lot of pain. One of the problems with transition is that you know what is supposed to happen, but it isn't real—you can't act on it—until it does happen.
>
> This transition, I believe, was particularly tough for Olson. He had every reason to expect to be named presi-

dent and COO when Bill Ellinghaus retired in 1984. He
finally was given that title in May 1985, but by then he
probably had some self-doubts about his future vis-à-vis
the leadership at AT&T—and the state of limbo that he
was in continued until early 1986, when Brown told him
that he would be recommended as the next CEO. Even
then, he was in no position to celebrate openly because it
was not announced until the end of May 1986.

During this entire period, I know that Olson was receiving strong positive signals from Brown and some of
the directors, but he still wasn't holding the brass ring.
That uncertainty probably hurt his effectiveness, even
though it was not a conscious behavior. He was a real vic-
tim of the transition process—and we all were. I could
feel the same uncertainty hanging over me, though I tried
not to let it affect me. Given the magnitude of the challenges we were facing, I would have to conclude that our
transition from one CEO to the next—prior to February
5—was expensive. But everything AT&T dealt with during this period was complex and expensive. Passing
through the trauma of divestiture and building a new business extracted large costs on every front. Deciding when to
roll out a new succession plan had to be evaluated in the
context of all we were living through—and the trade-offs
were most difficult.

Now, since February, Olson has assumed the CEO's
mantle and is much more comfortable. He's more relaxed
now, and has developed a longer-term perspective. I can
also sense that the board of directors has been more comfortable since then. Some directors have said to me that
we waited too long to close the loop.

On the positive side, these four months from February
through May have been a settling time—a time for thinking and planning. I'll be accepting responsibility for some
major activities that I know less about, including Bell
Labs, Network Systems, International Operations, Technology Systems, etc. The transition gives me a chance to do
my homework before the people who will soon be report-

ing to me even know that I will be their next boss. I've had a chance to think through how I will try to establish myself with each of them. What is my "theme" to be? What do I say when I finally start traveling around and have to address my new troops? Knowing the timing, I was prepared to call a meeting immediately after the announcement was made, inviting my new direct reports to help me shape the process of managing AT&T.

At the same time, I'll be giving up my direct responsibilities for the Information Systems Division, and Tobias and I and our helpers have really made a lot of progress on the consolidation since February. In effect, Tobias and I have been technically wearing our old hats while actually starting to think about the new roles we will have. In a sense, the transition really ended in February. Since then we're in sort of an interregnum, pretending as though nothing had really happened yet, while at the same time power is changing hands fairly rapidly.

The ambiguity of an interregnum is useful, particularly for the next fifty to one hundred managers below us. With the decisions made, but no announcement, the grapevine does its work quite effectively. The benefit of this is that each manager has a private opportunity to assess his own position in the new organization, particularly if it involves a change in reporting relationships to a new superior. For example, one key manager and I happened to be at a large reception sometime in mid-March, and I was sure that he knew at that time that he would be reporting to me in a few months. Normally, he and I would exchange a sentence or two at such an affair, but this time we chatted for nearly ten minutes—and neither of us referred even inferentially to the impending organization change. It may seem strange for grown men and women to behave this way, but it's not possible to develop mutual respect instantly, and so it is useful to have a chance to get to know each other better before it all becomes official.

Reg Jones at General Electric

When Reg Jones retired as chairman of GE in April 1981, he moved out of the corporate headquarters in Fairfield, Connecticut, and also resigned from the board. GE's practice, not uncommon, is to provide an office and secretarial support for retired chairmen and vice chairmen, and it has a suite of offices for that purpose in a wing of the GE Credit Corporation headquarters in Stamford, Connecticut. I visited Jones there in August 1984. My primary mission was to gather information about his succession road map and related items, but I also asked him to comment on the transition from his tenure to Welch's, and this is what he told me:

On December 19, 1980, the board of directors of General Electric Company voted that Jack Welch would become the next chairman and CEO effective April 1, 1981. The decision was immediately announced to the press, referring to Welch as "chairman elect," rather than resurrecting the presidential title that I had held during the similar interregnum before I became chairman. His induction began immediately, and the biggest event was the annual Management Conference that we hold in Florida each January for our top 500 executives.

Jack and I spent quite a bit of time together during the first three months of 1981. One thing that I did that he seemed to appreciate was to give him a detailed oral history of the management of the company—more detail than he had known about those who built the company. I would be leaving the ship, so it was time for the new skipper to know every last thing that he could about the organization he was about to lead.

Another step we took that turned out to be useful was to invite Peter Drucker, a wise and experienced consultant, to spend a day with us talking about the environment ahead and about changes that Welch might be making. Jack is young and energetic, and he intended to make some early moves fairly quickly. Both of us knew that Jack would be running the company and that I would no longer be on the board, but nevertheless we both felt very comfortable in talking about such topics. I believe that Welch really did want my views on those subjects, and I also was appreciative of the fact that I would have some sense of what was in his mind as he looked to the future.

And, of course, we also spent time together on the road as I took him around to introduce him to major customers and suppliers that he may not have met. During these months, we also made some trips to Washington, D.C., for several business meetings and social events where I could introduce him to the friends that I had made there during my tenure.

A so-called interregnum period can be very useful because conversations can be so open and direct and thus perhaps more helpful. But this period should be kept short; the outgoing CEO is a lame duck and the incoming CEO is anxious to get on with the job. In our case, three months proved ideal.

Comparative Analysis

Although these three stories yield few generalizations, it is useful to attempt to understand these complex situations because there is a process at work and the critical question is: Who is controlling the pace of events? I will comment briefly on three aspects of that issue.

When is the Heir Apparent? The answer to that question is clear at Chemical Bank, but far less so at the other two. At AT&T, Olson was (finally) named president and COO in May 1985. In an earlier era, that announcement would have identified him as the most likely candidate to become the next CEO. But a new wild card — divestiture — changed the game, and nobody knew that better than Olson. A major change was required, and AT&T's board had to think long and hard about bringing in an outsider as CEO to make it happen. Olson had good reason to worry even after he was named president. My speculation is that the board realized that even if it brought in an outsider, he would need to be supported by a strong chief operating officer, and so they passed that title to Olson, perhaps with a specific caveat that the CEO decision had not yet been made. It was not until February 1986 that the word began to spread among a broadening circle of AT&T executives that Olson would be the next CEO.

At GE it is even more difficult to pinpoint the date on which Welch became the heir apparent. The field of contenders in the horse race was pared from seven to three in August 1979, but the announcement naming Welch as the next CEO did not occur until December 1980. If there was conflict in the selection process at GE, as I surmise, then the decision about Welch was probably made sometime during the summer or fall of 1980. The explicit, prolonged transition interval that we have observed in companies using the duo mode simply did not occur at either AT&T or GE. Instead of a gradual transfer of responsibilities from one CEO to the next, in AT&T and GE the transfer was almost cataclysmic; suddenly, "The king is dead, long live the king." The risk in this process is mitigated by the new CEO's immediately having two or more colleagues to work with him as members of the top management team. We saw this process work well at Dow Chemical when Paul Oreffice was suddenly appointed the new CEO and immediately named two senior colleagues to work with him on the operating committee.

Gestation and Interregnum. Gestation can be an important interval in the succession process of top management teams because there frequently is no overt heir apparent until shortly before the selection of a new CEO is announced. For companies using the relay process, there is a gestation period just before the announcement of a new president, but it is usually brief. At Chemical Bank, Shipley was told that he would become president and heir apparent only six weeks before the public announcement. His selection was a major event, but he did not become CEO until two years later, and the organization had a transition interval long enough to absorb and adapt to the change of leadership.

At AT&T and GE, the situation was quite different. Olson

was told he would be the next CEO in January 1985 and the announcement was made five months later. At GE, I don't know when Welch was told, but my informed guess is that it was not long before the announcement. The gestation period in situations like these is awkward; as Allen says, "You know what is supposed to happen, but you can't act on it until it does happen." Nevertheless, the interval is clearly useful, particularly for the next two or three levels of managers as they become privy to the outcome, allowing them time to reassess their own situations and adjust their expectations.

The interregnum that occurs when the effective date of a CEO appointment is subsequent to the announcement date is usually not an important interval. The reason for the delay is often to accommodate the retiring CEO's pension entitlements. Announcing the appointment before it is officially effective allows the new CEO to "get his new show on the road"; the incumbent CEO is a lame duck from the moment of the announcement. I would speculate, however, that in some successions of top management teams the interregnum may serve the purpose of a gestation interval. As Jones describes what happened at GE during the three months after the announcement, his conversations with Welch could be characterized as passing the baton, discussions that would have occurred earlier in a relay process.

The Role of the Board. I will argue here that the pace of succession events at AT&T and GE was controlled by the board of directors. More broadly, in companies run by top management teams, the board expects the incumbent CEO to recommend who should be selected as his successor. When that recommendation is accepted, as it was at Chemical Bank, the relay process begins and the incumbent can control the pace of events.

At AT&T, I assume that Brown recommended Olson and the board demurred, thus causing the delay and pain that Allen described. At GE, more speculatively, I assume that the board was divided on the recommendation from Jones, thus triggering another lap of the horse race until a consensus emerged. The power of the board in selection flows from its ability to withhold its consent to the CEO's recommendation.

For companies using the duo mode of top management organization, the board can also withhold consent to the incumbent's recommendation for his heir apparent, but the incumbent will still be CEO for a few years, and almost has a "right" to select his junior partner. In the team mode, the incumbent will resign when his successor is named. From the board's perspective, the incumbent CEO is already a lame duck, insofar as his recommendation on his successor is concerned; he will depart, but the board will have to live with the new CEO that *it* selects. Inherently, the board in a company using the team mode has more power in selection than the board in a company using the duo mode.

Stepping Out; Leaving the Board

I will end this chronology with a brief discussion of the two decisions a CEO must make at the end of his career: retiring early from the position of chairman, thus stepping out as a full-time employee, and resigning from the board of directors. Neither of these decisions has much impact on the continuing succession process within the firm, but they are important personal decisions for the individuals, and were an important topic of discussion in each of my seminars. One of my colleagues at Harvard Business School has made a major study of retiring CEOs, and I recommend it highly if you are approaching that phase of your career.[2]

Stepping Out as Chairman

For companies using the relay process of CEO succession, the chairman/CEO can control the timing of when he passes the CEO title to his president/COO—if he doesn't delay too long. That event, stepping down as CEO, leaves him with the title of chairman and the status of lame duck. The next event, stepping out as chairman, is not solely his decision. The relay process works best when there is an interval for the new president/CEO to establish his leadership and to marshal a set of candidates from which he

2. J. Sonnenfeld, "Heroes in Collision: Chief Executive Retirement and the Parade of Future Leaders." *Human Resource Management*, Summer 1986, Vol. 25, Number 2, 305–333. John Wiley & Sons, Inc., 1986.

and the board can select an heir apparent. During this interval, the chairman is still holding on to the baton, and he lets go at the request of his successor.

This is what happened at Time Inc. when Munro decided to expedite naming Nicholas as his heir apparent, and Davidson relinquished the chairman's title to Munro. Davidson, still a year and a half from normal retirement, assumed the title of chairman of the Executive Committee. But the variations within this general pattern are endless; juggling a transition involving three people, the relay process can be used quite flexibly.

Most chairmen/CEOs step down three or four years prior to normal retirement, and at least half of that time is needed for a smooth handoff. But the prior CEO experiences a progressive diminution of authority and at some point considers taking charge of the remainder of his life by stepping out — resigning as a full-time employee. The exit barriers are enormous, and should be mitigated to the extent possible, but most chairmen stay simply because they "own" the company. They've given it their lives.

For companies using the team mode of top management organization, the final phase of a CEO's career is quite different. In most top management teams, the chairman/CEO relinquishes both titles to his successor, stepping down and out simultaneously. The timing of that event is frequently determined by the incumbent's normal retirement date, as we saw at GE and AT&T (treating Jones's early retirement as normal, given GE's traditions). Still, variations abound, as at Dow, where the CEO carries the president's title and, when his successor takes those titles, the prior CEO may become chairman but with an overtly "decelerated" role.

Leaving the Board of Directors

The issue here is simply put: should a prior CEO continue to serve on the board of directors after he has retired as a full-time employee? I hadn't given the question much thought, but it came up on the agenda in each of my seminars — and was quite controversial. I now acknowledge that it is an important issue in CEO succession, even though I'm torn on the right answer. First, I will present conflicting opinions from two of my collaborators, and then, I will attempt to sort it out.

Roger Birk at Merrill Lynch

In chapter 2 Bill Schreyer recounted his activities in 1984, his first year as the new CEO for Merrill Lynch. Those events were triggered by the early reitrement of Roger E. Birk, the chairman and CEO of the company at that time. I met with Birk in August 1985 and asked him why he decided to take early retirement. He commented:

> In 1974, Don Regan, then chairman, asked me to become the next president of Merrill Lynch. I was running the Operations Division at that time and was not even a member of the Executive Committee. His offer would mean that I would be jumping over some people, and in fact several of them did leave. I told him I'd like to think about it overnight.
>
> I accepted the next morning, in part because having been offered the job I felt a responsibility to the firm to accept it. In addition, I knew that we needed to make a lot of progress in bringing our management systems up to snuff and developing a comprehensive management development process. I like that kind of work, and we did make a lot of progress during the next two or three years.
>
> During the last three years of Regan's tenure, I was his overt right-hand man. We made a good team, I believe, because he trusted me and because we were complementary. Regan likes controversy, challenge, and authority. My preferences differ somewhat. We were different, but compatible, and, I think, very effective.
>
> After the national elections in the fall of 1980, Regan accepted an appointment in the Reagan White House. When Regan asked me to be his successor as chairman and CEO of Merrill Lynch, I accepted, but said that I would probably retire at fifty-five. He offered to bet with

me that I'd change my mind; that once I got into the job
I'd love it. And, in fact, he was partially correct.

I held all three titles, chairman, president, and CEO,
for a year. From the beginning, however, the board of directors knew that Bill Schreyer was my back-up if anything happened to me. At the end of that time, we decided
to make it official and named him president. Schreyer is
good; he likes to be where the action is, and he's a great
delegator—better than I am. Again, I think that Schreyer
and I made a very effective team.

Why did I decide to retire early? I guess it's really a
question of your philosophy of life. Most people don't
think about the issue of retirement. The question is, How
do you want to spend your life? I gave 100 percent of my
life to Merrill Lynch for thirty years, and that's enough.
There are just too many other things to do. I haven't made
any detailed plans for a second career or anything like
that, but I might take another job in some nonbusiness organization, and I have accepted some of the offers I'm receiving to join boards of directors. I'm not worried about
filling my days, but I did think the time had come to
change the routine.

Having decided that, it then seemed obvious that I
should begin the transition sooner rather than later. In
mid-1984 I recommended that the board transfer the CEO
title to Schreyer, and I would then stay on for another year
as chairman before retiring.

The last decision I had to make was whether to continue as a director of Merrill Lynch after I retired as chairman. Regan was not allowed to stay on any boards when
he became Secretary of the Treasury. I think staying on a
board after having been CEO is unfair to all concerned. If
you speak up in a board meeting, arguing with a recommendation from the CEO, I think that's wrong because
your opinion supposedly carries more weight than that of
an outside director. But if you don't speak up in such a
situation, that's also wrong. All in all, staying on a board
can only cause embarrassment for the retired CEO and/or

the incumbent. I think I can continue to be of help to Schreyer because of my knowledge of the business, but I don't need to be on the board to do that. In fact, I can help him more by not being a member of the board. Schreyer and I talked about that; it was clear that he was happy with my decision. So am I.

Don Platten at Chemical Bank

At the seminar he attended shortly after his retirement as chairman and de facto CEO at Chemical Bank, Don Platten listened attentively and then offered his opinion:

> I understand the pros and cons of the argument, but I think that commercial banks are a special case. It's true that banks are becoming more transaction-oriented, but there's still a lot of relationship banking in this country. A banker and a client who have worked together over many years develop a mutual confidence and trust that is hard to quantify but can be extremely valuable to both parties.
>
> If you accept that, then it's silly for a bank to, in effect, throw away a major asset — the relationships of the retiring CEO — by asking him to resign from the board of directors. Citicorp does just that, and I think they're wrong.
>
> I still serve as a director and chairman of the Executive Committee of Chemical Bank. Because I have that status, I'm in demand for speeches and other affiliations, and that's good for the bank. The cost of that benefit is the risk that my behavior as a director might somehow constrain Shipley's ability to function as CEO. I understand that, and I make sure that I don't bug Shipley.

Commentary. The demographic data from our population of companies does not shed much light on the issue. Of the CEOs retiring during the period 1960–1984, 70 percent continued to serve on the board for a year or more. The nontrivial minority suggests, however, that like most of the issues in this book, the solution is a reflection of the specific situation. I'll try to summarize the primary costs and benefits that affect the result.

The basic argument against having a retired CEO on the board is that he has an impossible role. If he tries "not to bug" his successor during board meetings, he fails to fulfill his responsibilities as a director. The retired CEO is, in effect, stifled, which means, at best, that he adds no value to the board's deliberations and, at worst, that he is behaving unethically by failing to provide data known only to him and the incumbent. If the retired CEO is too forthcoming, on the other hand, he runs the risk of upstaging the incumbent, embarrassing everybody and, alas, himself.

Substantively, the argument can be made that a retired CEO/ director can be a roadblock to desirable strategic change. At GE, for example, Jack Welch and the board he inherited from Jones decided to sell Utah International as one of Welch's early initiatives. Jones had engineered the acquisition only five years before, and the divestment surely was easier because Jones was no longer on the board, although it should be reported that Jones was very supportive of the divestment. Several CEOs at my seminars mentioned this aspect of the issue, but one disagreed, arguing that the support of his predecessor, endorsing a major change, made it easier for his board to accept it.

Finally, I would mention two benefits of keeping a retired CEO on the board, assuming that he wants to serve and is in good health. First, the retired CEO/director can be a valuable resource; he knows the company and its industry, and he wants the company to prosper, like Ron Cape at Cetus, for reasons both financial and psychic. Second, if the incumbent CEO turns out to be a disappointment, the man who championed his selection may be useful in correcting the error.

Honorable people may honestly disagree on the balance between these costs and benefits. In most situations, the decision is made by the retiring CEO; not many companies have a policy or tradition that prohibits him from continuing to serve on the board. My own opinion is that the retiring CEO is the best person to make that decision. If he decides to stay on the board, recognizing the somewhat awkward role, he will probably handle it well.

*   *   *

Early in my research, I anticipated that I would have a problem writing the final paragraph of this chronology, so I kept my ears open for a capstone comment. Don Platten at Chemical Bank phrased it just right:

> My last official act as chairman and CEO was a dinner in my honor in Washington, D.C., at the State Department, during the International Monetary Fund meeting in September 1983. Most of the central bankers whom I had gotten to know over the years, plus other friends, were there — it was a fine affair.
>
> The next morning, Peg and I packed up the car and headed toward Charlottesville, Virginia. About a half hour down the road I turned to her and said, "I really don't know what I had expected to feel on retirement, but all of a sudden I have a great feeling of relief!" It was a very tangible feeling and I could almost feel the weight coming off my shoulders. We both smiled.

8

Diagnosis, Prognosis, and Prescription

Finally, our chronology is complete. With the help of twenty-nine collaborators in twenty companies, I have carefully inspected the territory called CEO succession. These companies were, in effect, self-selected; their willingness to share their experiences with you is testimony to their belief that their succession process was handled "right," and I concur in that judgment in almost every case. But, the regimen of the chronology has occasionally been confining, and now I'd like to graze more broadly across the ground we've covered, and connect it to the broader topic of corporate governance.

I've used a medical analogy as my title for this chapter because it captures the objectives I set for myself in this research. A doctor, performing a routine physical examination of a new patient, knows the characteristics of a healthy human being. He inspects the "territory," looking for symptoms of abnormality. Using that set of symptoms, he then tries to diagnose the illness. He knows the common symptoms for a variety of illnesses, and classifying this patient's illness then allows him to prognosticate on the seriousness of the situation, and to prescribe what actions should be taken to restore the patient's health. The data base of codified medical experience that supports his analysis is massive.

My allusion to witch doctors in the first paragraph of chapter 1 was not meant in jest. Forget about medical science: we do not even have a published folklore about CEO succession. A "science" for this topic is not likely, because every situation is unique. All human beings have common anatomical characteristics: two arms, a brain, etc. Looking for such structural rudiments, I assumed that every board of directors would have someone who carried the title of chairman of the board — until I found a few companies that violated that rule. As a result, I have not even attempted to construct a prescriptive theory powerful enough to specify how the process of CEO succession should be managed in a particular company at a particular time.

Folklore, however, is better than nothing. In selecting my research sites, I sought collaborators who would say, implicitly or explicitly, "Here's how we did it. We're happy with the result. We're healthy." Even if these twenty companies are healthy, their collective experience is insufficient to yield a prescription for companies in trouble. Nevertheless, later in this chapter, I will attempt to identify the early symptoms in unhealthy companies as a starting point for, someday, prescribing how to deal with such situations.

For healthy companies, the stories I have told clearly show that many paths in the succession process will "get you there." On the other hand, I do not believe that any path will get you there as effectively as the path you carefully design for your situation. The stories were collected to demonstrate and expand the range of alternatives you might consider. I believe that these stories are my primary contribution to advancing the state of the art of CEO succession. What you see in them will be different from what I see, if only because we have different backgrounds and different perspectives. I have learned a great deal from this study, and in the preceding chapters I've shared my insights and opinions with you. I will conclude by discussing four important topics at a somewhat more general level. The first deals with the analysis leading to the selection of a new CEO, and the second reviews the selection process. The third section reflects my current assessment of the state of the art, and the final section offers some prescriptions for improving it further.

Continuity and Change

The tension between continuity and change has been a recurring theme in this book. Now, with all the stories having been told, we can address the issue head on. "Strategic change" is common business parlance; I will not define it at the moment. "Organizational continuity" is a more ambiguous term, and I'll start by describing what this concept means to me.

Sources and Benefits of Continuity

The sources of continuity lie in the past; the benefits lie in the future — if the continuity is sustained. The basic elements of the continuity equation are most easily seen in a microcosm. Quality Circles and other forms of work-force involvement in the production process have been widely tested in U.S. corporations, with varying results. When these work, the results are almost like magic. A small team, working together, produces innovative solutions that increase productivity and quality. Part of these improvements might be ascribed simply to team spirit. But the program is more substantive than that. Particular attention is paid to reducing work-force turnover and absenteeism; a team that stays together for a fairly long period continues to improve its performance. Replacing even one member means that the newcomer will have to be trained and acculturated into the group. When a team breaks up, the technological innovations may be passed on, but the momentum of progress has been ruptured.

At the level of top management, our focus, the synonym for continuity is corporate culture. Every corporation can be said to have a culture, but the spectrum is broad. At the corporate level at GE, Reg Jones described the company as a meritocracy, the epitome of the American Dream in a melting pot called the USA. IBM's culture, at the other end of the spectrum, is best described as a "family," having a set of explicit shared values and embedded beliefs that affect the behavior of all employees. The continuity of top management in the two companies, appropriately, reflects their vastly different cultures: the retiring chairman of GE does not stay on the board, while at IBM there are usually two prior CEOs still sitting on the board. I do not believe that IBM is better than GE in some sense; IBM is *different* from GE; I hope you will agree, but GE's cadre of managers are past the point of being a cohesive family. The relevance of this difference for CEO succession, is, I hope, obvious. Many companies do have a family culture, and regard it as a precious asset to be assiduously sustained. I will review the benefits of a family culture in a moment; here, I will simply assert that such companies have a strong bias toward selecting an insider to be the next CEO. These companies value the continuity that has sustained their success, and they work to keep it.

The wellspring of a corporate culture is a strong-willed founder with a clear vision of the future. In our set of companies, the best example is at AT&T. Early in this century, Theodore Vail, then president, proclaimed his vision of "universal telephone service," and fifty years later the company had a million employees with "Bell-shaped heads." Other companies in our set that have a family culture include Corning Glass, Cummins, Dow, Kellogg, and Time Inc. Continuity that sustains a corporate culture is provided by people—cadres of people at all levels in the organization whose ownership grows by "being there" over a long period. Lifetime employment is a watchword in such companies; one does not kick a cousin out of the house just because there was a crop failure this year. The reciprocal of that is an intense loyalty on the part of the work force—a sense of belonging. Continuity of personnel does not necessarily mean standing still in terms of "how things are done around here"; small, incremental adaptations to a changing environment are a necessity for continued good health, and innovations are easier to implement when there is no risk of losing your job.

Continuity at the top is important in sustaining a family culture because the CEO and his team symbolize the shared values and articulate them perennially for the benefit of both oldtimers and new recruits. More important, a discontinuity at the top—a new CEO from outside—can destroy the embedded beliefs. It takes decades to build a set of broadly shared values in an organization, but only a few months to dismantle it. The relay process of CEO succession, as we have seen, is designed explicitly to provide continuity at the top—and it works. The team mode of top management organization can be an even more powerful force for continuity. One person carries the title of CEO, but he has two or three near-peers who cannot be ignored because they also sit on the board of directors.

The benefits of a family culture, and the continuity that sustains it, cannot be measured in monetary terms. Managers all the way down the hierarchy understand the company's mission and share its vision of the future. As a result they know, innately, how to deal with today's brush fire. Communications between these managers are more efficient—they almost talk in code—and less needs to be said to reach an agreement and get on with it. These managers have a sense of personal competence that is reinforced by the excellence of their company—a sense of pride in their organization and trust in their colleagues. For the last twenty-eight years, I have worked in an organization with such a culture, Harvard Business School, and have closely studied the culture in several large, mature corporations. Culture is a major asset of an organization that has it, and is not to be dissipated casually.

Strategic Mandate and Source of Selection

I find the concept of a strategic mandate very useful in thinking about the issues of CEO succession. The mandate, usually more implicit than explicit, is a message to the new CEO concerning the magnitude, direction, and pace of change that is expected during his tenure. I find that, with a little information about the company and a little information about the candidate selected to be the next CEO, it is possible to make useful inferences about the mandate that led to that choice. Using my stories, I have attempted such an analysis, displayed in Exhibit 8.1.

Of the twenty companies that provided stories, five are omitted from this analysis because their stories contained no information about who was selected to be the next CEO. The Allied Chemical story, however, provided data on two selections: John Connor and then Ed Hennessy. In total this provides us with sixteen data points on the intersection between the strategic mandate and the source of the new CEO.

Looking first at the left-hand column of Exhibit 8.1, I have defined six strategic mandates that describe the magnitude of prospective change in the competitive environment over a relatively long period. I have attempted to array these mandates from the most sweeping (deregulation) to the most benign (stay the course). These definitions are not intended to serve as a taxonomy for major strategic change. The categories are not comprehensive—they do not embrace all situations—nor are they mutually exclusive: in any given situation, the CEO's agenda

EXHIBIT 8.1

Continuity and Change

Source of the New CEO or Heir Apparent

Strategic Mandate (Implicit or Explicit)	Outsider Named CEO	Recent Outsider; Director; Maverick	Insider (Ten Years or More)
Deregulation			AT&T Chemical Bank Merrill Lynch
Cultural Shift	Allied (Connor) Monsanto	Cetus General Electric	
Functional Shift	Emhart	Xerox	
Restructuring	Allied (Hennessy)	Avon	Time Inc.
Stay the Course			Corning Cummins Dow (Merszei) Jewel

would include two or more of the items listed. Nevertheless, I find these definitions useful as the starting point for analysis.

The other three columns in Exhibit 8.1 identify the source of the new CEO, and are arrayed from left to right with the greatest need for change resulting in the selection of a new CEO from outside and the greatest need for continuity resulting in promotion of an insider. The middle column will be explained in a moment. At this point, however, the important thing to realize is that the sixteen entries in the table are the data from which the definitions of strategic mandates and CEO sources were derived. More specifically, I did not invent the definitions and then go looking for stories; I collected the stories and used them to develop the definitions. In academia, we call that hypothesis creation, not hypothesis testing.

I did have a hypothesis, of course, that a company facing the need for major strategic change would be more likely to bring in an outsider to achieve it than to promote an insider. If that were true, then the entries in the table would cluster along a line from the upper left to the lower right corner. Such is not the case. More accurately, the case is not that simple. Some of my more scientific colleagues are quick to point out that it is impossible to make *any* inferences based on sixteen data points selected through a personal network and dealing only with what I call healthy specimens. So be it; I'm looking for insights, not theories.

For me, creating Exhibit 8.1 helped me think about the meaning of "massive strategic change." The best examples are industries that are going through deregulation: AT&T, and financial institutions like Chemical Bank and Merrill Lynch. I rank these situations as the most difficult because the change agenda has so many dimensions. Changing the culture of an organization is, in itself, a major undertaking, as we saw when Jack Hanley at Monsanto and John Connor at Allied tried to professionalize the management of those moribund companies. Changing the dominant functional orientation of an organization also requires time and patience, as we have seen at Emhart and Xerox. By comparison, restructuring the product-market portfolio of a company is almost easy; the stakes are high and the results are fast, but the actions to be taken are more surgical than psychological.

Why, then, do deregulating companies faced with all these problems select twenty-year veterans as the next CEO? One answer is that no one has the qualifications to accomplish what amounts to an almost impossible job. When a less beleaguered company perceives that a specific change is needed, and that its own pool of internal candidates are not qualified, it can find a CEO from outside who has the necessary experience and talents. Deregulating companies, faced with open-ended, long-term change on many dimensions at once, cannot simply hire a quick-fix expert. Someone is going to have to cope with the situation, and it might as well be someone who knows the current business very well and can help it evolve into the business that it will someday become.

One final comment on that middle column in Exhibit 8.1. If the highest priority on the change agenda is a cultural shift, and if the company has a long tradition of promotion from within, an insider may be selected to attempt the task. That, I believe, was part of Welch's mission at General Electric. He was a twenty-year veteran, but still a "maverick," and he succeeded far beyond my expectations. It's a tough assignment for anyone, and an impossible task for a purebred insider.

The Selection Process

The selection of a new CEO or heir apparent is the outcome of the entire process of CEO succession, but the selection process is the most important element because it provides answers to the questions of who and when. I am not really interested in the name and date as much as I am in the process—the why and how—that produced those decisions. I will briefly review here the two most common selection processes: the relay process as described by Henry Schacht at Cummins in chapter 4, and horse races, as described by Reg Jones at GE in chapter 6. Then, using these two examples as polar extremes, I will take ten other companies for which we have data about the selection process and create a spectrum of practice on this topic, focusing on the role of the incumbent CEO, and concluding with some advice for the candidates.

The Relay Process

The analogy of CEO succession to a relay race is apt, but only to a point. A relay race is a team event and the speed of each runner is important in winning. But the relay process—passing the baton at high speed—is even more important. Dropping the baton means that the whole team loses. In this sport, the team of four is carefully chosen, and the sequence of the runners reflects the game plan of the team.

In CEO succession, the race is perpetual, limited only by the survival of the corporation. Each CEO runs only one lap, and during his tenure he must both improve the position of his team *and* pick someone to pass the baton to. A good CEO tries to plan for two laps beyond his own. The next lap will be run by his successor, but he also attempts to develop a strong set of "comers" who can qualify to run the lap after that. The primary benefit of the relay process is that it almost ensures a smooth handoff of the responsibilities of the incumbent CEO to his successor. When the process works, the continuity is almost seamless.

At Cummins, the relay process is used pervasively to fill all managerial jobs, thus creating another major benefit. The relay process creates winners who can then do their jobs competently, and with dignity and self-respect, until they pass the baton to their successors. Some of those winners have more potential than others, and are selected to be trained for higher positions. But each person, topping out at whatever level, can look back on an unblemished, successful career. Compared with the jockeying for position that occurs in a horse race, the relay process is much more civilized.

Horse Races: Why and How?

The why is easy; the how is much more situational. Once the CEO and his board have decided that the next CEO should be selected from the pool of internal candidates, there is almost always a horse race of one sort or another. Even if the choice seems obvious to the CEO and his directors, there are likely to be two or more senior officers who believe they have a chance of gaining the top job. These expectations can be managed in a variety of ways, but the self-selected candidates have the right to expect that they will be treated equitably across the set of contenders — particularly if they are to continue to serve under the next CEO. Sometimes, the tradition and culture of the company almost dictate the selection process, as we saw at GE. A head-to-head race such as that does offer some benefits for the company, and it also serves to stake out the other extreme on our spectrum of selection processes.

That spectrum, displayed in Exhibit 8.2, is a continuum; nevertheless, I have defined two intermediate points across the scale. My objective here is to describe both the how and the why of the selection process, and the likely outcomes that result from using one process rather than another. The company names in each of the four columns now serve almost as code words; I have discussed each of the companies at some length in the preceding chapters, and I will not repeat all of the characteristics of each

EXHIBIT 8.2

The Selection Process

Deep, Early Selection	Pool of Candidates	Defined Contenders	Head-to-Head Race
Cummins	Chemical Bank	CIGNA	GE
AT&T	Corning	Emhart	RCA
	Dow	Jewel	
	Monsanto	Time Inc.	

Likely Outcomes

all winners	redefine "success"	a "visible process"	trauma
no "failures"	no losers	a polite horse race	several departures
most continuity			psychic cost to losers

Note: Eight companies in the set are excluded in this analysis. Three (Allied, Avon, and Cetus) selected an outsider. The other five lacked sufficient data: Bristol-Myers, Ex-Cell-O, Kellogg, Merrill Lynch, and Xerox.

situation. Basically, the spectrum, from left to right, ranges from a "quiet" selection to a "noisy" one, and the outcomes are calibrated in terms of an implicit "trauma index." Let me emphasize that I am being descriptive, not prescriptive; the Cummins process would simply not work for the meritocracy called General Electric.

Another useful way to think about the spectrum of selection processes is in terms of the candidates' expectations. Bob Allen knew that he was on the list at AT&T, but he also knew that at least two dozen others in his age group appeared to be equally qualified. Charlie Brown plucked Allen out of that set, put him on the board of directors, and guaranteed that he would have fifteen years as a member of AT&T's top management team, with a good shot at becoming the CEO some day. The other members of

Allen's cohort fully understood the implications of Brown's decision, but did not feel personally wounded because the field of contenders was so large and dispersed. More generally, in the middle two columns of the spectrum, I'm trying to draw distinctions concerning both the size of the candidate pool and the explicitness with which the contenders are defined. At Chemical Bank, Don Platten took a group of five contemporaries and assigned them the substantive task of creating a new strategy for the bank. Shortly thereafter, he selected Shipley as heir apparent, and the team barely missed a beat. In contrast, at Time Inc. there were three contenders for the role of heir apparent and at Emhart and Jewel there were only two. In a small, defined group of contenders, the expectations of each candidate are higher, and the risk of an embarrassing loss of face is greater. Recognizing this, we saw Dick Munro at Time Inc. compress his timetable by more than a year to mitigate the anxiety.

A final dimension of the selection spectrum is the timing of the decision. Generally, the earlier the decision is made, the lower the cost for the candidates, as illustrated in the two left-hand columns in Exhibit 8.2. The company also benefits because it is more likely that the entire cadre of candidates will stay in place, thus providing a team for the new heir apparent and strengthening the continuity of the transition. The only "cost" I can see in this situation is that there may be only one really good candidate — and then the question becomes whether he is good enough to be an effective CEO.

An overt contest involving two or more contenders over a period of a year or more does have heavy psychic costs for the individuals involved. For the company, however, the stakes are high — the custody of billions of dollars of assets is about to be transferred from one person to another — and it is very important to pick the best of the lot. Another benefit for the company is the effect that the horse race itself has on the candidates. One CEO whom I interviewed (his story is not included here) put it this way, "During the horse race I could almost see the competitors growing — sometimes two or three inches per week." To the extent that his statement is accurate, the effect is that the individual selected will be the best of a "better" set of candidates.

Which is the best selection process? Well, at least you know why I can't answer that question. Every situation is different, and we've known that from the start. There are a lot of idiosyncratic variables to be taken into account, not the least of which is the personality and style of the incumbent CEO.

Role of the CEO

In chapter 1, I stated that the incumbent CEO should "manage the process" of CEO succession, and in the intervening chapters you have seen that there are several steps along the way. Now, as the time for the selection decision approaches, we see that the CEO has two tasks: designing the selection process in terms of the spectrum presented above, and then implementing it. In this section, I shall restrict my comments to companies using the duo mode of top management organization. This means that the selection decision is to name a new president and heir apparent as the first step in a relay process that will ultimately produce a new CEO. The task for the incumbent CEO can most easily be described in terms of four questions that he must raise and resolve.

Appraising the Candidates. Do you have two or more insiders who are sufficiently qualified to become CEO? If you have only one good inside candidate, then you have a calibration problem; the best of a bad lot may not be good enough to be your successor. Your board of directors is no doubt concerned, and you ought to be a little embarrassed to find yourself in this situation. If time permits, you should bring in one or two outsiders at a high level so as to then have a choice. If time is short, you need to hire an executive search firm to cast up at least one candidate to compare with your internal contender.

Personal Choice. If you have two or more qualified candidates, do you know which one is the best? Are you sure? Does the board of directors agree with your appraisal? The answers to these questions will determine what happens next in the selection process. If you and the board do not agree, a horse race may be almost mandatory for you to reach a decision. If you and the board are agreed, it may still be desirable to run a more or less overt race.

Managing Expectations. If you and the board are agreed, how will you handle the expectations of the other candidates? The central message in Exhibit 8.2 is that the earlier you make the selection decision the easier it is to manage the expectations of the other candidates. Decide how you want to treat your candidates, in terms of winners and losers, look at the outcomes in Exhibit 8.2, and then use the selection process that is likely to yield the outcome you desire.

Controlling the Pace. How fast should you move in resolving the questions raised above? This is a complex issue, because the timing of the short strokes can be important for a smooth transition. You need to develop a timetable that starts with today and ends with the day you retire as a full-time employee of the company. In many relay situations you will be dealing with three generations of CEOs: your predecessor, still serving as chairman, yourself, and your successor, the incipient heir apparent. Your timetable will include a transition interval while the new president is brought up to speed before taking the title of CEO, and probably will include the final stage in your career when you serve as chairman and lame duck. The timetable is your private plan, but you will need to share it in such a way that your board of directors will know that your plans include a retirement date. The board will accept your recommendations regarding timing, as long as they are equitable for your predecessor and successor, thus permitting you finally to depart with dignity.

Advice for Aspiring CEOs

If you are a member of an operating committee chaired by the CEO, and are nine years (plus or minus three) younger than he is, you are probably a candidate to be the next CEO. Do your own strategic analysis of your company's situation, positioning it in terms of continuity and change as I did in Exhibit 8.1. What characteristics will the next CEO need? How does your own expertise fit with the future needs of your company? Can you design a program of personal development that will help position you better against those needs? Are other candidates, particularly recently hired outsiders, better qualified than you to meet those needs? If the answer to that last question is yes, you should take a deep breath.

The fact that 27 percent of new CEO appointments go to outsiders who have been with the company for five years or less is both good news and bad news. The bad news is that your loyalty to good old Company X may not pay off—an outsider may get the job. The good news is that there is a lot more mobility in the executive labor market these days. You, too, can move to another company that wants you to be a contender for CEO. Maybe you should get on with it, moving sooner rather than later. Or, maybe you should lower your expectations. Do you really want to become a CEO somewhere else? Being a member of the "first team" at good old Company X can be a rewarding career.

The candidates I talked with had already thought their way through these questions and had decided to play out their hands. Already members of the first team, each of them was relaxed and confident in his situation. Rick Miller at RCA put it well when he said, "I'm happy with my life." I interviewed two candidates, promising anonymity. One said, "Yes, I'd like to be the next CEO, but I'm not willing to kill for it." The other was even more am-bivalent: "A few years ago I was sure that I *didn't* want to become CEO—I didn't like the external relations part of what I saw in that job. I just wanted to do my thing. I like complex business problems where I can see that I really have an impact. If I became CEO, I'd have to let my subordinates come up with the solutions. But now the odds are increasing that I will be named heir apparent, and I'll probably be able to find that there are virtues in the art of listening rather than doing." All four of these men (including Bob Allen at AT&T), each in his own way, had managed to "quench the fire in his belly" in such a way that he would not be shattered by a temporary setback in his career. Four candidates are just a straw in the wind, but I'd like to think that maybe this is a sign that CEOitis is on the wane and that the future belongs to CEOs who are team players.

Finally, I will comment briefly on your behavior during a horse race. Again, you must be your own analyst, this time trying to understand the selection process the CEO has designed. The spectrum presented in Exhibit 8.2 may be helpful, particularly if you approach it with the perspective of the CEO rather than as a candidate. Knowing how the CEO is trying to manage the process may be a useful guide for your behavior—but perhaps not. One of my anonymous candidates described his situation as follows: "A couple of years ago our CEO set up a two-person horse race using Reg Jones as a model. I believe he thought that my counterpart and I would fight it out and that one of us would emerge as the winner, but we refused to do that. He and I are about the same age and we decided to work together rather than to compete with each other, which we were sure would politicize the organization. We talked about it a lot. The result is that we have frustrated our CEO by not helping him resolve his selection decision." At first glance, that seems rather weird, but it actually is not very different from the selection of an heir apparent at Jewel. The broader lesson here is the realization that you, the other candidates, and the CEO are working out the rules of the game as you go along. Your analysis should also anticipate a private "peer review" discussion with the CEO, and the stance you take should be worked out in advance. Don't say, "Pick me or else . . ." unless you are really prepared to find a new position. A much better choice is to be a team player, using Walter Shipley as a model. But do's and don'ts are dangerous; my best advice is be yourself and trust your instincts.

Diagnosis: The State of the Art

The selection of new CEOs in large U.S. corporations is being handled very well. Each year, the custody of billions of dollars of assets is transferred to new CEOs in an unregulated but orderly fashion. This aspect of our capitalistic society is effective for two reasons. First, given the stakes involved and the inevitability of the need for a new CEO, the incumbent CEO and his senior officers devote enormous effort to developing the talents of their younger colleagues. A new CEO appointed from inside is just one of a set of candidates who have been groomed for the job for twenty years or more. Second, over the last three or four decades, the mobility of top managers has increased dramatically. The meritocracy that attracted a nation of immigrants still functions, and we now have a national market for executive talent. Now, the "best" insider may have been with the company only a few years, and occasionally an outsider is hired directly into the CEO position. The process of CEO succession is basically healthy.

There are varying degrees of healthiness, of course, but every specimen in my collection is more or less healthy. In this section, I will define "good health" in three dimensions, illustrating what I mean by using examples from our set, and identifying symptoms that may indicate trouble. The three dimensions are the top management team, the board of directors, and sourcing the candidates.

The Management Team

A cohesive, collegial group of managers at the top, working effectively with the CEO on corporate problems, is the basic signal of good health, analogous to a normal heartbeat and body temperature. Although not directly related to the issues of CEO succession, such a team does say a great deal about the incumbent CEO, who created and chairs it. By definition, the existence of such a team means that the CEO is willing to listen to a variety of viewpoints on important issues. The result is likely to be better decisions. Another benefit is that such discussions are likely to broaden the perspective of all of the members, and that does have positive implications for the candidates to become the next CEO. The size and formality of such a group can vary widely, from the formal top management team at Chemical Bank or Corning Glass to the informal one at Cummins. At Dow Chemical, the group consists of the inside directors who have their discussions in the board meetings. Jack Hanley views the committee that he created at Monsanto as one of his major achievements. When it really works well, such a group can develop a strong sense of mutual respect and trust.

At the other extreme, the absence of such a team would be a major symptom of an unhealthy situation—an imperial CEO, keeping his own counsel. Less extreme, and more common, is the CEO who presides over a monthly "show and tell" with his senior officers. Such meetings do have some value, but they may also be symptomatic of an advanced case of CEOitis.

The Board of Directors

In similar fashion, the relationship between the incumbent CEO and his board of directors is a good barometer of the health of the organization, with major implications for CEO succession. The issues again are involvement and mutual respect, and we have several examples of healthy situations in our set. The gold star should go to Emhart—thanks to Mike Ford—followed closely by the boards at Time Inc. and Jewel. My speculations, based on anecdotal evidence, also suggest that the directors of GE and AT&T were actively involved in the selection process in those two companies. Useful involvement by the board of directors in succession, however, is rarely possible unless the board is also involved frequently in open discussions of major strategic issues.

The red flag that signals a nonproductive relationship between the board and the CEO can frequently be inferred from an examination of the board's composition and agenda. A "weak" board, with too few members who are independent peers of the CEO, is almost a sham—perhaps by design of the CEO. Board meetings are perfunctory: a few committee reports, a polished slide show—and no discussion.

Sourcing the Candidates

Another gauge of healthy practice in CEO succession can be defined by a simple question: Has one or more of the pool of candidates been employed by the company for less than ten years? Many companies have an excellent management development program, and believe they must validate its effectiveness by selecting a loyal, career employee as the next CEO. But for most companies, the national market is too big to ignore. Thus, taking examples from our set, we see Ron Cape at Cetus hiring an outsider as heir apparent, John Connor at Allied trying to groom successors for ten years and, failing that, bringing in an outsider, and Dave Mitchell at Avon turning to one of his outside directors to become the next CEO.

My criterion of having outsiders in the pool may be too strict. Certainly, I can believe that the strong culture at Kellogg justifies Bill LaMothe's prediction that the next CEO will come from inside. And CIGNA is a special case because it is still consolidating the top management teams of two large companies. But, searching for symptoms that may signal potential trouble, I believe that continuous inbreeding is a major red flag. Every large company should be hiring mid-career executives from outside. Companies that fail to accept that discipline must then shoulder the burden of proving that they are right.

*   *   *

By identifying the symptoms of aberrant behavior, I have also defined an implicit prescription for each. Stating the matter positively, a company that has an effective management team, an involved board of directors, and the practice of hiring mid-career executives from outside is well positioned to select the best possible person to be the next CEO. The incumbent CEO, the senior officers, and the directors are working together as partners, and the quality of the candidates has been calibrated against the national pool of executive talent. That's the way that healthy companies in the United States manage the process of CEO succession.

Prognosis and Prescription

Where do we go from here? I set out to identify and describe current good practice in the process of CEO succession and, having done that, I discover that I may have been overtaken by events. My demographic data base goes back to 1960, and the majority of the CEOs I interviewed were appointed before 1980. But think how much the business world has changed in the last half-dozen years! In this new context, I have concluded, my study is even more timely. The turmoil of unfriendly takeovers and "voluntary" restructurings has caused almost all companies to rethink the roles and responsibilities of the board of directors. The core issue is the independence of the board vis-à-vis the incumbent management. In this closing segment, I will face up to the new realities, speculating about the implications for corporate governance and offering some suggestions for boards of directors that want to stay at the forefront of evolving good practice.

Restructuring Corporate America

In the so-called good old days, a board of directors that found itself with a CEO whose performance was just barely tolerable would simply wait him out. The old prognosis in such a situation was that the institution will survive and the next CEO is bound to be better. The prescription was: Do nothing. This, too, will pass. Such is no longer the case! Now, the prognosis is that if you can't clean your own nest, a raider will buy your company and do it for you. The prescription is: If your incumbent CEO can't do it, select a new CEO, perhaps from outside. Hostile takeovers and the inevitable restructuring that results are brutal but effective, justified only by the law of the jungle: survival of the fittest. If the corporation of which you are a director is to survive (and *who* should decide that?), a failing CEO cannot be allowed to stay around very long.

Corporations that survive in this new, more demanding environment will earn their success by competitive performance in two external markets: product markets and capital markets.[1] Product markets are the source of profits, and corporate performance is driven by an effective competitive strategy that yields an acceptable return on investment in each market served. Current best practice suggests that a portfolio of markets should constantly evolve, expanding or acquiring businesses in attractive markets and pruning or divesting those in less attractive markets. An average rate of return that looks respectable is not acceptable if it masks the losers in some markets. Product markets can sometimes change rapidly, almost blind-siding the incumbent CEO. At Avon (chapter 1) we saw Dave Mitchell, totally inbred, become CEO in 1976, when the return on equity was 26 percent, and retire seven years later at fifty-six, when the return on equity had dropped to 10 percent. Recognizing that he couldn't handle the discontinuity, he took himself out and found an excellent successor. Today, an effective board of directors might move more expeditiously to remedy the situation.

1. Gordon Donaldson and Jay W. Lorsch, *Decision Making at the Top*, Basic Books, 1983.

The capital markets, in a very short span of years, have emerged as a source of discipline to monitor the portfolio decisions of corporate managers.[2] Aggressive investment bankers are focused on return on equity and "shareholder value," a new euphemism for higher immediate stock prices. The theory of the case is simple: mature companies that are well positioned in defensible product markets should be leveraged more like public utilities than like venture capital start-ups. The advice, offered at enormous fees, is to "provide value" by the massive repurchase of common shares, and many corporations have rushed to do so rather than find themselves acquired by a raider who uses their own debt capacity to provide the funds. In this way, our hyperactive capital markets have introduced an almost random variable that can thwart the survival of any company. Paul Casey at Ex-Cell-O (chapter 2) became CEO in 1981 and less than five years later had succeeded in changing his conglomerate's portfolio from a moribund set of machine tool companies to a collection of high-tech automotive and aerospace businesses. Before the security analysts could switch their classification of Ex-Cell-O's industry category, the analysts at Textron sensed an opportunity. Faced with the "bear hug" of an all-cash offer for 100 percent of the shares, Casey recognized the handwriting on the wall and proceeded to negotiate a "friendly" merger—but at a very hefty premium over the market. Even the best-run companies, these days, cannot be guaranteed that their institutions will survive.

How will this new environment affect the process of CEO succession? The external markets will continue to be less forgiving, and the board of directors, responsible for the survival of the corporation, will have to follow suit. An important distinction between capital markets and product markets is that a strategic move in the former is frequently executed as a single transaction, and the market reaction is almost immediate. A new strategic initiative in a product market must be implemented over a period that may run several years and involves dynamic interplay with a

2. Michael C. Jensen, "The Takeover Controversy: Analysis and Evidence," in *Takeovers and Contests for Corporate Control* edited by John C. Coffee, et al., Oxford University Press, 1987.

defined group of competitors in the industry. Using external advisors to cope with the capital markets, the board of directors,
above all else, looks to the CEO to design an effective strategy in
the product markets. This, then, creates a dilemma for the board
of directors. The CEO owns the strategy and is held accountable
for the results. But the board of directors, also accountable, must
live with the results, and so it "buys into" the strategy. Monitoring the performance of the CEO as events unfold is difficult
enough, given the long time horizon, but if the results are bad,
who is at fault? In retrospect, it is very difficult to distinguish
between a mediocre CEO and a mediocre strategy — which the
board approved. Replacing the incumbent CEO will become more
common, but there are some wrenching decisions ahead for
boards of directors.

Prescriptions for Boards of Directors

How will boards of directors handle their new, more rigorous
responsibilities? The performance standards for CEOs have gone
up substantially in this new era, and the performance standards
for directors must also escalate — not just for legal reasons —
because the survival of their corporations is more threatened than
in the past. Some boards will fail to meet that challenge, and
they, too, will not survive.

I have no magic solutions, but my basic recommendation is
that the board of directors must become more independent of the
CEO. A partnership board such as Mike Ford built at Emhart is
still the ideal, but the partners must be equal. The primary vehicle for increasing the independence of the board lies in the "committee on directors," more commonly called the nominating
committee. The committee would include all outside directors
and would meet several times per year, including at least one
executive session without the incumbent CEO present. The chairman of the committee should be a senior director who is clearly a
peer of the CEO in all dimensions. The name of the committee
should be broad enough to signify its expanded agenda. My recommendations for that agenda, below, are not unprecedented,
but I know of no company that embraces all of them.

Inside Directors. The committee on directors should determine the number of senior full-time officers who should be members of the board of directors, and, in consultation with the CEO, decide which officers should be elected as directors. The critical factor is to ensure that there are *enough* inside directors; they should account for one-third to one-half of the total membership of the board. I have discussed this topic at some length, in chapter 4. The benefits of inside directors are that they mitigate the unilateral power of the CEO, and by providing more points of contact for outside directors, reduce their dependence on the CEO.

CEO Appraisal. The committee on directors should perform an annual *formal* appraisal of the CEO's performance, and, at the end of the discussion with the CEO, should go into executive session to discuss its evaluation. Subsequently, the chairman of the committee should report privately to the CEO on the executive session. Most companies have an executive compensation committee that appraises the CEO's performance for purposes of bonus awards and salary increases; the mandate of that committee should continue, because it is important to have consistent compensation policies that embrace the entire officer group. The appraisal by the committee on directors should range more broadly. The process at Time Inc. is one model. There, the board reviews the CEO's nonfinancial objectives for the coming year, trying to understand and shape the items on his personal agenda, and then reviews his performance against those goals a year later. Again, one of the purposes is to reduce the board's dependence on the CEO by reminding him, at least once a year, that he is accountable to them.

The Management Team. The committee on directors should initiate three programs that would allow it to monitor the management team without preempting the CEO's executive authority. First, the committee should request an annual report on mid-career executives hired into the corporation from outside. This simple report should help prevent inbreeding. Second, the committee should ask the CEO to arrange one or two occasions each year, usually an on-site visit, where the outside directors will have a chance to rub shoulders with managers four and five levels down in the organization. This action is more symbolic than substantive, but the symbolism is important, and it may occasionally produce information that further reduces the outside directors' dependence on the CEO. Third, the committee on directors should inform the CEO that one of its members will conduct a private exit interview with any second- or third-level officer who resigns from the company, no matter what the nominal reason. This action does not impinge on the CEO's prerogatives—he has no doubt had such a meeting himself—and it might provide valuable information for the outside directors. It is not unusual for a member of the audit committee to have such an interview with a chief financial officer who resigns—for obvious reasons. But the practice should be used more broadly. As I said in chapter 3, it is almost impossible for a senior officer to blow the whistle on a CEO who he feels is failing, so he resigns and moves on. If such an interview does raise a red flag, the situation must be handled delicately—starting first with a conversation between the chairman of the committee on directors and the CEO.

Selecting New Directors. The committee on directors should take the initiative in identifying and nominating new candidates to join the board. This does not sound like a radical proposal, because that's what nominating committees were set up to accomplish. In practice, however, the initiative ends up in the hands of the incumbent CEO. He is the one who has the staff that prepares the list of prospective candidates that is then given to the nominating committee, frequently with the CEO's recommendations. Candidates are discussed, a short, ranked list is prepared, and the CEO is authorized to approach the candidates in that order, offering them a position on the board. Almost everyone, including me, believes that the CEO should have a right to blackball a candidate for the board simply on the grounds that the "chemistry" won't work. In every other respect, however, the process of selecting new directors should be turned on end. The CEO should not make recommendations for new directors, because he is already a lame duck; a new director is likely to have a tenure in office far longer than that of the current CEO. A staff should be retained by the committee on directors — an executive recruiting firm that can understand the criteria the committee wishes and then scan the national market for talented directors in order to prepare a short list. Then, the ranked list can be reviewed with the CEO to eliminate the candidates he would not feel comfortable with, and after that the chairman of the committee on directors should make the contacts. These minor changes could have a dramatic effect on the board's independence. Within just a few years, most of the directors would have been selected by the board and therefore would not be beholden to the CEO.

Evaluating Outside Directors. Finally, the committee on directors should devise a process for cleaning its own nest, weeding out members who are no longer productive. This is not a new proposal, but neither is it common practice today because it is an onerous task that must be handled discreetly. Here, again, to achieve this important objective the committee on directors will need external staff — the same recruiting firm, or perhaps a different consultant. With the knowledge and agreement of all outside directors, the consultant would conduct a private interview with each director (including inside directors) every year or two, soliciting an appraisal of each of the outside directors. No report of this survey would be presented to the committee on directors as a whole, but the chairman of the committee would be informed of members who were ranked relatively low by their peers in their contributions to the work of the board. The purpose is to create an ethic within the board that an outside director must add value to the company or depart. If that ethic can be established, the director who receives a poor rating would be expected not to stand for reelection when his or her current term expires. In this new era, it is increasingly difficult to attract talented people to serve on boards of directors. That task should be much easier if the prospective director understands that the board disciplines itself and is independent of the CEO on the important dimensions listed above.

I confess that I am not much of a believer in structural solutions that try to deal with messy interpersonal problems. I do not believe that the proposals offered here are radical, certainly not when compared with the magnitude of the task and the need to increase public confidence in the effectiveness of corporate governance. Whether these prescriptions will be useful depends, finally, on the quality of the people who try to make them work.

Demographic Data and Analysis

Introduction
by Richard F. Vancil

The genesis of the data base on CEO succession is described briefly in the preface, and it served me well, both as an icebreaker for interviews and in defining the three modes of top management organization. Beyond that, however, I think it is accurate to characterize the data base as a latent asset, waiting to be exploited. My hope is that academics at other institutions will participate in the exploitation. The data base is yours for the asking, and we haven't even scratched the surface of productive analysis.

I was fortunate in this study to have the assistance of Audrey L. Helfant. She worked with me for fifteen months, from June 1985 through August 1986, hiring a small crew to glean the data from public records, and then responding to my endless requests for statistics that might provide insights. My debt to her is immense, and to recognize her contribution, I asked her to write this appendix describing the survey, explaining the diagrams, and commenting on the analysis of CEO tenure.

Survey Design and Documentation
by Audrey L. Helfant

Selection of the Random Sample. The population from which the sample was drawn consisted of one thousand companies: the Fortune 500 Industrials of 1984 (*Fortune*, April 29, 1985) and the Fortune 500 Service of 1984 (*Fortune*, June 10, 1985). *Fortune* classified the one thousand companies into eight groups:

500 Industrials	50 Life Insurance
100 Diversified Financials	50 Utilities
100 Diversified Service	50 Transportation
100 Commercial Banks	50 Retailers
	1000 Total

Before sampling, three groups were reduced by dropping the companies in the bottom half (numbers 51 to 100) of the *Fortune* ranking: diversified financials, diversified service, and commercial banks. In addition, life insurance companies were eliminated, because a large proportion were mutuals (and so not required to meet the same standards of disclosure as the rest of the sample), or were owned by diversified financials.

These restrictions reduced the population to seven groups:

500	Industrials
50	Diversified Financials
50	Retailers
50	Diversified Service
50	Utilities
50	Transportation
50	Commercial Banks
800	Total

Next, individual companies were dropped from the eligible population if:

1. They were subsidiaries of another company (listed as such in Standard & Poor's Index).
2. They had not been publicly held as of January 1, 1960.
3. They were, or had been within the period of the study, organized in cooperative or mutual forms (subject to different disclosure requirements).
4. They were the product of a merger of equals that took place after January 1, 1960.
5. They had, within the period of the study, been controlled by court-appointed trustees rather than by a board of directors, as a result of bankruptcy proceedings.

These restrictions limited the sample to companies that had existed as independent, publicly held corporations since January 1, 1960. This ensured that the data sources — proxy statements and annual reports — would be available for each company for the entire period of the study.

In two groups, industrials and diversified financials, ineligible companies formed a substantial part of the original population. For these two groups, every company was examined — 500
industrials and 50 diversified financials — to determine its eligibility. The pool was then reduced by the number eliminated. The
most common disqualifier for industrials was that they had not
been publicly held as of January 1, 1960. The most common
disqualifier for diversified financials was that they had gone from
a mutual to a stock organization within the period of the study.
The resulting groups were:

Industrials	*Diversified Financials*
500 original	50 (reduced from 100)
−95 ineligible	−31 (ineligible)
405	19

In the other groups, only the companies randomly selected
for the sample were examined for eligibility. Ineligible companies were replaced by a random drawing of new ones. The
sample size was not recalculated, however, as the numbers involved were small.

At this point, the seven groups consisted of:

405 Industrials
 19 Diversified Financials
 50 Retailers
 50 Diversified Services
 50 Utilities
 50 Transportation
 50 Commercial Banks
674 Total

Each group was sampled independently to produce a propor-
tional stratified random sample. A separate section from the
RAND Corporation's table of "A Million Random Digits" was
assigned to each group, and companies whose *Fortune* ranks cor-
responded to the numbers reached in the tables were included in

the sample. Occasionally, a company that was eligible for our study could not be included because its proxies and annual reports were not available. In these cases, a replacement was determined by the next number in the appropriate section of the random-number table.

The final sample included approximately one-third of the eligible companies in each classification: 227 companies, divided into seven groups:

135	Industrials
7	Diversified Financials
17	Retailers
17	Diversified Service
17	Utilities
17	Transportation
17	Commercial Banks
227	Total

How to Read and Interpret the Succession Diagrams

A succession diagram for Avon Products, Inc. was presented in chapter 1. More generally, the CEO succession diagram for a given company displays information about the executives who held one or more of five top management titles over a twenty-five-year period (from the beginning of 1960 to early 1985). The titles (limited to officers of the parent company) are: chairman, vice chairman, president, CEO, and COO. Changes in these positions were generally recorded from public sources — for the most part, from proxy statements and annual reports. In some cases, the company supplied the data. Companies were asked to review the diagrams prepared from public sources, in order to ensure their accuracy. Depending on the titles used by a particular company, the number of individuals holding more than one title, the number of vice chairmen, and the number of inside directors, anywhere from one to a dozen executives might be included on the diagram at a given time.

Reading the Diagram. The names of all executives who held these positions over a twenty-five-year period appears to the left of the diagram. Under each name are four "key dates." These are the executive's year of birth, year of employment with the company, year of election to its board, and year of retirement. From these years can be deduced an executive's age and length of service with the company at any point. Age is printed on the diagram at each title change; tenure in each title with the company is easily calculated.

In addition to the five specific titles, two more general ones were added: officer and director. "Officer" does not include all officers. Instead it is used to record the date at which an executive who subsequently assumed one of the top five titles was elected to the board of directors. The criterion for an "officer" is not his or her specific title on the date of election to the board; it is solely determined by the officer's subsequent holding of one of the top five titles. The category "director" records the date on which an executive who held one of the five titles ceased full-time employment with the corporation, but continued to serve on its board. This includes chairmen emeriti, chairmen of the executive committee, etc.

The information displayed in the titles "officer" and "director" can also be deduced from the key dates. An executive is an "officer" from the time of election to the board until the assumption of one of the five designated titles. Likewise, an executive is a "director" from the time of relinquishing the last title until the year of retirement noted under "key dates." For greater simplicity, the officer and director designations have been left off the Avon diagram.

Each change in the title held by a top officer is an "event" on the succession diagram. During the twenty-five years included in the diagram, Avon had eleven such events. These are listed in the narrative chronology below. This narrative includes no information not captured in the diagram itself: its purpose is only to aid the reader's understanding of the diagram.

Succession Events at Avon

Date	Title Changes
Jan. 1, 1960	At the beginning of the chronology, Avon had a 73-year-old chairman, Mr. Clark, and a 59-year-old president, Mr. Ewald. Note that on the diagram's first entry, the age printed under each title is not the executive's age upon assuming that title, but simply his or her age as of January 1, 1960. Likewise, the titles given are titles held as of January 1, 1960: they could have been assumed at any point before that.
Dec. 6, 1961	Mr. Clark retired as chairman, but did not retire from the board. (This is apparent from the year of retirement included in his key dates.) Mr. Ewald took over as chairman, and Mr. Rooks was elected president. Mr. Rooks was then fifty-five. His age, reached by subtracting his year of birth from the year of the appointment, is printed on the diagram. He had been with Avon for thirty-five years. Employment tenure is not printed on the diagram, but is readily apparent from the year of employment, which appears under the key dates.
Mar. 7, 1962	Mr. Rooks died on January 31, 1962, but the "succession event" did not occur until Mr. Hicklin was named president a few weeks later. The year of Mr. Rooks's death is listed as his "year of retirement" under key dates, even though he had not actually retired. The reader should note that deaths are recorded on the diagram only when executives died while they were still employees or directors of the company. Deaths after retirement are not succession events.
Nov. 3, 1966	Mr. Ewald assumed the additional title of CEO.

Date	Title Changes
Dec. 8, 1967	Mr. Ewald retired, completing fifty years of service with Avon. Mr. Hicklin, heir apparent to Mr. Ewald for five years, was made chairman and CEO, and Mr. Fusee, fifty, was elected president.
Jan. 6, 1972	Mr. Hicklin stepped down as CEO, retaining the role of chairman. Mr. Fusee was named vice chairman and CEO at age fifty-four, and Mr. Mitchell, forty-three, was elected the youngest president in Avon's recent history.
Dec. 6, 1973	Mr. Hicklin retired as chairman, passing that title to Mr. Fusee. The CEO title was discontinued, but the diagram assumes that Mr. Fusee was the de facto CEO.
Dec. 4, 1975	Mr. Mitchell, continuing as president, was also named CEO.
Mar. 3, 1977	Mr. Fusee relinquished the title of chairman (and died a few months later). Mr. Mitchell became chairman and CEO, and Mr. Chaney, forty-five, became president and COO.
Mar. 4, 1982	Mr. Chaney relinquished the COO title, continuing as president.
July 25, 1983	Mr. Waldron, aged sixty, was named president and CEO. He had not previously been employed by Avon, but had served on the board of directors since 1980. Mr. Mitchell continued as chairman and Mr. Chaney became executive vice president.
Nov. 3, 1983	Mr. Mitchell retired as chairman, passing that additional title to Mr. Waldron.
Apr. 16, 1985	Mr. Waldron brought in an outsider—John S. Chamberlin—as president and COO. Mr. Waldron continued to serve as chairman and CEO.

Interpreting the Diagram. Working just with these data, it is possible to draw several useful inferences about CEO succession at Avon:

· Avon had depth in its management cadre in the early 1960s. When Mr. Rooks died suddenly, the company was able to replace him within a few weeks with Mr. Hicklin, five years younger than Rooks, but with thirty-four years of service with the company. Mr. Hicklin subsequently became chairman and CEO of Avon.

· The CEO title was first used by Avon in 1966, when Mr. Ewald added that title to his role as chairman. That title was just coming into vogue in American business, in part because it facilitated the succession process. In Avon's case, with Ewald only a year from retirement, the CEO title made it easier to clarify Mr. Hicklin's role as the new chairman and CEO when Mr. Fusee was elected the new president.

· When Mr. Hicklin passed the CEO title to Mr. Fusee, he apparently set a precedent that Avon's CEO should not serve beyond age sixty. One of the advantages of the CEO title is that it permits the chairman to continue in a signficant role, while passing major responsibility to a younger executive.

· The more important part of the event in early 1972 was that Mr. Fusee took the title of vice chairman, thus vacating the presidency and allowing Mr. Mitchell to assume that post. This was an unusual move for Avon, requiring three executives at the top. If Avon had followed its traditional practice, Mr. Mitchell would have been named president two years later when Mr. Hicklin retired as chairman. It seems reasonable to conclude that Mr. Mitchell was regarded as an exceptional talent who deserved early recognition.

· In 1975, Mr. Fusee reinforced Mr. Hicklin's earlier precedent. At age fifty-eight, he stepped down as de facto CEO by reviving that title for Mr. Mitchell.

- The team of Fusee and Mitchell was expected to stay in place for several years, but Mr. Fusee died in 1977. Avon named Mr. Chaney as the new president with the additional title of COO, further clarifying the division of responsibilities between the two executives at the top of the company.

- Mr. Chaney's loss of the COO title in 1982 cannot be explained without an additional piece of public information: Avon acquired Mallinckrodt, Inc. in a major diversification move, and the president of Mallinckrodt reported directly to the CEO. Mr. Chaney continued as president of the parent (Avon), but his position in the line of succession had become more ambiguous.

Analysis of CEO Tenure

The use of the CEO title has increased dramatically during the period covered by this study. As late as 1967, only half of the companies in the sample were using the title. Therefore, in order to include earlier data in the analysis of CEO tenure it was necessary to establish guidelines for determining the de facto CEO in every company in every year covered by the study. When the CEO title was used, when one person served as both chairman and president, or when only one of these positions existed, the assignment presented no problems. Ambiguous situations arose when the titles of chairman and president were held by two people, neither designated as the CEO. In these cases, it was decided after some experimentation to give priority to the title held by the first CEO upon becoming CEO. In other words, if the first titular CEO was the president of the company, then earlier presidents were assumed to have been de facto CEOs; similarly, if the first titular CEO was the chairman, earlier chairmen were assumed to have been de facto CEOs. For the few companies that still did not use the CEO title officially at the end of 1984, the de facto title was assigned to the chairmen. Although this method was inevitably arbitrary, it appeared to give reasonable results: comparison of the assigned CEOs with those who were unambiguously CEOs (by title or situation) revealed no significant differences on the dimensions of tenure, age at appointment, or age at retirement.

With this disposition of the earlier years, the data set yields 838 CEO tenures held by 820 CEOs. The CEOs who served more than once were excluded from the analysis: this reduced the data set to 802 executives who served as CEO during the twenty-five years. However, the number of years served for completed tenures is known for only 398 executives. Two hundred and twenty-eight CEOs were still in office at the end of the study. (The number 228 reflects the 227 companies in the sample, one of which—Golden West Financial—currently has dual CEOs.) Moreover, it was hard to obtain the dates of appointment for CEOs who were incumbents on January 1, 1960, the date on which the study began. The appointment date could be determined only when the incumbent was a titled CEO, or chairman and president simultaneously, and when the company provided additional data. Thirty-two cases met those conditions; for the rest of the sample—195 companies—the incumbent in 1960 had an unknown date of appointment, and so an unknown length of tenure. Nine companies were missing both beginning years and end years: in other words, a single CEO served for the duration of the study. The result is 398 completed tenures:

```
  802   CEO tenures
 -216   missing end year only
 -179   missing beginning year only
 -  9   missing both beginning and end years
 ─────
  398   Total
```

This set of tenures should not be regarded as a survey of corporate practice for the period we studied, because companies with short tenures are inevitably overrepresented. (A long tenure is more likely to extend beyond the study in one direction or the other, and so to be unknown.) Indeed, seventy-five of the known tenures (18.8 percent) were three years or less in length.

Short Tenures. The seventy-five "short tenures" were distributed among the sample companies as follows:

One short tenure:	48 companies
Two short tenures:	7 companies
Three short tenures:	3 companies
Four short tenures:	1 company

One hundred and sixty-eight companies had no short tenures.

It seems, then, that a tenure of three years or less is rarely, if ever, a matter of policy. Rather, it is a response to circumstances that are unusual enough not to have arisen in twenty-five years for most of the companies we studied. The section on career paths in chapter 3 discusses some of those circumstances.

A simple count of the number of completed tenures in the data base gives disproportionate weight to companies with short tenures. One way to rectify this bias is to look at the group of CEOs in office at a given time. In each group, a company is counted once only. For this analysis of tenure, the date that falls at the middle of the survey was most appropriate, because it keeps to a minimum the number of tenures whose beginning or end is unknown, and allows deductions even about those. Therefore, we looked at the 227 CEOs in office at the end of 1972.

CEOs of 1972. Of the 227 CEOs holding office in the surveyed companies at the end of 1972, sixty-five had tenures of unknown length. The sixty-five missing tenures must have been at least twelve years long, however (since the end of 1972 is twelve years from each chronological end of the study). Taking this into account, nearly half of the CEOs had tenures of more than twelve years. See Exhibit A.1 for a distribution of the tenure lengths.

The mean and median ages of appointment for the group were 51.4 and 52.3 years, respectively. (Age at appointment was known in 196 of the 227 cases.) The median of the known ages at retirement (174 known) was 64.2. Finally, the mean of the years of employment with the company before becoming CEO was 18.8. Nineteen percent had less than six years employment with the company before assuming the position of CEO; more than 50 percent had at least twenty-one years employment before their appointments. See Exhibit A.2 for the distribution.

How does this compare with the CEOs in office at the end of 1984? Age at appointment has remained constant: the mean and median ages in 1984 were 51.3 and 51.6 years (based on 211 cases). Length of completed tenure and age at retirement are not, of course, known yet for this group. The pattern of length of employment before becoming CEO has shifted: 27 percent had served less than six years before their appointments, and only 43 percent had served twenty years or more.

Finally, to obtain a distribution of the departure routes for CEOs (described in chapter 3), we used the retirements of CEOs whose tenure was known for all of the companies in our sample. The criteria for each career are defined in Exhibit A.3.

EXHIBIT A.1

Tenure (in Years) of CEOs in Office in 1972

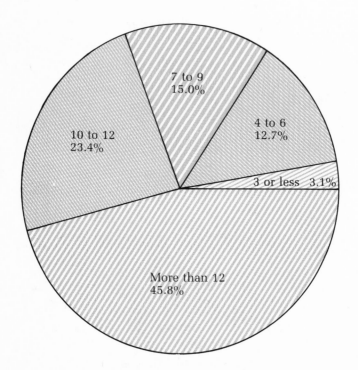

7 to 9
15.0%

4 to 6
12.7%

10 to 12
23.4%

3 or less 3.1%

More than 12
45.8%

CEOs: Years Employed by Company before Appointment as CEO

Number of Years	Percent of Sample*	Cumulative Percentage
Fewer than 3	13.8%	13.8%
3 to 5	5.4	19.2
6 to 8	5.4	24.6
9 to 11	5.8	30.4
12 to 14	6.5	36.9
15 to 17	4.3	41.2
18 to 20	5.4	46.6
21 to 23	7.7	54.3
24 to 26	7.4	61.7
27 to 29	10.6	72.3
30 to 32	9.0	81.3
33 to 35	7.4	88.7
More than 35	11.3%	100.0%

*n = 556

PASSING THE BATON

EXHIBIT A.3

CEO Careers: Departure Routes

The table below gives the specifications that were used in calculating the number of CEOs who fell into each "career." A blank under a given criterion indicates that no restrictions were imposed for it.

Tenure, age at appointment, and age at retirement are self-explanatory. One note on age at retirement: since we don't know executives' birth dates, the ages in our data base may be too high by one year. To compensate for this bias, and to arrive at a conservative estimate of CEOs retiring late, we have set the limit of "normal retirement" at sixty-six rather than sixty-five.

For a distribution of departure routes, see Exhibit 3.2. Note: In using retirement modes to determine career classification, we considered CEOs to remain as chairmen or directors only if they retained those titles for at least one year after resigning as CEOs.

Criteria for Career Patterns

	Tenure (in years)	Age Appointed	Age Retired	Retirement Mode	% of Sample*
Selection Error	LE 3	LT 58	——	Not Death	4.8
Two-Career	GT 3	——	LE 55	Not Death	6.2
Policy Retirement	GT 3	——	56–61	Chairman or Director	12.4
Other Exit (1)	GT 3	——	56–61	Left Board or Died	9.7
(2)	——	——	LE 66	Died	
Replacement	LE 3	GE 58	——	——	9.0
Mandatory Retirement	GT 3	——	62–66	Not Death	47.3
Late Appointment	4–12	——	GE 67	——	6.6
Curmudgeon	GT 12	——	GE 67	——	4.0

*n = 421. LE = Less than or equal to. GT = Greater than. GE = Greater than or equal to.

APPENDIX B

Biographical Profiles of Collaborators

Robert E. Allen born January 25, 1935 in Joplin, MO. Education: B.A., Wabash College, 1957.

Employment: With various telephone operating companies owned by AT&T, 1957–1978; Corporate Officer, Indiana Bell Telephone (Indianapolis, IN) 1971. Vice President, AT&T (Basking Ridge, NJ) 1978–1981. President, Chesapeake & Potomac Telephone Companies (Washington, D.C.) 1981–1983; Chairman, C&P Companies and President-Elect, Bell Atlantic (Washington, D.C.) 1983. Executive Vice President, AT&T (New York, NY) 1983–1985; Chairman and CEO, Information Systems, 1985–1986; President and Chief Operating Officer, 1986–.

Corporate Directorships: City Federal Savings and Loan (Elizabeth, NJ) 1979–1984. Riggs National Bank and Riggs National Corporation (Washington, D.C.) 1981–1984. Cluett Peabody, Inc. (New York, NY) 1983–1985. AT&T (New York, NY) 1984–. Manufacturers Hanover Trust and Manufacturers Hanover Corporation (New York, NY) 1984–. Bristol-Myers Company (New York, NY) 1985–.

Earle B. Barnes born July 14, 1917 in Pueblo, CO. Education: B.A., Texas Christian University, 1938. M.A., University of Nebraska, 1940.

Employment: The Dow Chemical Company, 1940–1982; Production Superintendent, Director of Research, General Manager of Texas Division (Freeport, TX) 1941–1966; Corporate Director of Manufacturing (Midland, MI) 1967–1969; President, Dow Chemical Company U.S.A. (Midland, MI) 1969–1975; Executive Vice President, 1975–1979; Chairman of the Board, 1979–1982. President, Earle Barnes Associates, Inc. (Jackson, WY) 1982–.

Corporate Directorships: The Dow Chemical Company (Midland, MI) 1966–1982. Dow Badische Company (Williamsburg, VA) 1966–1978. The Dow Corning Corporation (Midland, MI)

1972–1982. Asahi-Dow Chemical Company (Tokyo, Japan) 1979–1982. Comerica Bank (Detroit, MI) 1981–.

Roger E. Birk born July 14, 1930 in St. Cloud, MN. Education: B.A., St. John's University, 1952.

Employment: U.S. Army, 1952–1954. With Merrill Lynch, Pierce, Fenner & Smith, Inc., various positions, 1964–1974; President (New York, NY) 1974–1976. President, Merrill Lynch & Co., Inc. (New York, NY) 1976–1982; CEO, 1981–1984; Chairman, 1981–1985. Chairman, International Securities Clearing Corp. (New York, NY) 1986–.

Corporate Directorships: Merrill Lynch & Co., Inc. (New York, NY) 1974–1985. Federal National Mortgage Association (Washington, D.C.) 1985–. Mutual of America Life Insurance Company (New York, NY) 1985–. New Jersey Resources Corporation (Wall, NJ) 1985–. Hertz Penske Truck Leasing Inc. (Parsippany, NJ) 1985–.

Ronald E. Cape born October 11, 1932 in Montreal, Canada. Came to the United States in 1967, naturalized in 1972. Education: A.B., Princeton University, 1953. M.B.A., Harvard University, 1955. Ph.D., McGill University, 1967. Postgraduate, University of California, Berkeley, 1967–1970.

Employment: Merck & Company, Ltd. (Montreal, Canada) 1955–1956. President, Professional Pharmaceutical Corporation (Montreal, Canada) 1960–1967; Chairman of the Board, 1967–1973. Cetus Corporation (Emeryville, CA); President, 1972–1978; Chairman of the Board, 1978–.

Corporate Directorships: Cetus Corporation (Emeryville, CA) 1972–. Scientific American, Inc. (New York, NY) 1980–1986. Neutrogena Corporation (Los Angeles, CA) 1980–.

Edward Paul Casey born February 23, 1930 in Boston, MA. Education: B.A., Yale University, 1952. M.B.A., Harvard University, 1955.

Employment: Davidson Rubber Company (Dover, NH); Vice President, General Manager, President, 1955–1964. McCord Corporation (Detroit, MI); President, 1965–1978. Ex-Cell-O Corporation (Troy, MI) 1978–1986; President, 1978; CEO, 1981; Chairman, 1982–1986. Textron, Inc. (Providence, RI); Vice Chairman, 1986–.

Corporate Directorships: Manufacturers National Corporation (Detroit, MI) 1950–1964. Davidson Rubber Company (Dover, NH) 1950–1964. McCord Corporation (Detroit, MI) 1964–1978. Ex-Cell-O Corporation (Troy, MI) 1978–1986. Norton Company (Worcester, MA) 1978–1986. Uniroyal, Inc. (Middlebury, CT) 1984–1986. Textron, Inc. (Providence, RI) 1986–.

John Thomas Connor born November 3, 1914 in Syracuse, NY. Education: A.B., magna cum laude, Syracuse University, 1936. J.D., Harvard University, 1939. Bar: New York, 1939.

Employment: Associate with firm Cravath, deGersdorff, Swaine & Wood, 1939–1942. General Counsel, U.S. War Agency, OSRD 1942–1944; Air Combat Intelligence Officer, U.S. Marines, 1944–1945. Counsel with Office of Naval Research, also Special Assistant to the Secretary of the Navy, 1945–1947. Merck & Company, Inc. (Rahway, NJ); General Attorney, 1947; Secretary, 1947–1951; Counsel, 1947–1953; Vice President, 1950–1955; President and CEO, 1955–1965. U.S. Secretary of Commerce, 1965–1967. Allied Chemical Corporation (Morristown, NJ); President, 1967–1978; Chairman and CEO, 1968–1979. Schroders, Inc. (New York, NY); Chairman of the Board, 1980–1986.

Corporate Directorships: Merck & Company, Inc. (Rahway, NJ) 1955–1965. General Foods Company (White Plains, NY) 1962–1974. General Motors Corporation (Detroit, MI) 1963–1984. Allied Chemical Corporation (Morristown, NJ) 1967–1980. American Broadcasting Company (New York, NY) 1976–1984. Schroders Limited, P.L.C. (London, England) 1980–1987.

T. Mitchell Ford born April 27, 1921 in Albany, NY. Education: A.B., Harvard University, 1943. J.D., Yale University, 1948. Bar: Connecticut, 1948; Massachusetts, 1949.

Employment: Becket & Wagner (Lakeville, CT) 1948–1952. Assistant General Counsel, CIA, (Washington, D.C.) 1952–1955. General Counsel, Naugatuck Valley Industrial Council (Waterbury, CT) 1955–1958. Emhart Corporation and predecessor

American Hardware Corporation (Hartford, CT) 1958–1986. Secretary and General Counsel, American Hardware Corporation; Vice President, 1964–1967; President, 1967–1984; Chairman, 1976–1985.

Corporate Directorships: Emhart Corporation (Hartford, CT) 1965–. Veeder Industries (Hartford, CT) 1967–1972. Hartford National Corporation (Hartford, CT) 1967–. United Technologies Corporation (Hartford, CT) 1970–. Bliss & Laughlin (Chicago, IL) 1972–1977. Travelers Insurance Corporation (Hartford, CT) 1977–. Connecticut Natural Gas Corporation (Hartford, CT) 1984–. Quamco, Inc. (Hartford, CT) 1985–.

Lawrence Edward Fouraker born October 28, 1923 in Bryan, TX. Education: B.A., Texas A&M College, 1947; M.S., 1948. Ph.D., University of Colorado, 1951.

Employment: Instructor, University of Wyoming (Laramie) 1948–1949. Assistant Professor/Professor, Pennsylvania State University (State College) 1951–1961. Harvard Business School (Boston, MA) 1961–1983; Professor of Business Administration, 1963–1983; Director of the Division of Research, 1968–1970; George Fisher Baker Professor of Business Administration 1970–1980; Dean, 1970–1980.

Corporate Directorships: Citicorp (New York, NY) 1970–. RCA (New York, NY) 1973–1978. New England Mutual Life (Boston, MA) 1973–. Gillette (Boston, MA) 1973–. R. H. Macy (New York, NY) 1974–1986. Jewel Companies (Chicago, IL) 1975–1984. Texas Eastern (Houston, TX) 1977–. Alcan (Montreal, Canada) 1978–. General Electric (Fairfield, CT) 1981–. Ionics (Watertown, MA) 1986–.

Richard Lee Gelb born June 8, 1924 in New York City. Education: B.A., Yale University, 1945. M.B.A., with Distinction, Harvard University, 1950.

Employment: U.S. Army, 1943–1946. Clairol, Inc. (New York, NY) 1950–1964; President, 1959–1964. Bristol-Myers Company (New York, NY); Executive Vice President, 1965–1967; President, 1967–1976; CEO, 1972–; Chairman of the Board, 1976–.

Corporate Directorships: Bristol-Myers Company, (New York, NY) 1960–. Bankers Trust Company (New York, NY) 1971–1985. Cluett Peabody & Company (New York, NY) 1972–1985. New York Times Company (New York, NY) 1974–. New York Life Insurance Company (New York, NY) 1981–. The Federal Reserve Bank of New York (New York, NY) 1985–.

John W. Hanley born January 11, 1922, in Parkersburg, WV. Education: B.S., Pennsylvania State University, 1942. M.B.A., Harvard University, 1947.

Employment: Allegheny Ludlum Steel Corporation (Tarentum, PA) 1942–1943. The Procter & Gamble Company, (Cincinnati, OH); Field Sales Management, 1947–1953; General Office Sales Management, 1953–1960; General Manager, U.S. Soap Division, 1960–1967; Vice President, Group Executive, 1967–1970; Executive Vice President, 1970–1972. Monsanto Company (St. Louis, MO); President and CEO, 1972; Chairman, President, and CEO, 1975–1980; Chairman and CEO, 1980–1983; Chairman of the Executive Committee, 1971–1985.

Corporate Directorships: Armco Steel Corporation (Middletown, OH) 1965–1973. The Procter & Gamble Company (Cincinnati, OH) 1967–1972. Monsanto Company (St. Louis, MO) 1971–1985. Citicorp Bank (New York, NY) 1974–. Citibank, N.A. (New York, NY) 1974–. The May Department Stores Company (St. Louis, MO) 1976–. Southern Pacific and Southern Pacific Transportation (San Francisco, CA) 1976–1980. R.J. Reynolds Industries, Inc. (Winston-Salem, NC) 1981–.

James Alan Henderson born July 26, 1934 in South Bend, IN. Education: A.B., Princeton University, 1956. M.B.A., Harvard University, 1963.

Employment: Faculty, Harvard Business School (Boston, MA) 1963–1964. Cummins Engine Company, Inc. (Columbus, IN) 1964–; Assistant to Chairman, 1964–1965; Vice President-Management Development, 1965–1969; Vice President-Personnel, 1969–1970; Vice President-Operations, 1970–1971; Executive Vice President, 1971–1975; Executive Vice President, COO, 1975–1977; President, 1977–.

Corporate Directorships: Hayes-Albion Corporation (Jackson, IN) 1972–1986. Cummins Engine Company, Inc. (Columbus, IN) 1974–. Indiana Bell Telephone Company, (Indianapolis, IN) 1978–1983. Inland Steel Company (Chicago, IL) 1978–. Ameritech (Chicago, IL) 1983–.

James Richardson Houghton born April 6, 1936 in Corning, NY. Education: A.B., Harvard University, 1958; M.B.A., Harvard University, 1962.

Employment: Goldman, Sachs & Company (New York, NY) 1959–1961. Corning Glass Works (Corning, NY) 1962–; Production and Finance (Danville, KY and Corning, NY) 1962–1964; Vice President, Area Manager-Europe (Zurich, Switzerland and Brussels, Belgium) 1964–1968. Vice President, General Manager, Consumer Products Division (Corning, NY) 1971–1983; Chairman of the Board and CEO, 1983–.

Corporate Directorships: Corning Glass Works (Corning, NY) 1969–. Dow Corning Corporation (Midland, MI) 1972–. The Sperry and Hutchinson Company (New York, NY) 1972–1981. Metropolitan Life Insurance Company (New York, NY) 1975–. CBS, Inc. (New York, NY) 1977–. J.P. Morgan Company, Inc. (New York, NY) 1982–. Corning International Corporation (Corning, NY) 1966–1980; 1983–.

Reginald H. Jones born July 11, 1917 in Stoke-on-Trent, England. Education: B.S., University of Pennsylvania, 1939.

Employment: General Electric Corporation (Bridgeport, CT); Vice President, 1961–1968; General Electric Corporation (New York, NY); Vice President-Finance, 1968–1970; Senior Vice President, 1970–1972; Vice Chairman, 1972; President, Chairman, and CEO, 1972–1981.

Corporate Directorships: Federated Department Stores (Cincinnati, OH) 1980–. General Re Corporation (Stamford, CT) 1980–. ASA Limited (Madison, NJ) 1981–. Bethlehem Steel Corporation (Bethlehem, PA) 1981–. General Signal Corporation (Stamford, CT) 1981–. Merck & Company, Inc. (Rahway, NJ) 1981–. Morgan Guaranty International Council (New York, NY) 1981–.

Robert Donald Kilpatrick born February 5, 1924 in Fairbanks, LA. Education: B.A., University of Richmond, 1948. Postgraduate, Harvard Business School, 1973.

Employment: Connecticut General Life Insurance Company (Hartford, CT) 1954–; Vice President, Chief Administrative Officer, Aetna Insurance Company (affiliate), 1968–1973; Senior Vice President, Group Insurance Operations; President and CEO, 1976–1982. Cigna Corporation, (Philadelphia, PA) 1982–; President and Co-CEO, 1982–1983; Chairman and CEO, 1983–.

Corporate Directorships: Scovill Inc. (Waterbury, CT) 1978–1983. Federal Reserve Bank of Boston (Boston, MA) 1978–1981. Allied-Signal Corporation (Morristown, NJ) 1980–.

William E. LaMothe born October 23, 1926 in Brooklyn, NY. Education: A.B., Fordham University, 1950.

Employment: Kellogg Sales Company (Battle Creek, MI) 1950–1960; Product Development Coordinator, 1958–1960. Kellogg Company (Battle Creek, MI); Assistant to President, 1960–1962; Vice President, 1962–1965; Vice President, corporate development, 1970–1973; President, Chief Operating Officer, 1973–1979; President, CEO, and Chief Operating Officer, 1979–1980; Chairman of the Board, CEO, 1980–.

Corporate Directorships: Kellogg Company (Battle Creek, MI) 1972–. Kimberly-Clark Corporation (Neenah, WI) 1981–. Burroughs (Unisys) Corporation (Detroit, MI) 1985–. The Upjohn Company (Kalamazoo, MI) 1986–.

Charles Peter McColough born August 1, 1922 in Halifax, N.S., Canada. Came to United States, 1951; naturalized, 1956. Education: Student, Dalhousie University, 1943; LL.B., 1947; LL.D., 1970. Osgoode Hall Law School, Toronto, 1945–1946. M.B.A., Harvard University, 1949.

Employment: Lehigh Coal Navigation Company (Philadelphia, PA); Vice President Sales, 1951–1954. Xerox Corporation (Chicago, IL) 1954–; Vice President Sales, 1960–1963; Executive Vice President of Operations, 1963–1966; President, 1966–1968; President and CEO, 1968–1971; Chairman and CEO, 1971–1982; Chairman executive committee, 1986–.

Corporate Directorships: Xerox Corporation (Chicago, IL) 1961–. Rank Xerox Ltd. (London, England) 1966–. Fuji-Xerox Company Ltd. (Tokyo, Japan) 1966–. Citicorp, NY (New York, NY) 1971–. Union Carbide Corporation (Danbury, CT) 1979–.

Alonzo L. McDonald born August 5, 1928 in Atlanta, GA. Education: A.B., Emory University, 1948. M.B.A., with Distinction, Harvard University, 1956.

Employment: Westinghouse Electric Corporation (Staunton, VA); Assistant to sales manager (air conditioning division), 1956–1957; Western zone manager (St. Louis, MO) 1957–1960. McKinsey & Company, Inc. (New York, NY); Associate, 1960–1964; Principal (London, England) 1964–1966; Managing Principal (Zurich, Switzerland) 1966–1968; Managing Director (Paris, France) 1968–1973; Managing Director, Firm (New York, NY) 1973–1976. Deputy special trade representative, also ambassador in charge of U.S. delegation that concluded the Tokyo Round of Multilateral Trade Negotiations (Geneva, Switzerland) 1977–1979. Acting STR, 1979. Assistant to President of the United States, White House staff director, (Washington, D.C.) 1979–1981. Faculty, Harvard Business School (Boston, MA) 1981. Bendix Corporation (Southfield, MI); President, 1981–1983. Avenir Group, Inc. (Bloomfield Hills, MI); Chairman and CEO, 1983–.

Corporate Directorships: American Stock Exchange (New York, NY) 1981–1986. BSN Groupe, S.A. (Paris; International Advisory Board) 1981–. Dannon Company (New York, NY) 1981–. J. Henry Schroder Bank & Trust Company (New York, NY) 1981–. Lafarge Corporation (Dallas, TX) 1983–. Chicago Pacific Corporation (Chicago, IL) 1985–. Scientific Atlanta (Atlanta, GA) 1985–. Diamond-Bathurst (Malvern, PA) 1986–.

J. Irwin Miller born May 26, 1909 in Columbus, IN. Education: B.A., Yale University, 1931; M.A., Oxford University, 1933.

Employment: Cummins Engine Company, Inc. (Columbus, IN) 1934–; Vice President and General Manager, 1934–1942; Executive Vice President, 1944–1947; President, 1947–1951; Chairman of the Board, 1951–1977. Irwin Union Bank & Trust Company (Columbus, IN) 1947–; President, 1947–1954; Chairman, 1954–1976. Irwin Union Corporation, (Columbus, IN); Chairman Executive Committee, 1976–.

Corporate Directorships: Cummins Engine Company, Inc. (Columbus, IN) 1935–. Purity Stores, Ltd. (San Francisco, CA) 1935–1939. Irwin Union Bank & Trust Company (Columbus, IN) 1937–. American Zinc, Lead, and Smelting Company (St. Louis, MO) 1944–1945. United Electric Coal Companies (Chicago, IL) 1944–1953. Indiana National Bank (Indianapolis, IN) 1953–1959. Indiana Bell Telephone Company (Indianapolis, IN) 1953–1959. AT&T (New York, NY) 1959–1980. Chemical Bank (New York, NY) 1962–1972. The Equitable Life Assurance Society (New York, NY) 1962–1969.

Richard Wesley Miller born November 22, 1940 in Buffalo, NY. Education: B.B.A., Case Western Reserve University, 1967. M.B.A., Harvard University, 1970.

Employment: National City Bank (Cleveland, OH) 1961–1968; Credit Officer, 1966–1968. Penn Central Corporation (New York, NY) 1970–1982; Arvida Corporation (Boca Raton, FL); Vice President-Finance, then Executive Vice President, 1972–1979; Corporation Senior Vice President and CFO, 1979–1982. RCA Corporation (New York, NY) 1982–1986; Executive Vice President and CFO, 1982–1985; Executive Vice President, Consumer Products and Entertainment, 1985–1986. General Electric (Fairfield, CT); Senior Vice President, 1986–.

Corporate Directorships: Arvida Corporation (Miami, FL) 1971–1982. Sav-A-Stop Inc. (Jacksonville, FL) 1975–1980.

David W. Mitchell born January 14, 1928 in Pasadena, CA. Education: High School Diploma.

Employment: Avon Products, Inc. (New York, NY) 1947–1984. President, 1972–1976; President and CEO, 1976–1978; Chairman and CEO, 1978–1984.

Corporate Directorships: Avon Products, Inc. (New York, NY) 1965–. J.P. Stevens (New York, NY) 1977–1978. Manufacturers Hanover Trust Company (New York, NY) 1977–1980. U.S. Industries (New York, NY) 1974–1977. A.M.F. (White Plains,

NY) 1980–1984. Dry Dock Savings Bank (New York, NY) 1975–1984. U.S. Trust Company (New York, NY) 1973. New York Life Insurance Company (New York, NY) 1974–.

Richard J. Munro born January 26, 1931 in Syracuse, NY. Education: B.A., Colgate University, 1957. Graduate work, Columbia University.

Employment: Time Inc. (New York, NY) 1957–. Business Manager, *Sports Illustrated* (New York, NY) 1962–1967 and General Manager, 1967. President, Pioneer Press (subsidiary of *Time*) (Chicago, IL) 1969. Publisher, *Sports Illustrated,* 1969–1971; Vice President, Time Inc., 1971–1975; Deputy to Group Vice President in charge of book publishing, cable television, and film operations, 1972; Group Vice President for video, 1975–1979; Executive Vice President, 1979–1980; President and CEO, 1980–1986; Chairman and CEO, 1986–.

Corporate Directorships: Time Inc. (New York, NY) 1978–. IBM Corporation (Armonk, NY) 1979–. The Rand Corporation (Santa Monica, CA) 1984–.

Paul Fausto Oreffice born on November 29, 1927 in Venice, Italy. Came to the United States, 1945, naturalized, 1951. Education: B.S. in Chemical Engineering, Purdue University, 1949.

Employment: Dow Chemical Company (Midland, MI) 1953–. Mediterranean Sales Manager, 1955; Manager, Dow Brazil, 1956; Manager, Dow Spain, 1963; President, Dow Latin America, 1966; Director-Financial Services, The Dow Chemical Company (Midland, MI) 1969–1970; Vice President Finance, 1970–1975; President, Dow Chemical U.S.A., 1975–1978; President and CEO, 1978–. Chairman, President, and CEO, 1986–.

Corporate Directorships: Dow Corning (Midland, MI) 1976–. CIGNA Corporation (Philadelphia, PA) 1979–. Northern Telecom Ltd. (Mississauga, Ontario) 1983–. The Coca-Cola Company (Atlanta, GA) 1985–.

Donald S. Perkins born March 22, 1927 in St. Louis, MO. Education: B.A., Yale University, 1949. M.B.A., Harvard University, 1951.

Employment: U.S. Merchant Marines, 1945–1946. U.S. Air Force, 1951–1953. Jewel Companies, Inc., 1953–1983. Retired Chairman.

Corporate Directorships: G.B.-Inno-BM (Brussels, Belgium) 1959–1980. Jewel Companies, Inc. (Chicago, IL) 1962–1983. Aurrera, S.A. (Mexico City, Mexico) 1965–1983. Inland Steel Ind., Inc. (Chicago, IL) 1967–. Eastman Kodak Company (Rochester, NY) 1970–1978. Corning Glass Works (Corning, NY) 1972–. Cummins Engine Company, Inc. (Columbus, IN) 1974–. AT&T (New York, NY) 1979–. LaSalle Street Fund, Inc. (Chicago, IL) 1979–. Time Inc. (New York, NY) 1979–. Freeport-McMoRan, Inc. (New York, NY) 1980–1984. G.D. Searle & Company (Skokie, IL) 1981–1985. TBG, Inc. (Monaco) 1981–. Firestone Tire & Rubber Company (Akron, OH) 1982–1986. The Putnam Companies, Inc. (Boston, MA) 1982–. Combined International Corp. (Chicago, IL) 1983–. Springs Industries, Inc. (Fort Mill, SC) 1984–. K Mart Corp. (Troy, MI) 1986–.

Donald C. Platten born September 18, 1918 in New York City. Education: B.A., magna cum laude, Princeton University, 1940.

Employment: Chemical Bank New York (New York, NY) 1940–. Senior Vice President, 1964–1967; Executive Vice President, 1967–1970; 1st Vice President, 1970–1972; President, 1972–1973; Chairman of the Board, 1973–1983. Chairman of the Board, Chemical New York Corporation, 1973–1983; Chairman, Executive Committee, 1983–.

Corporate Directorships: Thomson Newspapers, Inc. (Toronto, Canada) 1968–. CPC International, Inc. (Englewood Cliffs, NJ) 1973–. Associated Dry Goods Corporation (New York, NY) 1976–1986, now The May Department Stores Company (St. Louis, MO) 1986–. Consolidated Edison Company New York, Inc. (New York, NY) 1979–. The Reader's Digest Association, Inc. (Pleasantville, NY) 1980–. Cleveland-Cliffs Inc. (Cleveland, OH) 1981–. Texas Oil & Gas Corporation (Dallas, TX) 1984–1986.

Henry Brewer Schacht born October 16, 1934 in Erie, PA. Education: B.S., Yale University, 1956. M.B.A., Harvard University, 1962.

Employment: Irwin Management Company (Columbus, IN);

Investment Manager, 1964–1966; Vice President and Central Area Manager-International (London, England) 1966–1967; Group Vice President-International and subsidiaries (Columbus, IN) 1967–1969; President, 1969–1973; President and CEO, 1973–1977; Chairman and CEO, 1977–.

Corporate Directorships: Cummins Engine Company, Inc. (Columbus, IN) 1969–. CBS (New York, NY) 1971–. AT&T (New York, NY) 1981–. Chase Manhattan Bank (New York, NY) 1982–.

William Allen Schreyer born January 13, 1928 in Williamsport, PA. Education: B.A., Pennsylvania State University, 1948.

Employment: Merrill Lynch, Company, Inc. (New York, NY) 1948–; President and Chief Administrative Officer, Merrill Lynch, Pierce, Fenner & Smith, Inc., 1978–1980; CEO, 1980; Chairman, 1981; President and Chief Operating Officer, 1982; CEO, 1984; Chairman and CEO, 1985–.

Corporate Directorships: Merrill Lynch & Company (New York, NY) 1979–. New York Stock Exchange, Inc. (New York, NY) 1985–. Schering-Plough Corporation (Madison, NJ) 1986–.

Michael S. Scott Morton born August 25, 1937 in Mukden, Manchuria. Education: Engineering, Glasgow University, Scotland. B.S., Carnegie Mellon University, 1961. D.B.A., Harvard University, 1967.

Employment: Massachusetts Institute of Technology-Sloan School of Management (Cambridge, MA); Faculty member, 1966–; Professor of Management, 1975–.

Corporate Directorships: Index Systems (Cambridge, MA) 1971–. Emhart Corporation (Hartford, CT) 1976–. ICL PlC (London, England) 1983–1984. ICL North America (Stamford, CT) 1985–.

Walter Vincent Shipley born November 2, 1935 in Newark, NJ. Education: B.S., New York University, 1960.

Employment: Chemical Bank (New York, NY) 1956–; Executive Vice President in charge of International Division (New York, NY) 1978–1979; Senior Executive Vice President, 1981; President, 1982–1983; Chairman of the Board, Chemical New York Corporation (New York, NY) 1983–.

Corporate Directorships: Champion International Corporation (Stamford, CT) 1983–. NYNEX Corporation (New York, NY) 1983–.

Richard F. Vancil born September 17, 1931 in St. Louis, MO. Education: B.S., Northwestern University, 1953. M.B.A., with high Distinction, Harvard University, 1955; D.B.A., 1960.
Employment: U.S. Army, 1955–1958. Harvard Business School (Boston, MA); Full-time faculty member, 1958–; Lovett-Learned Professor of Business Administration, 1977–. The MAC Group (Cambridge, MA); Founder and Chairman, 1964–.
Corporate Directorships: Rochester Capital Leasing Co. (Rochester, NY) 1962–1966. Arvida Corp. (Boca Raton, FL) 1971–1974. Great Southwest Corp. (Los Angeles, CA) 1973–1978. Connecticut General Corp., now CIGNA Corp. (Philadelphia, PA) 1976–. Ausimont NV (The Netherlands) 1985–.

Hicks Benjamin Waldron born October 31, 1923 in Amsterdam, NY. Education: B.S., University of Minnesota, 1944.
Employment: General Electric Company, 1946–1973; Vice President, Group Executive Consumer Products group, 1971–1973. Heublein, Inc. (Farmington, CT); President, CEO, 1973–1982; Director, 1982–1983. R.J. Reynolds Industries, Inc. (Winston-Salem, NC); Executive Vice President, 1982–1983. Avon Products, Inc. (New York, NY); President and CEO, 1983–.
Corporate Directorships: Connecticut General Insurance Corporation, now CIGNA (Philadelphia, PA) 1974–. Connecticut Bank & Trust Company (Hartford, CT) 1975–1985. Avon Products, Inc. (New York, NY) 1980–. R. J. Reynolds Industries, Inc. (Winston-Salem, NC) 1982–1983. Allegheny International, Inc. (Pittsburgh, PA) 1984–1985. Sea-Land Corporation (Menlo Park, NJ) 1984–1985. Bank of New England (Boston, MA) 1985–.

Index